To Frank Espinosa —
I hope the book brings
back some exciting
sports memories.

Best wishes,
Joe McGiff

Why Me?
Why Not Joe McGuff?

Why Me?
Why Not Joe McGuff?

By Joe McGuff

Joseph McGuff
Prairie Village, Kansas

Grateful acknowledgment is made to the
Kansas City Star for permission to reprint the
columns that appear in this book

Published by Joseph McGuff
9 LeMans Court
Prairie Village, Kansas 66208

ISBN 09632306-0-3

Printed by Herald House, Independence, Missouri

Printed in the United States of America

Jacket photo by Roy Inman

Jacket design by Barney Newcom

Contents

CONTENTS

Acknowledgments

So many people have been helpful to me in putting this book together that I can't name all of them, but there are a few who deserve special recognition. Dale Bye, who runs *The Kansas City Star* sports department, and my wife Kay are principally responsible for bringing this project to a conclusion. Dale not only urged me to do the book but personally went through hundreds of columns, chose the ones he thought were of special interest and had them stored on computer disks. The idea was to publish the book on my 40th anniversary at *The Star*. Unfortunately, I could never find the time to go through the columns, make the final choices and do the final edit. Kay took over from Dale, alternately encouraging and harassing me until until I capitulated and finished the project. Then she took over many of the time-consuming tasks that are involved in publishing a book. I want to thank Terri Wiley who entered numerous columns into *The Star* computer system, and Rob Perschau, the newsroom computer guru, who led me through the complexities of the computer age. I also would like to thank Jim Hale, the publisher of *The Star*, who offered encouraging words about my writing and then gave me an opportunity to spend the last six years of my career as editor of *The Star*.

Introduction

There are no rules that stipulate how introductions should be written, but in most cases I think an introduction should serve two purposes. First, if a title is not self-explanatory, the reader should be told what the significance of it is and how it came to be chosen. Second, the reader is entitled to know the reason, aside from avarice, why the book was written.

I will proceed immediately to these two points.

Some book titles almost suggest themselves. That was the case with "Winning It All," a book I wrote about the Chiefs' 1969 season and their Super Bowl victory over the Vikings. The title for this book was chosen after a lot of discussions that began, "What would you think about..."

Titles such as "The Sports World of Joe McGuff," "The Joe McGuff Anthology" and "Joe McGuff Writes About Sports" were discarded as snoozers. "Gone With The Wind" would have been a dandy but it seems to have been spoken for.

The title that was chosen is taken from a 1980 column. The Royals had returned from Philadelphia after losing the first two games of the World Series to the Phillies. George Brett was in agony. He was suffering not from a pulled hamstring or a torn tendon but from a severe case of hemorrhoids. To add to his discomfort, everybody was writing and talking about George's ailment.

Having your hemorrhoids held up to public scrutiny is close to the ultimate invasion of privacy.

Through the years Brett has suffered from an unusual variety of injuries and I asked him if he ever wondered why all of these things kept happening to him.

George thought a moment and in replying he said, "I keep saying, 'Why Me? Why not Joe McGuff?' "

The line struck me as both funny and insightful. Anyone could have said, "Why me?" That is an eminently forgettable quote. But whenever we say "Why me?" we are implying that we would rather our misfortune be transferred to someone else. George identified that someone else.

It was a funny line uttered with wry good humor in a bleak moment. It is the sort of humorous line you hope to get in an interview and rarely do. It was part of the give and take of a friendly working relationship. We both laughed and George went off to St. Luke's Hospital where he said he was going to get the same room he had occupied five years in a row.

When people made reference to the column, the first thing they mentioned was Brett's quote.

The sports section is supposed to provide some relief from the calamities of our times. Sports should be fun and I hope the title of this book sets the tone for the pages that follow.

This brings us to the reason for doing the book.

Yesterday's newspaper is of little interest to anyone with the possible exception of your neighborhood recycler. As time passes, however, old newspapers and old columns assume a historical quality. Some of the columns in this book are offered in the hope that readers will find them interesting or entertaining or both. Others offer a record of people and events that are part of the sports history of this area.

I spent almost 38 years in the sports department of *The Kansas City Star* and it was my good fortune to be writing about sports in an extraordinarily eventful era. I covered the arrival of major league baseball, the loss of the Athletics and the acquisition of the Royals. I wrote about the coming of the Chiefs and the construction of the Truman Sports Complex.

This book contains accounts of the Royals' two appearances in the World Series and the Chiefs' two trips to the Super Bowl.

I have been fortunate enough to cover the exploits of many great athletes and coaches--George Brett, Len Dawson, Tom Watson, Hal McRae, Jim Ryun, Dan Devine, Hank Stram and Don Faurot, just to mention a few.

The most unsettling part of putting this book together was deciding what to leave out.

Compiling the material for this book has been an unusual experience because at times I have had the feeling of reliving much of my adult life. My work has taken me to many exciting events and enabled me to meet many fascinating people. I hope the reader will feel a part of those experiences.

CHAPTER 1

PERSONAL FAVORITES

The Legacy of Charles O.

Baseball without Charles O. Finley? Goodness, this is going to take a bit of getting used to. Who will be left to denounce Bowie Kuhn and call him the village idiot? Who will promote orange baseballs, pinch-running specialists and tout the merits of albino kangaroo shoes?

Baseball without Charles O. will be like a rose bush without thorns, politics without Howard Jarvis, Canada without Margaret Trudeau.

There are those in Kansas City who would have been delighted if Finley had gotten out of baseball shortly after purchasing the A's in the winter of 1960-61. Abusive, vindictive, shrewd, erratic. Finley was all of those things and more, but even his critics will concede he was never dull.

Baseball, Finley style, should have been performed in three rings to the accompaniment of dancing bears and a steam calliope.

The first indication Finley was not going to operate in the tradition of Connie Mack or Branch Rickey came shortly after he purchased the A's. He met with Ernie Mehl (former sports editor of *The Star*) and myself and informed us that even before the season opened he would have a sellout for every game at Municipal Stadium.

How was he going to perform this miracle with a wretched team that reached only a .377 level the year before? With a mail-order campaign, that's how. Finley was going to sell baseball the same way he sold insurance.

His first season here was an unforgettable experience. He nearly came to blows with his manager, Joe Gordon, in spring training and later fired him. He hired Frank Lane as his general manager and fired him. He bought an old school bus and burned it, proclaiming he had burned the shuttle bus to Yankee Stadium, and there would be no more deals with the Yankees. Before the season was over he traded his star pitcher to the Yankees.

In July of his first season, Finley went to Dallas and explored the possibility of moving his team there and playing in the Cotton Bowl. He presented a poison-pen award to Mehl, who broke the story, and when Commissioner Ford Frick apologized to Mehl, Finley rebuked the commissioner.

Then there was the great Mercedes caper. When Finley hired Lane, he gave him a Mercedes and a 10-gallon hat. Lane assumed both items were his property. He was half right.

When the time came to get a new license for the car, Lane wrote to Finley for the title. Finley refused to send it. With no proof of ownership, Lane could not get a license.

The impasse was resolved when Joe Brown, then general manager of the Pirates, bought the title from Finley and the car from Lane.

One of the highlights of Finley'second season in Kansas City was the Manny Jimenez home-run edict.

In late July, Jimenez ranked second in the American League in hitting and had a chance to win the batting title. His average was .337. At that point, Finley called his manager, Hank Bauer, and told him he wanted Jimenez to start swinging for the fences.

"I don't pay Jimenez to hit singles," Finley declared. "Jimenez is a smart Cuban and he's going for singles and a better average."

Jimenez actually was from the Dominican Republic but then it's easy to get those Caribbean countries confused.

"What he say make me mad," Jimenez said. "I no go home, but I plenty sad."

Jimenez's batting average also became plenty sad, falling to .301 by the end of the season. He hit 11 home runs.

Finley was a frequent critic of Bauer's managing, sometimes exhorting him with telegrams. On one occasion, Finley sent the following wire: "Henry, for your sake and my sake, I wish to pass on to you an old adage which has meant so much to me. It is simply this: A man who wakes up and finds himself a success has not been sleeping. We did not play to win tonight."

Another time Bauer received a wire that read: "Please, please, please, please, please, please, please, please, please, please, please, please play the game to win."

Baseball will be quieter without Charles O., but after 20 years of him we can use a little peace.

The Vaughan
Exchange

FORT MYERS, FLA.—In 1955 Kansas City acquired an American League baseball franchise that had come upon hard times in Philadelphia and as a result people immediately began to say that Kansas City had gone major league.

Precisely why a baseball franchise should determine whether a city is major league, triple-A or what have you is something that has long puzzled me, but it is a standard by which cities are judged and who am I to tinker with the great American scheme of things.

Maybe we seize upon sports as a measuring device because it is much more difficult to classify orchestras, the performing arts, school systems and sewer districts. For all I know Kansas City's refuse collection may be double-A, but I doubt there would be any great outpouring of public support if a Greater Kansas City Trash Commission were organized and a civic drive were started to make Kansas City major league trashwise.

But I digress.

The purpose of today's column is not to examine the system whereby we rate our cities but to comment on the work of a local artisan who I would call the poor man's Jeane Dixon were I not afraid that Jeane might see a libel suit in my future.

The first year that the Athletics played in Kansas City Bill Vaughan, *The Star's* resident wit and the man who provides the sugar that makes the editorial page go down, wrote a column picking the A's to win the pennant, the old gonfalon, all the marbles and whatever else comes your way when you finish first.

In the beginning I accused Bill of poaching on the preserves of the sports department and suggested that he confine his ink-stained typewriter keys to Congressman Sludgepump, Cousin Fuseloyle and the School That Doesn't Pay its Players. After all, I was picking the A's to finish last or thereabouts. If by some weird series of circumstances Bill

4

happened to be right, there was going to be a huge credibility gap at 1729 Grand Avenue. Besides, Bill and I usually eat lunch at the same saloon and an A's victory would have left me with a terminal case of indigestion.

Sure, the chances of the A's winning the pennant were remote, but then who thought that Jim (Catfish) Hunter, a tobacco-chewing pitcher from Ahoskie, N.C., would be named to the Best Dressed list by the Fashion Foundation of America.

In recent years I have mellowed regarding Bill's annual intrusion into the sports prognosticating business. After all, it's a column for him, a column for me and when you're in the columning business a subject idea is an all-important consideration.

Last year I even tried to encourage Bill to add a little more pizzaz to his column. I suggested that the annual rite of picking Kansas City's baseball team to win it all should become a public event. I proposed that we assemble a crowd around his desk, get Kate Smith to sing "God Bless America" and as Bill began pounding the keys the audience could shout, "Way to go, Bill. Pick 'em again."

At the conclusion there would be favors for the ladies, autographed copies of his column for the men and everybody could join in a chorus of "Everything's Up to Date in Kansas City." In time I could foresee moving the event to Kemper Arena.

Like most great ideas this one seems to have been ahead of its time, but now I have come up with a better idea, one that will revolutionize prognosticating just as McDonald's revolutionized the hamburger business. It is based on the premise of making Bill available on a nationwide basis to pick teams—your team, my team, anybody's team—to win a pennant.

There are some people who probably will fail to see a need for this type of service, but their lack of vision will only be a source of embarrassment to them in the years ahead.

To explain why this is an idea whose time has come, let's take the case of Ray Kroc. He is chairman of the board of McDonald's, owns the San Diego Padres and is worth from $200 million to $500 million depending on how the stock market is fluctuating on a given day.

Kroc's baseball team is engaged in what we in the sportswriting business like to call a rebuilding program or a youth movement. What this means is that he has a lousy team. Let's say that after a hard day of turning out fries and Big Macs Kroc is relaxing at home and decides that it would be nice if somebody would pick the Padres to win the pennant.

He goes to the phone, rings up the folks at the Gallup Poll and asks what it would cost to have them predict that the Padres will win all the marbles. He will quickly find the Gallup folks' services are not for sale on this basis, and besides Gallup is still trying to live down the Truman-Dewey thing.

Where does Kroc turn next? Well, he might try Jimmy the Greek, who handicaps everything from Mexican jumping bean races to paper towel absorbency tests on TV commercials. But versatile as he is, there is no possibility that The Greek would pick the Padres to win the pennant. If he did he would be the laughing stock of Las Vegas and he would not care for his predictions to become the centerpiece of a Johnny Carson monologue.

Would the *Sporting News* do it? Such a suggestion would be heresy to a publication known as the Bible of Baseball. Could you get a columnist such as Red Smith to pick the Padres? Sure Red would—the day after Marvin Miller is named commissioner of baseball.

Clearly there is only one thing left for Kroc to do—turn to a syndicated columnist with 21 years of experience, a man pre-eminent in his field, someone so fearless that he picked Kansas City to win the American League pennant even in 1968 when it did not field a team.

Take the case of Tampa Bay, which is getting a National Football League expansion franchise. The old fashioned way, Tampa Bay might not be picked to win it all for 10 years, but now Tampa Bay would not have to feel inferior to the Steelers or Dolphins. Little leagues, minor leagues—no job would be too big or too small.

Beautiful, isn't it? And with a little luck Bill might even get federal funding.

Thanksgiving, 1982

Some things to be thankful for when we sit down Thursday to celebrate Thanksgiving with generous helpings of turkey, dressing, mashed potatoes, gravy, vegetables, rolls, cranberry sauce, three kinds of pie and coffee:

The opportunity to enjoy another Thanksgiving with friends and family in a country where freedom makes us the most privileged nation in the world even even when times are hard economically.

A bowl trip for the Kansas State Wildcats, who won only eight games in the previous three seasons and who went through a 12-year span from 1956 through 1967 when they won only 20 games.

A wood fire crackling and spraying sparks up the chimney on Thanksgiving morning.

The first snowfall of the year, even if it does tie up traffic and make you late to work.

Being able to sneak a taste of dressing right after the turkey comes out of the oven.

A hot biscuit covered by a thin layer of butter topped with honey that runs down the side.

Muhammad Ali has not announced that he is coming out of retirement.

Motion picture theaters where all seats are $1.

The Thanksgiving tradition of making a civic celebration out of turning on the Plaza Christmas lights.

A granddaughter asking you to please read her favorite book just one more time.

The genius who first looked at a pumpkin, wondered what to do with it and decided that it would make good filling for a pie.

Bear Bryant's squinty look when things are going badly for the Crimson Tide.

The taste of real whipped cream.

A World Series without George Steinbrenner.

The lack of willpower that allows you to go back for a second helping of turkey, dressing, mashed potatoes, gravy, vegetables and rolls even though you don't need them.

Leaves swirling and skimming along the ground on a windy autumn morning.

Not having to spend Thanksgiving alone.

Royals Stadium on a hot summer night when the fountains are a soothing sight and the home team is winning.

Reading in bed on cold winter nights.

Children getting to eat all the desert they want and finding that they can't hold as much as they thought they could.

Ed Nealy, the 166th choice in the National Basketball Association draft, beating the odds and making the Kings' roster.

The smell of fresh baked bread.

Frank White making the pivot on a double play.

A cook who operates on the theory that you can't put too much brandy in a mincemeat pie.

The sight of smoke curling from a chimney at dusk on a cold winter day.

Those words that wives and mothers most like to hear on Thanksgiving: "Never mind, I'll do the dishes."

A medical checkup that ends with the doctor saying he can't find anything wrong.

The impatience of a child while grace is being said before Thanksgiving dinner.

The invention of the video cassette, making it possible for us to watch Tom Watson's dramatic wedge shot on the 71st hole of the U.S. Open as often as we choose.

Memories of other Thanksgivings.

Formation of the Kansas City Symphony to fill the gap left by the demise of the Kansas City Philharmonic.

The genius who first thought up the recipe for creamed onions.

The sight of a powdery ski slope gleaming in the morning sun.

A trip to the refrigerator just before bedtime to sample the leftovers from Thanksgiving dinner.

The sight of runway lights when the pilot is making an instrument landing after a rough flight.

Those who had the wisdom to set aside a day for the nation's citizens to join together in giving thanks.

Stenerud's Biggest Miss

Eleven days have passed since the Chiefs' 27-24 loss to Miami in the longest professional football game ever played, but the calendar is irrelevant to Jan Stenerud who finds himself a prisoner of time. In his mind it is still Christmas day. At times he almost breaks free into the present, but like a prisoner in a science fiction story he is restrained by an invisible barrier.

Over and over he returns to the 31-yard field goal he missed, a field goal that would have enabled the Chiefs to defeat Miami in regulation time. He sees the ball soaring toward the goal post and then angling outside the upright by a matter of inches. As he relives the scene, all of the anguish of his failure wells up again in his mind and body.

Stenerud has kicked 143 field goals, many of them under extreme pressure, but the only kick he can remember today is the one he missed. Wherever he goes he is reminded of it.

On New Year's Day he watched the Rose Bowl game. With 12 seconds left Rod Garcia came in to attempt a field goal for Stanford. Ironically the distance was 31 yards.

"It was the same place I kicked from," Stenerud said. "I know how he felt. I was really pulling for the poor guy."

Garcia made his field goal and for a few moments Stenerud rejoiced with him, but suddenly it was Christmas day again: Bobby Bell makes the snap from center. Len Dawson positions the ball. The kick is up, but a little higher than it should be. Now it's curving, curving...

"I think about the game all the time," Stenerud said yesterday at the Country Club bank, where he is a vice-president. "I still can't get over it. It's bad enough letting the fans down, but the thing that bugs me is letting down the players and the coaches. I didn't really come through in the clutch. They talked about the first kick I missed and all of the other things that happened, but the only thing I think about is the kick I missed with a half minute left.

9

"When Ed Podolak made his run I got up and started to get loose. I felt nervous and a little tense, but I always do before I go in to kick. When I got in there I felt there was no way in the world I could miss. I thought I hit the ball reasonably well, but I got under it. The field may have been a little rough. You're always looking for a high spot.

"The ball was only inches wide. How many inches? I don't know but definitely less than six. But there was no doubt that it was wide. I didn't even look at the referee. I'm willing to accept the good things and the bad things that go with pro football, but I've never felt as bad about anything.

"On Sunday I didn't think I'd watch the Miami-Baltimore game but finally I did. After seeing Miami handle Baltimore I began thinking that we could have won and the misery started all over again."

The public attitude toward Stenerud has been almost entirely sympathetic, a somewhat surprising development considering that most football fans exhibit a low tolerance for failure.

"I've probably received 150 letters," Stenerud said, "and only a few of them are nasty. Those are from people who are just disappointed and mad. I honestly wouldn't blame anyone for getting nasty with me. They're kind of right in being mad and disappointed.

"I really appreciate all of the nice letters I've received. All you can do for those people is try to prove yourself. It's nice to know people have faith in you."

In his present tormented state Stenerud finds himself even worrying about failing the people who have befriended him.

"If something goes bad in your business you can work 15 hours a day and chances are you can get it straightened out," Stenerud said, "but it's different in athletics. Just because you work hard that doesn't necessarily mean you'll be successful. There's no guarantee that I'll have a good season in 1972 but I'm going to try my best.

"I can't get over how nice people have been. A good friend of mine wants to have a big party for me. He wants to print tickets and have hundreds of people. It gives you kind of a funny feeling. This guy is just great. I can't tell you how many nice things he has done for me, but I wouldn't feel right about a party.

"Hank (Stram) always stresses that we win as 40 people and lose as 40 people. As much as I appreciate the thought I don't think a party would be quite right and I know Hank wouldn't want it, but it's hard to say no when people are so thoughtful.

Stenerud's most painful experience on Christmas day came in the immediate aftermath of the game.

"The hardest part was coming in the dressing room and looking around at the other players," Stenerud said. "Jim Lynch came over and said something like, 'You didn't lose the game.' "A couple of the other guys came around and said something.

"I was really disappointed in myself. It hurts when you know you have the ability to do something and don't do it. I refuse to believe that the pressure got me. It was just a matter of inches. A couple of inches the other way and everything would have been different."

Stenerud drove directly home from the stadium and was scarcely inside the door when the phone rang. He debated whether to answer. The ringing continued ominously. It could have been a lynch mob giving him five minutes to get out of town. Obviously it was not President Nixon.

As it turned out the caller was Jim Turner, the former Jets' place kicker who is now with Denver.

"Jim is an old friend of mine," Stenerud said. "He just wanted to let me know he had been through the same thing. He said he had missed three big kicks like mine. I know he's missed some kicks but there couldn't be a more crucial kick than mine. It was worse than missing the same kind of kick in the Super Bowl. If you're in the Super Bowl you've already accomplished something and you're assured of some money, but this way we missed out on everything.

"Jerry Mays called that night. He said that knowing me as he did he knew I'd take the loss harder than I should. Dawson called. So did Johnny Robinson and Ed Lothamer. At the time I didn't know Robinson was hurt so bad. That's something that he would take the time to call me when he was in so much pain.

"My first thought when I got home that night was to have a few drinks, but I only had one beer. The first night wasn't so bad. I was so exhausted I fell asleep with my clothes on. The next night was much worse. They had the rerun of the game on television that night. I wanted to see the whole game. I guess I thought maybe I deserved the punishment. But my wife didn't want me to. I guess she was worried about what it would do to me. So I saw the first half but I didn't see the bad part."

Stram called Stenerud the day following the game.

"We had our Christmas on the 26th," Stenerud said. "Our kids are so young they don't really know the difference. Hank called and said he wanted to remind me that I had a lot of things to be thankful for. He said the most important thing was that I had a wonderful wife and fine children. He said that I shouldn't let this get me down, that we had to look ahead to next season. I've found there aren't many coaches like Hank. He has been patient with me at times when I didn't deserve it. I'm sure he knows how I feel. He's just been great."

At present Stenerud's mood fluctuates from anguish and self doubt to a positive attitude toward his plans for next year.

"It's going to be the most famous kick of all until someone comes along and misses a bigger one," Stenerud says in one of his grimmer moments. "It will be a long time before anyone forgets it. I can kick a hundred field goals next year, but this thing will still be in my mind. I hope it won't ruin me. I don't think it will. I know I'll have to live with it but I don't think it will hurt my performance. It's just awful to work that hard that long, get so close and then lose.

The thing that gets me is the uncertainty about coming back. I'm going to work hard but that's no guarantee. The week before the game I knew things were not going well but when I got in the game that was not on my mind. I was thinking like I always do. I didn't hear the crowd. I looked at my spot, looked at the goal post and then watched the ball.

"If we had lost 40-0 it wouldn't have been so bad. The two teams that are in the Super Bowl are excellent teams. The only better game would have been Kansas City and Dallas. We should be there.

"When I walked up the runway to the dressing room after the game I told myself I'd never go through this again. I felt it just wasn't worth it. But now, looking back over the last five years, I know I'd do it all over again regardless of the agony I've gone through.

"When I think of all the people I've met, the experiences I've had and what football has meant to me I know it's all worthwhile even though after the game I had said, 'Never again.'"

Turning Off the Flame

LOS ANGELES—A diary of the day they turned off the flame, closed the Olympics and sent everyone home:

Walk into hotel parking lot. Reflect on fact that the weather has been astonishingly good throughout the Olympics. Natives claim that when the national television cameras are on Los Angeles weather always gives an Oscar-winning performance. They are right.

Drive down the San Diego Freeway and turn right on Harbor Freeway to Main Press Center. After 24 days it is all becoming as familiar as the Southwest Trafficway.

Walk into Main Press Center. Guard stares at my badge. Sit down next to Jack Kahn of *The New Yorker* magazine. He is on page 30 of a 9,000-word Olympic story. Offer thanks that I am not Jack Kahn. He explains his editor wants the piece by Monday even though it may not appear for a month.

Go to concession stand for 24th straight morning. Woman smiles and automatically gets me a small Sanka.

William Simon, president of the United States Olympic Committee holds his final press conference. Says he may be "immodest" and "specious" but thinks these are the best Games ever. Occurs to me that in this context "specious" is not a good choice of words. What he is talking about is the possibility of being prejudiced. Where is William Safire when we need him?

Simon makes passionate defense of flag waving and U.S. boosterism at the Games. Says he's proud to be an American. Minneapolis columnist says he's as patriotic as the next guy, but this outpouring of patriotism is like standing on a street corner and telling everyone how religious you are. He has a point.

Simon criticizes Jimmy Carter's decision to boycott the Moscow Games. Make mental note that kicking Jimmy Carter has become an Olympic demonstration sport. Simon says in the future Olympic boycotters should be severely punished, that no matter what happens the athletes should not be deprived of a chance to play their games.

Find myself thinking of Avery Brundage, the late president of the International Olympic Committee, who didn't even want to stop the Games for one day after the Israeli athletes were killed in Munich.

Go back to work area. Kahn says he has about nine pages to go. Give thanks again that I am not Jack Kahn. Can't stand thought of writing another Olympic column. Start writing one anyway.

Carl Lewis press conference announced. Amazing thing happens. Lewis arrives early. Ranks as major Olympic upset.

Lewis says there are a lot of challenges left for him. He wants to run faster and jump farther. Says he had a ball at the Olympics. Didn't read newspapers so he was able to remain in good spirits. Answers questions thoughtfully and articulately. Gives all the right answers.

Says he can understand being booed after making only one legitimate jump in winning long jump. Explains a lot of athletes didn't stay in the Olympic Village, but all the attention was focused on him. Says ABC was justified in not providing live coverage of the relay race in which he won his fourth gold medal.

Explains he answers all of his mail and responded to all 267 messages from other athletes that he received through the Olympic computer system. Defends the strong U.S. bias of ABC coverage.

Impressive performance, but when he is through the smile leaves Lewis' face and he rushes past Los Angeles Olympic Organizing Committee volunteers who want autographs. Thought occurs that public probably thinks reporters are unfair to Lewis, but what the public sees is his stage personality. Off stage there is a different Carl Lewis.

Have lunch in Press Center restaurant. Thought comes to mind that other Olympics have been more enjoyable to cover than these, even Lake Placid in its own strange way. Maybe Los Angeles is too spread out and Games lose their identity. Maybe covering six Olympics is the problem. Not sure why, but aside from the winners, nobody here seemed to be laughing a lot.

Reflect on a scene Saturday night when a young man and a young woman stood in the fountain in front of the press center holding another young woman and threatened to drop her in water. It was nice to see them having fun.

Go back to work on column. Kahn says he has three pages to go. Suggest he deserves a gold medal for marathon Olympic writing.

Finish most of column. Leave for Coliseum and closing ceremony. British writer holds up copy of headline in *Los Angeles Herald-Examiner* and says it reflects American view of these Games. Headline reads, "Scott pushes Coe to second medal." Another British writer laughingly claims British papers should run a head saying Allan Wells pushed Carl Lewis to four gold medals.

Parking lot directly across from the Coliseum that was charging $100 on the day of the opening ceremonies is charging $15 for the closing ceremonies. Games have not been quite the financial bonanza they were supposed to be for Los Angeles businessmen.

Carl Lopes wins marathon. John Treacy of Ireland, the silver medal winner, is so fatigued he can hardly climb the steps to the stage where the victory platform is located.

Equestrian winners also receive their medals. One of the horses does what horses sometimes do, but the LAOOC is ready. Rushes cleanup crew to the spot.

Athletes' march gets a little unruly. Policy in riot helmets appear in Coliseum tunnel, but later withdraw as athletes calm down. Peter Uberroth, president of the Los Angeles Olympic Organizing Committee, is introduced and gets standing ovation. Thought occurs that California politicians are lucky he is becoming commissioner of baseball instead of running for mayor or governor.

International Olympic Committee President Juan Antonio Samaranch declares Games closed. Crowd groans. The Olympic flag is lowered and the flame is extinguished.

Flying saucer appears overhead. Laser lights stab through the night. Red lights come on in peristyle and smoke billows up. Expect Major Indoor Soccer League game to begin. Fireworks display follows. Sounds like re-enactment of the Normandy invasion. A tough act for Lionel Richie to follow.

Ceremonies end with more fireworks. Sounds like Normandy invasion and Battle of the Bulge combined.

Get on bus, return to Press Center and finish column. Reflect on Games, which are a great organizational triumph for Uberroth and his staff. Feel great sense of relief that no one was shot or killed.

Watson a Compassionate Winner

TROON, SCOTLAND—The significance of Tom Watson's British Open victory Sunday at Royal Troon was of such magnitude that he could not help but be happy even though he identified too closely with the torment of Nick Price and Bobby Clampett to be jubilant.

He had walked in their shoes, he had cried their tears and as his career carried him to heights occupied by the immortals of this ancient sport, he revealed himself as a compassionate champion in a game where sympathy is not a common emotion.

Watson had expected to win his fourth British Open championship Sunday by shooting a low score—a 68 was the number he had settled on—and outplaying the strange bag of multi-nationals who were in contention on the last day of golf's oldest major championship.

His old rival, Jack Nicklaus, was too far back to join this fight, and the other stars of the American tour had done so poorly that a British paper had run a headline that read: "Yankee Doodle Not So Dandy."

But history reveals that major championships are not always won with heroic rounds. This was to be the case Sunday, a day when old Troon gleamed in the sunlight and sea breeze of a Scottish afternoon.

In this respect it is worth noting that Byron Nelson, one of Watson's golfing gurus, won his only U.S. Open in 1939, the year Sam Snead needed only a 5 on the closing hole to win and instead took an 8. Billy Casper won the U.S. Open in 1966, but it would be more accurate to say that Arnold Palmer lost it, throwing away a 7-shot lead on the last six holes.

On this occasion Watson shot a respectable 70 and won by one stroke because his rivals grew faint and strangled on the pressure. It was not a tournament long on artistry, but it offered a fascinating insight into the human psyche.

Clampett, 11 under par after the first two rounds and leading by 1 shot when the final round began, was jauntily attired in gray plus-twos (knickers) for his Sunday outing at Troon. But he was a bedraggled figure at the finish after shooting a 77 to go 11 over par on the final two days and finish in a tie for 10th.

It was a performance that took Watson back to the 1975 U.S. Open at Medinah. It was there that he shot 135 in the first two rounds, had a 3-shot lead after the first day and a 6-shot lead after the second. Then he collapsed, shooting a 78-77. Watson recalled crying after that tournament.

"After Medinah I told myself I sure wasn't going to let that happen to me again. I won some tournaments, and it gave me confidence. I wasn't a winner when I started on the pro tour. I wasn't like Lanny Wadkins, who had won a lot in college.

"I didn't know if I was going to win or not (at Medinah). I knew what I had to do. I had a manufactured swing. It worked for two rounds, but it didn't work when the heat was on. In 1977, I turned the corner."

Watson also identified with Price, who came into No. 13 with a 3-shot lead over Watson, who at the time was playing 16. Watson shot par on the final three holes and disgusted himself by leaving a putt short at 18. Price obligingly fell apart down the stretch. He bogeyed 14, took a double bogey at 15 and bogeyed 17.

It was a finish that took Watson back to the 1974 U.S. Open at Winged Foot when he went into the final round with a 1-shot lead after shooting rounds of 73-71-69. On the infamous final day he shot a 79 and finished in a tie for fifth.

Watson's wife, Linda, remembers Sunday at Winged Foot as her lowest emotional point, although Watson calls Medinah his personal low.

"It was raining," she recalled, "and I was standing outside the clubhouse. I don't know why, but they didn't let the wives in. They were tearing down all of the banners, and Tom was inside feeling sorry for himself and talking to Byron Nelson.

"I remember standing there and getting wet and wondering, 'Is this what it's going to be?'"

Sunday Watson expressed his sorrow for Price.

"It's a sinking feeling," he said, "But you have to learn from it. You have to learn to win. I had to learn to win when I came out on the tour.

I learned by leading at Medinah for two rounds and shooting 155. I've been in the position Price is in. I lost the Tournament Players Championship and Heritage that way. I learned from it. I cried, and I imagine there might be a little crying going on by these fellows."

The most difficult part of professional golf is learning to win, and Watson spoke of acquiring his competitive nature early in life.

"I was always competing with my older brother (Ridge)," Watson said. "He taught me to be competitive. He's three years older than I am, and he was bigger and stronger and better at everything than I was.

"I remember playing basketball in high school, and we were four for nine at the start of the season. We lost to a tough team, but we played a good game. They probably were better than we were. It was my freshman year. I cried and said, 'Coach, when are we going to win?' We went to the quarterfinals of the state championship that year.

"Sometimes losing will hurt you. I think Ed Sneed's loss in the Masters hurt his career. Medinah was a very low point for me, but I knew what I had to do."

Watson's failures had become so publicized that at one time he was known as a choker, and at one tournament fans shouted at him, "Remember Winged Foot."

Watson led the Hawaiian Open by 4 strokes after three rounds in 1973 and shot a 75, finishing third. In the 1973 World Open, a tournament that stretched over parts of two weeks, he went into the final two rounds with a 6-shot lead and finished 76-77, falling to fourth place.

His first tour victory was in the 1974 Western Open. He was 6 strokes off the lead coming into the final round, but he shot a 69 and won when the leader, Tom Weiskopf, shot a 77.

Such is the fickleness of golf.

Although Watson's fourth British Open victory, all of them accomplished in Scotland, was made possible by the failures of others, it would be a mistake to overlook the quality of golf he played at Royal Troon, a course whose length, pot bunkers and narrow fairways proved unusually difficult even though the weather was pleasant through the final two rounds.

Watson's putter worked well only in the opening round when he shot a brilliant 69 on a wet, cold, windy day. This was the same day Nicklaus shot himself out of contention with a 77.

Watson's putting touch left him through the final three rounds, but rarely has he played better from tee to green. He shot a 71 on Friday, and a 74 on Saturday when the only winner was the stark, scruffy golf course at old Troon.

Watson, who is sometimes erratic off the tee, had one of the finest driving days of his career Sunday. He missed only three fairways, the sixth, ninth and 15th, and was never far enough off line to be in trouble.

In the years to come, when the failures of Price and Clampett are no longer so fresh in the mind, this will be remembered as the tournament Watson won with his eagle at 11, the par-5 railroad hole where Nicklaus once took a 10. The hole is not as narrow as it once was, but it is lined with whin bushes and rough and is an intimidating sight from the tee.

Watson, by his own measurements, hit a 278-yard drive and a 203-yard 3-iron that bounced on the green and stopped, three feet from the pin. He finished his round with one bogey and six pars, but the eagle enabled him to survive even though he walked off the 18th green thinking he would not be the champion.

Watson celebrated his victory with a few drinks and dinner Sunday night at a hotel that overlooks the back nine holes of the old course and as he left, he said, "I've never been handed a championship before."

The work ethic runs strong in Tom Watson, but not all golf tournaments are won with improbable chip shots at 17.

Brett's Search
for the Sweet Spot

Ted Williams, regarded by many authorities as baseball's greatest hitter, claims that hitting a round ball traveling 90 miles an hour or more with a round bat is the single most difficult accomplishment in sports.

Perhaps he is right, but since the start of the season George Brett has been swinging the bat in a manner that makes hitting look about as difficult as breathing.

Brett is baseball's hottest hitter, leading the American League with a .466 average, and he is swinging with such concentration and purity of timing that watching him imparts a feeling of sensual enjoyment, assuming, of course, that you are not 60 feet, 6 inches away with only a leather glove for protection.

The experience is not unlike that of watching Mikhail Baryshnikov leap across a stage and hang weightlessly in space or following Jack Nicklaus in the 1965 Masters when he shot a 271, leading Bobby Jones to observe, "He plays a game with which I am not familiar."

These are splendid occasions when the mind and body become one and in some mysterious manner produce performances of extraordinary dimensions. No one has yet put together a comprehensive explanation of how an athlete reaches this elevated state where, for a time, he performs at the ultimate level of his ability, but there are two experiences that are common to all athletes who have gone through these periods. They have total concentration, along with the sensation that everything happening around them has slowed down and they are aware of what is happening each millisecond.

"It's just like when the ball leaves the pitcher's hand, I see it so great," Brett said. "It's almost like it's in slow motion. I'm not usually a good spring hitter, and almost every day I come to the park I wonder when it's going to end. But it keeps on happening. I can't remember the last time I didn't hit the ball semi-hard.

"To hit like this, you almost have to be in a trance. All of your fundamentals have to be right. I don't even think about it when I'm on the field. All I see is the ball coming to me. I'm not aware of anything else. I'm not aware of whether it's cold or hot or raining."

Last Sunday at Royals Stadium, Brett broke his favorite bat, but his concentration was so extraordinary even that mishap did not disturb him.

"I loved that bat," Brett said. "I had worked the pine tar on it, and it was caking in the right places. It was just perfect. After I broke the bat I didn't feel comfortable, but when I went up to hit I forgot all about it. At other times it would have bothered me."

"When you're going bad, you feel like you're swinging at marbles, but right now the ball is big and it looks like it's coming in slow motion."

John Jerome has noted this phenomenon in his book, *The Sweet Spot in Time*. The title of the book has to do with that magic moment all of us have experienced when, on rare occasions, we are conscious of having hit the perfect golf or tennis shot. Jerome believes that athletes and musicians, especially the great ones, have the ability to perceive things and react within a minuscule time frame.

"Within that span of microseconds lies room that I never believe existed," Jerome writes, "room wherein the good performer can place the note, the beat—or the movement—with delicate control.

Jerome recalls throwing rocks as a youngster and the rare occasions when he threw the rock precisely where he wanted it to go.

"It was a moment when the amount of time between letting fly the rock and seeing it arrive at the bottle seemed to stretch out forever," Jerome writes.

The best hitters have the ability to wait until the last possible instant to commit themselves. A 90-mile-an-hour fastball reaches the plate in 0.4 second. The batter has 0.1 second to determine what kind of a pitch it is and where it is going and 0.15 second to decide whether to swing. Thereafter he loses sight of the ball and is swinging at where he thinks it will be. The sooner he commits himself, the more likely he is to make a mistake. Thus Brett's feeling that he is seeing the ball in slow motion helps to explain why he is hitting so well.

Unfortunately, these periods of phenomenal performance go as suddenly as they come, leaving behind no clues as to how they can be recaptured.

Cotton Works the Crowd

As game time approaches, most basketball coaches take on a stricken look suggesting the possibility that they may be suffering simultaneously from migraine headaches and bleeding ulcers. Not Cotton Fitzsimmons.

Before the start of Kings' game with Atlanta Wednesday night Cotton gave the appearance of a man who had just announced his candidacy for political office. While the Kingsmen played and the Glitter Girls glittered, he talked with the officials, kidded with the opposition and worked the press table. He smiled when Channel 9 wired him for sound. If someone had held a baby close enough, he would have kissed it.

"There was a time when I couldn't do that before a game," Fitzsimmons would say later, "but there are more important things in life than a basketball game. I used to put on a game face, but you know what? That didn't help."

When the game begins, Fitzsimmons assumes a kneeling position in front of the press area just to the midcourt side of the Kings' bench. Fitzsimmons explains that his unorthodox coaching position is not an act. His principal reason is to get a better view, but he has also found that the officials deal less harshly with a man in a supplicant position.

"I cannot sit on the bench very long, but if you jump up you start getting more technicals," Fitzsimmons explains. "If you're down low, you don't seem to bother the officials as much." From his kneeling position, Fitzsimmons exhorts his players, shouts instructions, critiques the work of the officials and agonizes when the defense breaks down or one of his players is guilty of a careless turnover. He is rarely silent for more than a few seconds at a time.

In the early stages of the game with Atlanta he urged Phil Ford to move the ball, shouted for Otis Birdsong to slow down Armond Hill and scolded Bill Robinzine for failing to get a rebound.

"You know what you're supposed to do, Bill," Fitzsimmons called. "Get on the boards."

Hubie Brown, the Atlanta coach, was assessed a technical foul early in the game by Dick Bavetta, a balding man with something of a Don Knotts appearance. Later the Kings were whistled for two three-second violations and Fitzsimmons waited until Bavetta came within range.

"Hey, Dick!" Fitzsimmons called. "I'm gonna take the next 'T' (technical foul) if I can get two three-second violations in a row."

When Sam Lacey began to berate Jack Niles, a rookie official, Fitzsimmons shouted, "Sam! Win the game. I'll handle him."

In the third quarter Fitzsimmons urged the defense to move the ball, grumbled because none of the three officials saw a traveling violation and warned his players to "execute and get your shot."

Atlanta was unable to come closer than 12 points in the final quarter, but even with 24 seconds left Fitzsimmons was shouting.

After the game, Fitzsimmons was talking with reporters when he saw Skip Caray, an old friend who broadcasts the Atlanta games and who is the son of broadcaster Harry Caray.

"Isn't Harry Caray a great announcer," Fitzsimmons said in a loud voice. "The offsprings don't do as well."

Although defeat wounds Fitzsimmons, he is a fast healer and earlier in the season he needled his players because their dressing room was so somber the night following a difficult defeat.

There are those who say that Fitzsimmons is as much a salesman as he is a coach. Fitzsimmons makes the same point, but in a different manner, saying that his greatest improvement as a coach has been in dealing with people.

"My basic principles are the same as they've always been," Fitzsimmons said. "I believe you win with defense, rebounding and discipline. But you have to have players to win. I like to think that I can deal with people better than when I was coaching in junior college or at Kansas State. At each level you give more leeway to people.

"I have great respect for Hubie Brown. He's a fine coach. Hubie is a pusher and a driver. I used to be the same way, but I began to loosen up more at Kansas State and I've continued that way in the pros.

"When I coached at Moberly, we won 80 percent of our games and I thought I could walk on water. I treaded water at Kansas State and in the pros I drowned. I'm not on an ego trip. It takes people to win. I haven't been on an ego trip for a long time."

Kansas City
Welcomes the GOP

Those of us in the sports writing business have a reputation for being a little free with our metaphors. For example, we might be inclined to mix sports jargon with politics by saying that the Republicans are ready to kick off their convention tomorrow at Kemper Arena.

Purists will frown at such cuteness and insist that the Republicans are simply opening their convention. Those who see themselves as realists will argue that neither description is acceptable because what the Republicans are actually doing in the aftermath of Watergate is turning suicide into a spectator event.

Whatever your preference in descriptions, the gathering of the Grand Old Party has brought many first-time visitors to Kansas City and those of us in the sports department would like to do our part to acquaint them with local history, geography and customs.

Despite the efforts of the city fathers, the Chamber of Commerce and a New York advertising firm, there are certain misconceptions about Kansas City that have an enduring quality.

By now our visitors undoubtedly are aware that regardless of what Republic Studios may have led them to believe, Kansas City is not flat and barren. I suspect that Republic was responsible for a lot of kids getting Fs in geography. I lost my faith in Republic at an early age when I watched Randolph Scott or some leathery hero ride into Dodge City and there across the horizon was a magnificent mountain range.

As for the cattle drives from western Kansas, well, they aren't much fun to watch because the trucks go by rather fast.

So much for misconceptions. Perhaps the most important thing for a newcomer to realize is that Kansas City is not located in Kansas even though after landing at the airport the flight attendant may have said, "Have a nice day in Kansas or wherever your final destination may be."

Actually, there are two Kansas Cities, one on each side of the state line. Clearly a potential for confusion exists, but we have a well thought-out method for identifying the two. The Kansas City that is located in Kansas—where you naturally would assume Kansas City to be—is always identified by its full name, Kansas City, Kansas. In abbreviated form it is known as K.C.K. The Kansas City that is located in Missouri and is responsible for all of the confusion is merely called Kansas City.

Once the visitor has grasped this ingenious method of identifying the two Kansas Cities he or she will have no trouble understanding that when trying to drive downtown from the airport he should not necessarily follow signs that have the word "Kansas City" on them, unless he wants to go the long way around. The shortest route to town is on an exit marked "Broadway."

Kansas City is named after the Kansa Indians who inhabited the area until they made a tactical error and signed a treaty of peace and friendship with the federal government. The Kansa Indians kept signing treaties and losing more land until eventually they wound up on a small reservation near Arkansas City, Kan. This experience would tend to support the view of conservatives who claim that the less you have to do with the federal government the better off you are.

Most cities engage in the practice of citing facts and figures and extolling certain virtues to bolster the municipal ego. Kansas City is no exception. In our municipal advertising we refer to this as one of the few livable cities left. Hopefully the Republicans will find this claim to be reasonably true, assuming that nothing happens to the air conditioning in Kemper Arena.

In support of our progressiveness we often point out that Kansas City is the largest market in the world for winter red wheat, that we rank first in the production of envelopes and greeting cards and that we are second only to Detroit in the manufacture of automobiles. We also claim to have more fountains than any city except Rome.

In regard to the latter point, I have read this statement so many times that I have come to accept it as fact, although I sometimes wonder what agency is responsible for making world-wide tabulations of fountains. For example, who do you go to in Newark to get an up-to-the-minute count on fountains? Besides, it seems only fair that a big fountain should be worth say five points while a cherub with water squirting from his mouth should be worth only one.

I have a feeling that Kansas City may also rank right up with the leaders in Dutch Elm disease, sod web worms, slush and other categories in which the Chamber of Commerce does not choose to keep score.

Sports activity in Kansas City is abundant. The Royals and the Chiefs play at the Harry S Truman Sports Complex, the nation's only dual-stadium facility. The Kings of the National Basketball Association play at Kemper Arena. The city's National Hockey League team also played there before moving on to Denver. Before departing, the Scouts set a league record for unpaid bills and most games without a victory.

Our visitors this week may find that Kansas Citians are a little pushy when it comes to talking about the Royals, but your indulgence is asked because it is not every day that Kansas City is in first place on Aug. 15. In fact, Kansas City has yet to win a league or a division championship since entering the American League in 1955.

To fully explain the extent of our baseball misfortunes, Kansas City did not finish higher than sixth the first 13 years it was in the American League. In addition, Charles O. Finley selected Kansas City as the site of his first major league baseball venture. When Charles O. moved to the shores of the Pacific, one city councilman said he didn't mind, except that he wished Charlie had kept going until his hat floated.

The late Casey Stengel is among the most famous of the city's sports personalities and was first known as K.C. Stengel before the name evolved into Casey. Not long before his death Casey was asked to name the best manager he had ever seen. "I was the best manager I ever saw," Casey said, "and I tell people that to shut them up quickly and because I believe it." And then Casey probably winked.

If Casey were still with us he would make a great keynote speaker for the Republicans. He could unite the party because it is difficult to take issue with someone when you're not quite sure what he is saying.

Wrestling Goes Gorgeous

They are the sort of names that P.T. Barnum would have loved: Brutus Beefcake, Kamala the Ugandan Giant, the Missing Link, Rowdy Roddy Piper, Nikolai Volkoff, the Iron Sheik, Andre the Giant, Big John Studd and the Junk Yard Dog.

Among other things, professional wrestling is the theater of the absurd, and some of the above-named gladiators have routines, costumes and hairdos as outlandish as their names.

They follow an earlier generation that gave us the likes of Abdullah the Butcher, Man Mountain Dean, Wild Red Berry, Strangler Lewis, the French Angel, Gorilla Monsoon, the Mongolian Stomper, Ivan Rasputin, Lucky Simunovich, Haystack Calhoun, the Super Swedish Angel and Chief Jay Strongbow.

Not only does this sport abound in colorful names and characters, but the ever resourceful heroes and villains have invented such terrifying holds as the abdominal stretch, the spinning toehold, the atomic drop, the cobra twist, the Sicilian Sledge, the tomahawk chop, the Indian death lock, the shillelagh swing, the Russian hammer and the Irish whip.

There have been cage matches, lights-out matches, mud matches, molasses matches and matches conducted under Texas death rules. In 1938, Joe Reno and Roughhouse Ross wrestled in 250 gallons of vanilla, chocolate and strawberry ice cream.

History fails to record whether the ring posts were topped with whipped cream and maraschino cherries.

Masked marvels go back at least to the early 1900s and have had such captivating names as Dr. Death, the Red Phantom, The ? and the Masked Terror.

And then there was the infamous Count Dracula who suddenly would produce a handkerchief and a bottle labeled "chloroform" and anesthetize his opponent while fans screamed at the referee, who for some strange reason could neither see nor smell what was happening.

Out of economic necessity professional wrestling always has resorted to a show-biz approach to hype the gate, but these days the theatrical aspects of the sport are in the ascendancy because of Vince McMahon, who runs the World Wrestling Foundation.

Despite McMahon's success, the man who exerted the strongest influence on professional wrestling as we see it today was a Nebraskan named George Wagner. As his fame spread, Wagner had his name legally changed to Gorgeous George.

"I do not think I am gorgeous," George would say, "but what's my opinion against millions of others?"

The Gorgeous George act evolved over time, but once it was perfected, it was the most-publicized and profitable routine pro wresting ever had seen. Wagner earned an estimated $2 million in a pre-inflation era, but drink destroyed his health and his marriages. He squandered his money, and when he died at the age of 48, friends had to pay for his funeral.

Wagner began his pro career as a preliminary wrestler, and not an especially good one. He had short hair and was the clean part of the act. The pay was small, and he was smart enough to recognize that he needed a gimmick. Supposedly the genesis for his new personality can be traced to a night in Eugene, Ore., when George took special care folding a robe his wife had made for him. He discovered that his deliberate actions incensed the fans.

I first saw George when I was working at *The Tulsa World*. Monday night was wrestling night in Tulsa. That was usually my night off, and wrestling was a powerful attraction because the tickets were free and I was broke.

In those days George was known as Gorgeous George Wagner. He had let his hair grow and showed up with a valet who first sprayed the ring with a perfumed disinfectant and then held up a silverplated tray with a mirror on it so George could check his appearance. When the referee checked the wrestlers for greasy substances, George would protest and his valet would spray the referee's hands.

Oh how the folks in Tulsa hated Gorgeous George Wagner. Once the match began he inflamed them further with gouging, choking and all the other tricks of the artful villain.

As George refined the act, he bleached his hair, acquired a collection of fur-trimmed robes and became known as "The Human Orchid, the toast of the coast." When George made his entrance, the arena was darkened and a spotlight followed him while "Pomp and Circum-stance" was played over the loudspeaker. Appropriately, the full de-velopment of the Gorgeous George act took place in Los Angeles. George was a villain everywhere but in Hollywood, where show-busi-ness people loved his act.

McMahon is given credit for originating the idea of combining wrestling and show-business personalities, but George wrestled in a celebrity circus for charity with Bob Hope as his valet and Burt Lan-caster as his opponent. Songs were written about George, and he ap-peared in a movie.

George even carried his act into restaurants, where he sometimes insisted that the patrons be sprayed. He was driven in a purple Cadil-lac, and his hair was kept in place by gold-plated "Georgie Pins."

George purchased a turkey farm and had one robe made with thou-sands of lavender turkey feathers.

In his book, "Whatever Happened to Gorgeous George," Joe Jares recounts an incident in Texas when George was giving free orchids to the ladies. George was to award one special orchid, and he called for an elderly woman to come to the ring. As she approached, George threw down the orchid, crushed it under his foot and sneered at the old woman. The crowd all but rioted.

Gorgeous George was a man who understood the art of villainy.

George developed a liver ailment in 1962 and had to quit wrestling. Doctors warned him to quit drinking, but he ignored them. On Christ-mas Eve in 1963 he had a heart attack and died.

His friends saw to it that he wore a silk robe, his coffin was covered with orchids and there were no hairs out of place.

Out Damned Tack

The time is January 1981. The scene is the New York Baseball Writers Dinner. Rick Honeycutt, Seattle pitcher, appears on stage in the garb of Lady Macbeth. The audience grows quiet as he begins the following soliloquy:

"Out, damned tack! Out I say. One, two: why then is time to do't. Hell is murky. Fie, my lord, fie. What! Will these hands ne're be clean? All the perfums of Arabia will not sweeten this little hand."

While the attention of the baseball world was largely focused on the three remaining division races, Rick Honeycutt was gaining a bit of baseball immortality Tuesday night in Royals Stadium. Not that he wanted it, you understand. It's just that it kind of stuck to him.

Honeycutt, a 26-year-old left-hander, was caught cheating. He had securely taped a tack and a piece of sandpaper to the index finger of his glove hand and was cutting the ball to make it perform strange acrobatics in flight.

The fact that Honeycutt was cheating was not unusual. Many pitchers cheat. The astonishing thing is that he was caught.

Bob Lemon, the Yankee scout who has spent 43 years in baseball, most as a pitcher and manager, never could recall anyone being apprehended with the evidence intact. Neither could Royals' Manager Jim Frey nor umpire Bill Kunkel, the investigator who cracked the case.

"That's got to be a little embarrassing getting caught that way," Lemon said.

"It was really funny," said Royals' pitching Coach Billy Connors. "He could see Kunkel coming. He was trying to get the thing off his finger, and it wouldn't come loose."

Honeycutt's inability to dispose of the evidence has cost him a 10-day suspension, which was announced by American League President Lee MacPhail.

"It's cheating, it's wrong and it should be eliminated," MacPhail said.

How prevalent is cheating in baseball? Well, at times almost everyone seems to be doing it.

Baltimore's Steve Stone makes an interesting comment on this point in the current issue of *Inside Sports*. Stone relates the following experience he had with Gaylord Perry, the master of the spitter:

"It was my first year there (with the Giants). Gaylord said, 'If you want to be a successful major league pitcher, I'll ensure that you are. I'll teach you my pitch for $3,000.' I said 'Gaylord, I'm only making $8,000.' And he never did teach me."

Whitey Ford, the former New York Yankee pitching star, confessed that he wore a wedding band with a rasp on it and cut the ball on occasion when a big out was needed. Ford said he struck out Willie Mays in an All-Star game with a cut ball to win a bet from Horace Stoneham, then president of the Giants.

MacPhail, general manager of the Orioles earlier in his career, recalled an incident involving Jim Bunning, then pitching for Detroit.

"Bunning pitched against us one day and we collected 17 balls that had been sliced," MacPhail said. "We raised hell with the league office, and the next time Bunning pitched against us they sent a special observer. As I recall, Bunning beat us with either a no-hitter or a 1-hitter. We found out later that Dick Brown, their catcher, had been cutting the ball on his belt buckle."

Kunkel says umpires have an almost impossible job in trying to stop cheaters.

"Everyone complains that we're not doing anything," he said. "We're the last ones in the world who would let anyone get away with anything illegal. But if someone is throwing a spitball the only way I can get the evidence is to catch it in flight. The ball is going 90 miles an hour and my reflexes aren't that good.

"We find balls that have been cut and scuffed, but we can't find what's doing it. This is the first time I've ever caught a pitcher with the evidence on him. I told him, 'Son, get out of here,' and he took right off."

Considering the embarrassment Honeycutt has suffered, perhaps he will want to invest in the Gaylord Perry course of applied cheating.

Thanksgiving, 1984

Some things to be thankful for when we sit down to celebrate Thanksgiving with generous helpings of turkey, dressing, mashed potatoes, gravy, vegetables, rolls, cranberry sauce and three kinds of pie followed by coffee and bicarbonate of soda:

Waking up on Thanksgiving morning and spending a few quiet moments anticipating a joyous day with your family and friends.

The sight of a child's face at the kitchen door reflecting wonderment at all of the activity and the food.

Getting the first taste of dressing when the turkey comes out of the oven on the pretext you want to see if it needs more salt.

Arrowhead Stadium on a sunny day when the teams are warming up and the fans are just starting to come in.

A Thanksgiving table set with "the good" china.

The thrust of Don Shula's chin.

Going to the grocery store on Thanksgiving morning for a pint of whipping cream and discovering there is exactly one left in the dairy case.

Memories of skinny Bret Sabergagen pitching a three-hit shutout against the California Angels in a game the Royals had to win.

The fact that Americans can criticize their country even though it provides more freedom and a higher standard of living than any other society in the history of the world.

Sparky Anderson's enthusiasm.

Biting into a hot roll dripping with honey and getting the honey on your fingers and chin.

The ability to enjoy Thanksgiving almost as much as children do.

The knowledge that even your doctor, your dietician or the founder of Weight Watchers wouldn't have the heart to fuss at you for eating too much on Thanksgiving.

The word that Ewing Kauffman's vascular surgery went well.

The memories of other Thanksgivings.

A flag snapping and popping in a brisk wind.

The first mouthful of mashed potatoes and gravy.

Watching a 10-year-old eating a turkey drumstick.

Settling back in a comfortable chair in front of the fireplace to watch a TV football game that is being played in a snowstorm.

Those immortal words, "How about another helping?"

Memories of Bill Johnson winning the Olympic downhill skiing while the Austrians, who had belittled him, sulked and complained about the course.

The genius who developed the broad-breasted turkey.

Laughter at the dinner table.

Opening one of your favorite vintages of wine and discovering it is just as good as you remembered it.

A call from a family member who couldn't get home for Thanksgiving.

Walking in the cold air after dinner is over and the dishes are done.

Watching George Brett follow the ball all the way into the catcher's mitt just as Ted Williams used to do.

The people who collect our trash, deliver the mail, throw the paper, repair our cars and never get any recognition for the work they do.

A cook who decides there should be a little more brandy in the brandy sauce.

Hearing a child say, "No thank you, I don't want any more pie."

The Plaza lights.

The opportunity to ask someone to dinner who is a long way from home and would have spent the day alone.

The understanding that the real joy of Thanksgiving is to be found in the faces of children, the embrace of a family member and the return of everyone who celebrated this holiday a year ago.

Hurrah
for the Kings

When you stop to think about it, the whole idea was sort of crazy. But for a while the Kings had us believing a team held together by guts, Ace Bandages and a coach slick enough to work the shell game on a Las Vegas pit boss could reach the NBA finals.

The Kings were short of players and they were forced out of their normal fast-break game, but they were so convincing in defeating Portland and Phoenix in the playoffs that they had an entire city wondering if something funny might be going on in the stockyards district.

Sure, we knew better, but like a child on Christmas Eve we almost were afraid not to believe. If the Mets could win the 1969 World Series and if the U.S. could win the Olympic Hockey championship, then why couldn't the Kings go limping into the NBA title round?

When the Houston Rockets took a 3-1 lead in their Western Conference title series with the Kings, most of us pretended we knew all the time the Kings didn't really have a chance. But then for a while Wednesday night, darn if they didn't have us believing again.

Phil Ford was back running the fast break and darting through the Rockets for layups. The Kings opened an early 11-point lead and after three quarters they led 77-73. The crowd was cheering and Cotton Fitzsimmons was exhorting his team to greater effort.

A few minutes later the Rockets quieted the crowd by going ahead, and as the quarter wore on the Rockets took control of the game. Slowly the crowd realized the Kings were running out of time and miracles.

The Kings called a final timeout with the Rockets leading 94-86 and 16 seconds remaining. When the horn blew for play to resume, Sam Lacey looked at the scoreboard and winced. The end had come.

The reason for the Kings' loss is simple to explain. In none of the five games were they able to score more than 89 points. They needed to run a fast break to have a chance against Houston, but they did not have enough bench strength, and Ford was not in condition to run for an entire game after being out of the line-up two months because of an eye injury.

The Kings gave a remarkable performance to survive as long as they did in the playoffs, and Fitzsimmons turned in the coaching job of his life. Though the Kings were disappointed about losing, their dressing room was not somber.

"We needed some extra bodies coming off the bench," Lacey said. "Everybody was physically beat. The guys played so hard against Phoenix, everyone was getting worn down.

"Next year we can do better if we just keep adding some players. I think the fans really appreciated the way we played. I know we'll be better next year. We're just a couple of players away."

Fitzsimmons had the Kings come out in the fast break hoping to improve his club's scoring. For the first half the strategy worked.

"We just didn't have enough people to sustain it," Fitzsimmons said. "You've got to knock some shots in, too, and we didn't do it. But I'm prouder of this club than any club I've ever had. I know we built something with this city. I think it is going to carry over next year."

There was nothing pretty about the game, which Houston won 97-88. Instead it resembled a street fight.

"Dog determination is what won it," commented the Rockets' Billy Paultz. "That and a few rebounds at the end. We didn't have one of our better games, but we were just determined not to let this one get away.

"I don't think they could play their normal game. They're not in shape yet. We made some adjustments on Ford after the first half, but let's face it, the guy had to wear out sooner or later. We're lucky they weren't 100 percent. They had to play our style and we're bigger and able to outrebound them."

The Kings' success in the playoffs clearly has created a new attitude toward pro basketball in Kansas City, and it was evident as Lacey walked through a cluster of fans and left the arena to the chant of "Lacey, Lacey, Lacey."

How to
Make a
Bookie Tremble

Law enforcement officers look on bookies with the same sort of affection that Kansas wheat farmers have for grasshoppers.

The FBI can tap their phones, the Internal Revenue Service can ensnare them in tax laws, the local police can harass them, but somehow there is always a bookie no more than a phone call away.

In the bookie's view he is a necessary part of American life, a small businessman catering to the greed and risk-taking impulses that are at the heart of the capitalistic system.

To the police he is a lawbreaker, period. Never mind the line in the parlay cards that reads "For information only."

Although the police may have despaired of stamping out the bookie, there is reason to believe that help is on the way. By the end of football season, the bookie will have gone the way of the dodo bird, the passenger pigeon and pithecanthropus erectus.

What's that you say? Who can dare to do what J. Edgar Hoover failed to do? The answer is simple. Destruction is coming from within. Skeptics will demand some sort of authority for this statement, but actually there is no reason to fool around with authorities and the like. The reason for the demise of the bookie is obvious to anyone who has picked up certain football publications and read the ads therein.

Yes sir, football fans, retirement on the French Riviera is no more than just a few Saturdays away.

As a first step, it is necessary to get the Las Vegas line. An organization in Detroit advertises that it will provide the line for $75 a month or $175 for the season. It is available on Sunday night and twice daily Monday through Friday.

The $75 service is the most prudent since the bookies will be out of money long before the season is over.

The next steps are relatively simple. All you do is select the advisory service of your choice, call your neighborhood bookie and wait for the money to come in.

Selecting an advisory service might seem to be a bit complicated, but it isn't in view of the fact that all of them are winners.

In his ad, Mike Warren, who professes to be America's leading racing and sports handicapper, offers to turn $200 into $13,000 in 16 weeks.

"Winning at football is a piece of cake," according to Warren. "I'll show you how to knock down the Las Vegas spread week after week and multiply your money 50 times over."

The cost for the season is $125, which seems a reasonable fee to pay for whipping inflation.

Or maybe you'd rather do business with a service called The Prophet. According to its ad, The Prophet has maintained a 70 percent winning percentage against the spread over the last five years.

"We don't promise success...we guarantee it," the ad states. The cost for the full service is $175.

The Las Vegas Sports Service offers to let you win first and pay later. It is owned and operated by H.R. Jones who states that he has "never had a losing football season in 15 years vs. the point spread."

And then there is Danny Sheridan whose ad states that he is the only football prognosticator "honest and accurate enough to appear on national television every year."

According to Danny, he has a winning percentage of 70 against the spread from 1964 through 1978 and was 76 percent against the spread last year for all of his college and pro picks

The price for Danny's overall service is $600.

Buckeye Sports confesses it was only 66 percent against the Las Vegas line last year and was not happy so it has hired Lee Stryker, calling him "the nation's best football handicapper."

The foregoing clearly establishes that the bookie has become an endangered species. Of course, there is reason to wonder why the folks who run the advisory services are not already in retirement on the French Riviera.

Who knows, maybe they are allergic to French cooking.

Ali Can't Fight
Any More

Before the bell rang for the first round, he was Muhammad Ali, the greatest show on earth. He snarled at Larry Holmes. He shouted. He held up four fingers, apparently signifying the round in which the fight would end. He made lunges at Holmes only to be restrained by his handlers.

The capacity crowd of 5,000 that gathered in Bartle Hall for the closed-circuit telecast loved it.

"Ali, Ali, Ali."

The chant began in Las Vegas and was picked up in Kansas City and probably every smoky arena where the fight was being shown.

Then the bell rang, and to the amazement of everyone Ali went through most of the first round without throwing a punch. Holmes followed him around the ring, jabbing tentatively and trying to figure out what was happening.

Ah, but the crowd knew. Ali, that clever, old rascal, had devised a new version of the rope-a-dope. What they were seeing was a box-scam. Ali was psyching out Holmes. Perhaps in time he would unleash a variation of the old cosmic punch that Lou Nova used against Joe Louis. Another round or two and Ali would let us in on his gambit.

The second round passed and the suspense grew. Ali still was throwing no punches. He looked like a man who had converted to passive resistance. The tempo picked up a little in the third round and the crowd sensed that at last Ali was ready to make his move, but then the fourth round came and went and nothing happened. Ali threw a few punches, but they were weak and clumsy.

Suddenly the crowd realized something was wrong. No fighter, whatever his tactics, intentionally throws away four rounds. There was going to be no box-scam. Ali was like a swaying tightrope walker who was actually falling. Something had gone wrong with the act.

The fifth and sixth rounds came and went and still Ali was not punching. Now Holmes was emboldened. He began to jar Ali in the seventh. In the eighth, ninth and 10th, he gave him the worst beating of his career.

In the 10th round, Ali was a man moving in slow motion. He could not get his arms up to ward off Holmes' blows. At times he tried to twist away from punches like a terrified schoolboy turning from a bully's blow. Only pride kept him going. The announcement that Ali would not come out for the 11th round brought expressions of relief.

Ali collected $8 million for his appearance, but even so it was an embarrassing end to a great career. When Joe Louis made his ill-advised comeback at the age of 37 and was stopped by Rocky Marciano, he at least was able to put up a fight. Ali was helpless.

At times he looked as if he wanted to throw a punch, but there was no coordination of mind and body. He was like a golfer who no longer can bring the putter back, or a hitter who is unable to get around on the fastball.

In truth, Ali has been through for four years. He was never the same fighter after his brutal bout with Joe Frazier in 1975, the so-called Thrilla in Manila. The deterioration in Ali's reflexes was obvious when he defended his title against Ken Norton in 1976. His friends urged him to quit after that bout and confirmation of their judgment came in February 1978, when Ali was defeated by Leon Spinks. Ali regained the title in September of that year, but only because Spinks did not prepare for the fight and was so inexperienced.

Boxing is a sport that ages men prematurely. Jack Dempsey was only 32 when he ended his active ring career. Aside from exhibitions, he had only two fights through the last four years of his career, both resulting in losses to Gene Tunney.

Tunney was 31 when he retired. Jack Sharkey was 34, Max Baer 32, Marciano 32, Frazier 32. Louis was 34 when he retired the first time. Jack Johnson, perhaps the greatest heavyweight champion of all time, was 37 when he was knocked out by Jess Willard and lost his title.

With all boxers, the time comes when the mind rebels against absorbing more pain and punishment. And so it was Thursday night with Muhammad Ali.

Ja, Wasser Verboten in München

MUNICH—If the Olympics have stimulated your interest in visiting München by all means come ahead. The climate is delightful, the buildings look as if they have been done in gingerbread and people go out on the street at night without getting mugged. But if you decide to visit Munich there are two things you should do. First, bring marks—lots of marks. Second, bring a canteen.

Your travel agent probably will poo-poo this latter suggestion, but ignore him. He will argue that Munich is located in Bavaria, not the Sahara Desert. He is right. The only sand I've seen around here is in the long jump pits. But bring a canteen anyway.

Munich has an unusual water problem. It is similar to the one that developed when Walter O'Malley threw open the doors of Dodger Stadium and the public discovered there were only four water fountains in the joint, one for every 14,000 customers. Walter was criticized severely for his craftiness, but by German standards Dodger Stadium is a veritable Niagara Falls.

Not only is the Olympic Stadium (capacity 80,000) without a drinking fountain, but there may be none in all of Bavaria.

At the bars in the Olympic press center beer, wine and booze are available at a price, but a request for "Wasser" brings a puzzled look unless you ask for "Scotch mit Wasser." The idea that anyone would drink unflavored water seems incredible to a German.

If you ask for "Wasser" in the press center dining hall the attendant calls for a supervisor. They discuss the matter in animated German. Soon a bus boy will emerge triumphantly with a bottle of sparkling water. Burping your way through breakfast may be great when you are 6 months old but the only thing it does for a grown man is to attract a lot of dirty looks.

The other night several of us visited Schwarzwalders, a fine old German restaurant with dark walls and big paintings. One member of the group asked for water. The maitre d' looked pained. We waited. The maitre d' looked pained again. It was the sort of expression you associated with someone having ordered a cheeseburger and a side of fries at Maxims.

Finally he left and returned with a small pitcher and a small glass. Not two glasses, not three glasses, but one glass. If any of us were going to get sloshed at Schwarzwalders it obviously was not going to be on water.

I am beginning to suspect that if anyone in Munich is caught driving home at night without the smell of beer or wine on his breath he runs the risk of being stopped and subjected to a test to determine if there is an excessive amount of water in his bloodstream.

Even ABC, which likes to brag about it's ratings and the efficiency of its Olympic coverage, has been unable to whip the water problem. ABC made a request for a water cooler at its TV center. The Germans gave ABC a lot of "ja, jas" and promptly delivered the cooler. ABC is still waiting for the water.

In the buildings where the press is housed a steward is provided for every two floors. He makes the beds, brings towels and can produce a corkscrew for opening wine bottles. However, no cups or glasses are furnished, apparently in the fear that someone will sneak off to the lavatory and draw a liter of water.

Francie Hellmich, a charming German girl who works in the newsstand at the press center and who has relatives in Pratt, Kan., says the Germans are suspicious of anyone who drinks water.

"When you go into some place and ask for water they are afraid you will leave without buying anything," Francie explains. "When I visited the United States I was amazed. Everywhere I look there are water fountains. I ask myself, 'What do they think I am, a camel or something?' "

The lack of drinking water is best explained by the fact that there are 1,000 breweries in Bavaria. Munich, which is approximately the size of Kansas City, has seven major breweries. Their product is marketed under the names of Augustinebrau, Hackerbrau, Hofbrau, Lowenbrau, Paulanerbrau, Pschorrbrau and Spatenbrau.

If a city is going to support seven major breweries it obviously can't afford to let the populace get addicted to water, ja?

Golf?
There's Nothing to It

The average golfer, so we are told, is an elite member of society in terms of educational background, occupation, personal income, disposable income and all of the other things so prized by merchants who are selling yachts, Rolls-Royces, 20-year-old scotch and Caribbean cruises.

Although they are an elitist group, golfers have a surprisingly high degree of larceny in their makeup. Usually it manifests itself in match-making on the first tee, but it also is directed toward the game itself.

Golfers, it seems, are unusually susceptible to gimmicks that promise to lower scores, lengthen drives and improve their game without the drudgery of taking lessons and spending hours on the practice tee.

It is unlikely a pianist would buy a Vladmir Horowitz metronome on the assumption it would enable him to play like the master in three weeks. There are no typewriters that promise the writer a shortcut to riches or a Pulitzer Prize. But golfers, well, they just can't seem to resist a visor, a glove or a titanium putter that offers hope of helping in their struggles against one of mankind's most frustrating games.

The other day a flyer came to my desk from some folks in Chicago who want to assist me with my golf game. For a nominal investment, they propose to lengthen my drives by 20 yards and improve my score by 5 strokes. All I have to do is buy either the 2-ounce or 6-ounce bottle of their product, rub it on a few golf balls and hurry to the course to enjoy the results.

According to the manufacturer, the product makes golf balls "superclean and friction-reducing to achieve these potent results for less than a dime a golf ball."

And what if this product turns me into the new Tom Watson? Well, don't look for me on the tour because Frank Thomas, technical director of the United States Golf Association, says this product and others like it have been disapproved by the USGA.

Thomas said the USGA did not test the product so he is not prepared to comment on its efficacy, but in the eyes of the USGA applying any type of a "foreign substance" to a golf ball is a no-no.

"Any foreign material or product that changes the playing characteristics is prohibited," Thomas said from USGA headquarters in Far Hills, N.J.

Approximately 60 devices or products designed to improve the lot of golfers are submitted to the USGA every year, and virtually all are disapproved. According to Thomas, most devices have to do with putting, a part of the game that bedevils everyone from Sam Snead to the hacker.

One of the oddest devices submitted to Thomas was a gyroscope putter. The contraption consisted of batteries, a motor, a rotor and a gyroscope. All the golfer had to do was line up his putt, push a button to activate the batteries and his gyroscope did the rest.

If the gyroscope putter seems a bit far out, you might prefer a U-shape putter that was submitted to Thomas.

The U-shape frame is placed over the ball. A pendulum with a putter head attached to it hangs down from the top of the frame. The golfer lines up his putt, holds the frame with one hand, pulls the pendulum back and releases it with the other.

"I sometimes ask people who send these things in what they are trying to do," Thomas said. "Usually they tell us that if the game of golf were easier then more people would play and they are only trying to make the game more attractive. That bothers me because it goes against the psychology of the game. Golf is supposed to be difficult. If we wanted to make putting easier, all we'd have to do is enlarge the size of the hole."

Oh, well, if the USGA won't let me use a gyroscope putter or apply foreign substances to the ball, other shortcuts to success are available. For details, all you have to do is read your favorite golf magazine.

For example, the "secret of perfect putting, can be obtained from Gene Autry enterprises for only $3. Also available are shank-proof clubs, the "extraordinary wonder glove" and self-hypnosis lessons. Let the USGA do what it will, but if I can learn the secret of perfect putting, add 20 yards to my drive and eliminate my shank, I'll be ready for the new season.

Thanksgiving, 1985

Some things to be thankful for when we sit down to celebrate Thanksgiving with generous helpings of turkey, dressing, mashed potatoes, gravy, vegetables, rolls, crabnerry sauce and three kinds of pie followed by coffee and a belt that has been let out one notch:

Hearing the doorbell and the voices of family members who have just arrived from out of town.

A treasured family recipe that has been lost and then rediscovered just as the preparations for Thanksgiving dinner are beginning.

Watching the Detroit Lions play again on Thanksgiving even if they aren't very good.

A 4-year-old anxiously inquiring how long it will be until dinner is ready.

The smell of a wood fire on Thanksgiving morning.

The sight of real butter melting on a hot roll and turning the roll from white to pale yellow.

The sound of children laughing

Discovering that no one at our house paid any attention to the article in *The Times* promoting such unusual Thanksgiving dishes as sauerkraut bake, sweet potato and pineapple soufflé, roasted red peppers and anchovies, artichoke bottoms with mushroom puree and spiced banana relish.

The genius who discovered you could take bread, seasoning and a few other ingredients, stuff them into the cavity of a turkey and produce something as delicious as dressing.

Having a reason to put the extra leaves in the dining room table.

A yard totally carpeted with leaves.

The understanding that love means you are more interested in someone else's happiness than you are in your own.

The price of turkeys.

Pictures from other Thanksgivings so that grandchildren can see their parents when they were youngsters and had mashed potatoes and gravy smeared on their faces.

The tranquility of an early-morning Thanksgiving church service.

Memories of the seventh game of the World Series when the Royals took an early 5-0 lead and the fans at Royals Stadium suddenly realized the Cardinals were not going to make a comeback.

A granddaughter showing the family members her newest crayon masterpiece.

A stretch of interstate without orange traffic barrels.

People who sell me my groceries, cut my hair, repair my house, wait on me in restaurants and get little or no recognition for the work they do.

Willie Wilson catching up with a fly ball hit to deep right center.

The realization of how extraordinarly and inexplicably fortunate we are to be living in Kansas City instead of Beirut.

The rebirth of basketball enthusiasm at the University of Kansas.

Knowing that no one will discuss the dangers of cholesterol at the Thanksgiving table.

Speakers who have invested a lot of thought in what they have to say.

Those who work so hard in the holiday season to gather money for the less fortunate.

The clerk who says "Thank you" and really means it.

The wisdom of our forefathers who set aside a day to give thanks and established the most distinctive of American holidays.

The rare alumnus who says he is more interested in the honesty of his college's athletic programs than in winning.

Leftovers. All kinds of leftovers.

Nick Lowery sending a driving kick through the uprights from the 50.

The genius who developed the recipe for pecan pie.

The defiant look of Al Davis.

The understanding that the real joy of Thanksgiving is not to be found in food and drink but in family and friends and a willingness to help those less fortunate than we are.

CHAPTER 2

PLAYOFFS
AND
WORLD SERIES

At Last
a World Series

New York—Life is measured not only in days and years, but in terms of historic events. Wars, floods, heat waves, Super Bowls, political conventions—these are elements of the human experience that become reference points in the relentless passing of time.

For Kansas Citians Friday night was one of those occasions. The Royals defeated the Yankees 4-2 to win the championship of the American League. After 97 years of major and minor league baseball, the World Series is coming to Kansas City.

The city celebrated as if there never would be a victory to equal it. The funny thing is, there never will be. This was a first, and no matter how many playoffs and World Series the future holds, the emotional impact will not be the same.

There were those who said the Royals were carrying a monkey on their backs because they had lost to the Yankees three times in the playoffs. In truth, they were carrying George Steinbrenner, Reggie Jackson, the Empire State Building and the city of New York.

In 1976 Chris Chambliss hit a home run in the ninth inning of the fifth and deciding game to defeat the Royals. The following year the Yankees scored three runs in the ninth inning of the fifth game to win. In 1978 the Royals lost in four games, and afterward the players complained bitterly about the club's inability to sign free agents.

Before the playoffs opened in Kansas City Wednesday, the Yankees appeared confident of winning.

"If we play 10 years, one of these years they'll luck out," Ron Guidry, the Yankees' first-game starter, said condescendingly.

Even after losing the first two games, the Yankees seemed to feel that the sight of Yankee Stadium would bring a swelling to the Royals' throats.

"They're gonna be in for a surprise tonight," the Yankees' Lou Piniella said before the third game.

There was a surprise, all right, but it was scarcely the kind the Yankees had in mind.

After six innings the Yankees led 2-1. Willie Wilson doubled with two out in the seventh, but to the Yankees this was only a minor annoyance. Rich Gossage is known to deal quickly with late-inning trouble makers and he was summoned from the bullpen. This was his first appearance of the playoff and a rested Gossage would be an overpowering Gossage.

U.L. Washington was overmatched, but he kept the Royals' hopes alive by beating out an infield hit. This was just what Gossage didn't want because now he had to pitch to George Brett. Baseball's best hitter was facing baseball's best relief pitcher.

The crowd grew tense in anticipation of this shootout at 60 feet, six inches. What happened next occurred so swiftly, so explosively that it almost was too much for the eye to follow.

The ball was a white blur as it left Gossage's hand. Brett's bat uncoiled as if released by a giant spring. The explosion was awesome. The ball soared on a high arc, climbing through the night sky until it reached its apex and plunged into the third deck in right field.

For all who saw it, the scene will remain a moment frozen in time.

In 1976 Brett hit a home run in the eighth inning of the fifth game to tie the score at 6-6, but the Royals lost. He hit three home runs against Catfish Hunter in the third game in 1978, but Thurman Munson hit a game-winning homer in the eighth and the Yankees went on to win in four games. But this time the scenario was different. This time the Yankees could not recover.

Brett had not only shot down Gossage, he had stolen the month of October from Reggie Jackson.

On Saturday morning, Mrs. Ewing Kauffman, the wife of the Royals' owner, said she still hadn't fully comprehended the events of the night before.

"I still can't believe it's happened," she said.

Her reaction is probably typical of most Kansas Citians. They have endured so much adversity where baseball is concerned that success is difficult to comprehend.

Kansas Citians have had a long love affair with organized baseball dating to 1894, when Kansas City was a member of the Union Association. Rarely has this love been reciprocated.

The Union Association team folded after two years. Later a Federal League team folded. Kansas City had the Blues of the American Association from 1901 until 1955 when Arnold Johnson purchased the Philadelphia Athletics and moved them to Kansas City.

Johnson was a business associate of Dan Topping, one of the co-owners of the Yankees, and the two clubs began to make so many trades with each other that Kansas City was sneeringly referred to as a Yankee farm club. The two clubs made deals involving 55 players in a period of five years. Not surprisingly, most of the deals benefitted the Yankees.

The A's finished sixth their first year in Kansas City. The franchise remained 12 more years, but the A's never again finished that high.

Johnson died while the club was in spring training in 1960. A bid for local ownership failed, and Charles O. Finley acquired the team in 1961. By the middle of his first season, he was attempting to move to Dallas.

For the next six seasons Kansas City struggled to keep its team, and Finley maneuvered to move.

In 1967 Finley was given permission to move to Oakland, and Kansas City obtained an expansion franchise for the 1969 season. The team was awarded to Ewing Kauffman. The Royals have proved to be the most successful expansion franchise in the history of baseball, but their three playoff losses to the Yankees became a source of frustration.

Kansas City fans have sometimes been criticized for not being more demonstrative. Before the start of the playoffs Gossage observed that playing in Kansas City was not like playing in Boston or New York.

"The fans are different," he said. "They're great fans and they're fair, but they're much quieter."

Having experienced 25 years of adversity in the American League, Kansas City fans had good reason to be restrained. Then on Friday night one swing of Brett's bat released all of their emotions.

The Yankee farm club years, the battles with Finley and the playoff losses were a thing of the past. George Brett owned October, the Royals were champions of the American League and the World Series was coming. It was time to raise a glass and celebrate.

Why Me? Why Not Joe McGuff?

After a wait of 26 years, the World Series has come to Kansas City, but it has arrived in damaged condition.

George Brett, suffering from the world's most widely covered case of hemorrhoids, is in St. Luke's Hospital for treatment. He rested on the charter flight home from Philadelphia by stretching out across three seats in the coach section. Brett was in pain and for that matter so were the Royals.

Until Tuesday everything had seemed so easy for them. They won the American League West from here to Seattle. They won the American League Championship Series from the New York Yankees in three games and left a sulking George Steinbrenner working on a Yankee hit list.

Now, for the first time this season, the Royals are dealing with adversity. They trail the Phillies two games to none and if they lose Friday night at Royals Stadium the tournament to determine the best team in the world of Bowie Kuhn will be all but over.

In 76 years of World Series competition, no team ever has lost the first three games and come back to win. Only seven teams have lost the first two games and survived to enjoy a champagne celebration.

"It's nice to go home for three straight," declared Ewing Kauffman, owner of the Royals. "We'll win 'em all." Chuck Tanner, baseball's foremost managerial optimist, couldn't have said it better.

Who knows, maybe the Royals will come back to win. After all, the Yankees lost the first two games to the Dodgers in 1978 and then won four straight. But if the Royals are going to get back in this World Series, quite a few positive things must happen. Above all, the Royals will have to get better pitching.

"We've got to hold a lead," Hal McRae said. "We can score runs, but we've got to hold 'em when we get in front. The pressure is on us

51

now, but if we win Friday the pressure will be on them because they won't want to see us even it up."

The Royals have had some baserunning problems and they botched a rundown play in the opening game, but to blame their 0-2 deficit on these lapses would be like blaming the energy crisis on Jimmy Carter because someone left the lights on in the White House.

The Royals had a 4-0 lead in the opening game, but Dennis Leonard, who pitched brilliantly against the Yankees in the playoffs, was unable to hold it. Wednesday night the Royals went into the last of the eighth with a 4-2 lead. Dan Quisenberry, who led both major leagues on the basis of victories and saves, wound up a 6-4 loser.

"I thought we had the game won," Willie Aikens said. "We get leads and can't seem to hold them."

The Royals also need to get Brett back in the lineup. He left the game in the sixth inning Wednesday night after getting two hits and drawing a walk against Steve Carlton, the Phillies' best pitcher. His status for the third game probably will be in doubt until shortly before game time.

It is ironic that Brett, widely acclaimed as the best hitter in baseball, might be forced out of his first World Series by an ailment everyone jokes about except the sufferer. Brett said he is frustrated, but still hopes to play.

"I just want to get the damn things taken care of," Brett said.

"I've done everything they've asked me to do. I feel disgruntled. I keep saying, 'Why me? Why not Joe McGuff?' "

Brett grinned wryly and added, "I'm going back to the same room I always have at the hospital. I've had it five years in a row."

If the Royals are looking for encouragement, perhaps they can draw on the fact that the World Series of 1980 has a look of unpredictability.

After all, who could guess that three days into the Series the nation's columnists and baseball writers would be interviewing not Pete Rose or Mike Schmidt but a proctologist. In a World Series that has brought hemorrhoids out of the closet, almost anything is possible.

Dr. John Heryer,who spoke at the press conference, not only proved to be informative about hemorrhoids but revealed himself as a man with a sense of humor. As he finished his press conference he was asked about the pronunciation of his name.

"It's hurrier," he said. "Like the hurrier I go the behinder I get."

While it is wonderful to discover as proctologist with a sense of humor, the good doctor provided only limited diversion from the Royals' problems.

Even if the Royals' pitching improves and Brett returns, the Royals still must find some way to cool off the Phillies. The Phillies are so hot they should overfly Kansas City and stop in Las Vegas. The Phillies have won four consecutive come-from-behind games, including the playoffs. They are high rollers who can't wait to get the dice.

"We keep coming back because these guys are good hitters," Pete Rose explained. "The thing is they're going to score some runs."

According to Mike Schmidt, the Phillies are full of confidence. "We just feel this is a good team," Schmidt said. "It's just a feeling of confidence. That's why teams are in the World Series. They do these types of things late in the year."

It is indicative of how well things are going for the Phillies, that they won the second game even though Carlton was not at his best and they made some mistakes. Carlton gave up 10 hits, six walks and threw a wild pitch. He also managed to log four double plays and induced the Royals to leave 10 men on base. They added an 11th in the ninth inning against Ron Reed.

Perhaps playing in the friendly setting of Royals Stadium will change the dynamics of the Series or maybe the Royals can play some mind games and con themselves into thinking they are playing guys named Reggie and Graig and Goose.

My,
What a Lovely
Home Run

Willie Aikens an oak of a man, stood at home plate and watched the flight of the ball as it soared majestically toward the bullpen area in right field. Satisfied with the quality of his masterpiece, he jogged slowly around the bases while the crowd at Royals Stadium cheered his genius.

Aikens' home run, his second in as many at bats, gave the Royals a 5-1 lead over the Phillies in the second inning and was obviously viewed by the crowd as the clinching bit of evidence that the Royals of summer had replaced the imposters who occupied their uniforms in Philadelphia. The World Series was no longer just an oddity to be gawked at in Kansas City. It was something to be won or lost, something you could lose your composure over. The team that looked as if it might expire in four games was alive and well and even with the Phillies after finishing the day with a 5-3 victory.

After the Royals defeated the Phillies Friday night, Hal McRae said he thought the Royals would go on to win the World Series. Asked for his rationale he said, "Because we have the best team."

The only problem at that point was that the Royals had succeeded in keeping their ability well camouflaged. Even in winning the third game, the Royals did not play as well as they are capable of playing. Through the first three games they were only a so-so team. Having conquered the Yankees, the Royals seemed a bit indifferent to the importance of conquering the world.

On Saturday, though, the Royals were the team that had dominated the American League West and swept the Yankees in the playoffs. McRae ran two singles into doubles. Dan Quisenberry relieved Dennis Leonard in the eighth and stopped the Phillies. Willie Wilson was on base twice and made a Willie Mays catch on a 400-foot drive to left-center in the seventh.

Among the spectators was Mrs. Lucille Webb, Aikens' mother, who saw her son play for the first time in a major league game. The Royals' only regret is that she stayed away so long.

Aikens hit a home run into the water spectacular in the first inning with Brett aboard. His second home run landed deep in an open area adjacent to the Royals' bullpen.

The Phillies are discovering that maybe there is something amiss with their scouting report on Aikens. Aikens hit two home runs in the first game of the Series and singled home the winning run in the 10th inning Friday night.

"He's had good pitches to hit,"commented Bob Boone, the Phillies' catcher. "But that's to his credit. We all get good pitches, but he's hit them."

Aikens has a relatively simple explanation for his success.

"I think I'm a pretty good hitter," he said. "I'm a streak hitter."

At present, Willie is on the streak of his life. Saturday was Mother's Day, the World Series and touch of New Year's eve all tied together.

Not only did the fourth game bring out the best in the Royals, but it brought out a little belligerency on the part of Dickie Noles, the Phillies' second pitcher. He knocked down Brett on an 0-2 pitch in the fourth, and Jim Frey, the Royals' manager, came running to the plate to protest to umpire Don Denkinger. Frey shouted at Noles, had to be restrained from going to the mound and exchanged words with Pete Rose.

After the game, the debate continued as to whether Noles had thrown intentionally at Brett. Frey said he had. Noles said he hadn't.

"He's the only guy who knows," Brett said. "I'm not going to accuse him of anything."

Mike Schmidt, the Phillies' third baseman, spoke on behalf of the accused.

"A pitcher doesn't like a hitter standing up there relaxed and hitting a line drive every time he goes up," Schmidt said. "I've been knocked down, but I've never had a manager go out there pleading for me. Jim Frey loves George Brett. I understand why."

Schmidt, illustrating Brett's batting stance, added, "When a guy stands at the plate like this, a pitcher has got to say 'Whoa.' He's not putting a quarter in the pitching machine out there. He's got a chance to be one of the greatest hitters of all time, and he's going to be brushed back a few times."

The Phillies, who rallied to win the first two games of the Series, attempted yet another comeback Saturday but were thwarted in the seventh inning by Wilson and thereafter by Quisenberry.

In the seventh, with one run home and Larry Bowa on second, Boone hit a drive to deep left-center that Wilson hauled in with an over-the-shoulder catch.

"When he first hit the ball it looked like it was off the wall or out," Wilson said. "It got caught in the crosswind, and Amos Otis kept talking to me all the way. He kept telling me I had room and wouldn't run into the wall."

Quisenberry relieved Leonard in the eighth when the Phillies added their third run. In the ninth, the Phillies did an uncharacteristic thing. They went down in order.

Today the Royals will try for a sweep of the three games in Kansas City.

"If we get this one, I think things definitely will have turned around," Wilson said.

"It's going to be two out of three now,"Rose said. "I don't know if this means Sunday's game is important for us because they've won twice or important for them because we're going back to Philadelphia. It's getting in high gear now. It's getting exciting.

"We're in the kind of position we've been in all year. We make it exciting. Give them credit. They played good."

Whatever happens in the rest of the Bowie Kuhn fall festival, the Royals are playing like the Royals, and World Series has become the World Series.

The Agony
of a World Series Loser

PHILADELPHIA—The reasons the Royals lost to the Phillies in the World Series are numerous and consequently go beyond any one individual, but in the first flush of misery that followed the sixth and final game, Willie Wilson had the horrible feeling the world was pointing at him.

Never mind his regular-season batting average of .326. Never mind his 230 hits. Never mind his 79 stolen bases.

In his tormented state, Wilson was convinced only the World Series would be remembered. They would talk of his .154 batting average, the few times he reached base and his record 12 strikeouts, the last one coming with the bases loaded and two outs in the ninth.

In another dressing room, Tug McGraw, the Phillies' pitcher who struck out Wilson in the ninth, was laughing and spilling champagne. Wilson was drowning in agony.

The predominant emotion in the Royals' clubhouse was disappointment. For the most part, the devastation that marked their three playoff losses to the Yankees was missing. They had beaten the Yankees, they had brought a World Series to Kansas City for the first time and they felt a strong sense of accomplishment despite losing to the Phillies. Having conquered the Big Apple, they would get around to the world at a later date.

Only Wilson was suffering the anguish of overwhelming failure.

"Nobody wants to get here and play bad," Wilson said in a low voice that had reporters straining to catch his words. "This is the worst offensive series I've ever had. I wish I could say what I did wrong.

"I put pressure on myself by reading that we were losing because I wasn't getting on base. We had a four-run lead and lost (game one). We had a two-run lead in the game we lost in the eighth (game two.) We gave it to them Sunday (game five). This game was the only game they took from us.

"I'm disappointed I didn't get on base. I think other people are say-ing I'm responsible for what happened. I don't like it because they're saying the Royals lost because I didn't get on base. They keep talking about if you stop me, you stop the Royals, but we had leads in the eighth and ninth. Granted, when I get on base it's easier."

Earlier, George Brett had said that despite losing, playing in the World Series had been fun for him. His perspective of the Series is one Wilson does not share.

"It stopped being fun for me when I didn't get any hits or get on base," Wilson said. "Everyone talked to me about negative stuff, not positive stuff. To me, if I was having fun, the people here would have been yelling and screaming at me. They weren't saying anything. I didn't have anybody yell one thing at me.

"Things just didn't go our way, and they didn't go my way. If you want to say I lost it, you can say it. What it all boils down to is we lost. I'm a bad loser."

None of Wilson's teammates was blaming him. The players were, in fact, speaking of their season in positive tones.

"It's hard to describe how I feel right now," Brett said. "Losing to a team like Philadelphia is nothing to be ashamed of. I thought we played well. Someone has to lose, and unfortunately we lost. It would have been a lot sweeter to win."

Dennis Leonard, who started the first and fourth games, was philo-sophical.

"I'm not going to go home and cry," He said. "I'm going to think we accomplished a lot of things this year. It would be great to be No. 1, but there's no shame in being No. 2."

Amos Otis, one of the Series stars with three home runs and a .478 average, thought the Royals could have won just as easily as the Phill-ies.

"I thought we should have taken the first four," Otis said. "We had leads in the two we lost. The fifth game, we should have won that, too."

Paul Splittorff, who earlier was angry because he did not get to start, said he had made peace with Manager Jim Frey and expressed a positive view of being in the Series.

"I think we played a pretty good Series," said Splittorff, who pitched in relief Tuesday night. "The thing that stuck out for me was the competition. These were two strong-willed teams that didn't ex-pect to lose. It was like two bulls charging at each other."

For the most part, the Royals said they played well in the Series and, though they didn't win, this was a good season.

They would not have felt that way had they lost to the Yankees in the playoffs.

Conversely, the Phillies believe their season would not have been successful without winning the World Series.

The most obvious pattern regarding the Royals' losses to the Phillies was an inability to hold leads, with the Phillies coming from behind in their first three victories.

Tuesday night, the Royals were the team attempting to come from behind, and they failed despite having opportunities in the eighth and ninth innings.

Hal McRae came up in the eighth with the bases loaded, two out and one run home. He grounded out. The Royals had the bases loaded with one out in the ninth, but McGraw retired Frank White on a foul pop and struck out Wilson.

"We can walk across this country or walk around the world with our chins up and say we're No. 1," McGraw said.

The Royals had a very good season, but as time passes their regret over losing the World Series is likely to grow deeper rather than diminish.

Brett
Saves the Royals

If you weren't there Friday night for game three of the American League Championship Series, you should have been. If you were there, you saw a performance that will become a part of baseball's post-season lore along with Babe Ruth's called-shot home run and Reggie Jackson's three home runs in the sixth game of the 1977 Series.

There are rare and wonderful moments when a great athlete throws aside the limitations humanity places on him and plays at a level that fills us with joy and awe. Friday night was one of those occasions.

Perhaps never has one player so dominated a big game as George Brett did. The Royals were gasping for life in their playoff series with Toronto. They had lost the first two games and were at risk of losing their 11th straight game in post-season play.

Brett hit a home run over the right-field fence in the first inning. He hit a double that was two feet from the top of the right-field wall in the fourth. He hit a home run to deep left-center in the sixth. In the eighth, he singled and scored the winning run in a 6-5 victory.

He also executed a defensive play reminiscent of Brooks Robinson's vacuum-cleaner performance in the 1970 World Series. In the third inning Brett made a back-hand stop of Lloyd Moseby's sharply hit ball down the third-base line, leaped and threw across his body to retire the fleet Damaso Garcia, who attempted to score from third.

Saturday night the Royals lost to the Blue Jays 3-1 and trailed in the series three games to one, but in years to come the series between the Royals and the Blue Jays will be remembered not so much for who won or lost, but because of what Brett did in the third game. It was a performance that makes the spirit soar.

Big games in post-season play are nothing new for Brett, but the totality of his performance in such a desperate situation goes beyond anything he has done before.

"We are awed by his talents," said Jamie Quirk, the Royals' reserve catcher and one of Brett's close friends. "When I came up to him after the game, I told him, 'I don't know what to say. You are unbelievable.' I'm glad that when I'm 50 I'll be able to say I played with George Brett."

John Wathan, shaking his head in wonderment, recalled a scene on the bench in the sixth.

"When George came up," Wathan related, "Jamie said, 'If he hits a home run, I'll take my clothes off and run on the field naked.' Jamie didn't do it, but I had his top two buttons off. Every time there is a big game, George is phenomenal."

Manager Dick Howser talked about the difficulty of pitching to Brett, who hits to all fields and has no obvious weakness.

"One club had five scouts who all happened to meet here to look at George," Howser said. "And they all disagreed on how to pitch to him."

Howser refused to identify the club, but another source with the Royals said Toronto had five scouts following the club.

"When I managed the Yankees and we played the Royals in 1980, nobody could really agree on how to pitch to George," Howser continued. "We had Bob Nieman, Birdie Tebbetts, Jerry Walker and Harry Craft scouting the Royals that year. One was a catcher, two were outfielders and one was a pitcher, and no one could agree. That is the ultimate compliment."

Saturday night the Blue Jays showed the type of respect rarely accorded to a hitter when they walked Brett in the sixth with the score tied 0-0 and runners on first and third. A subsequent walk to Hal McRae forced in the Royals only run.

Why is Brett so good in big games?

"I think he enjoys having people rely on him," Quirk said. "He likes to carry the team. His concentration is phenomenal. He has greater concentration than anyone I've ever played with."

Brett said he felt confident and relaxed coming into Friday night's game.

"I don't get nervous, and I don't get excited," Brett said of his approach to big games. "I'm confident because I've had success. I'm not cocky, but when I'm hitting good, I feel very, very confident.

"A lot of hitters look for a certain pitch. I just look for the ball. If it's up and in, I have a chance to hit a home run to right. If it's low and away, I hit to left. If your fundamentals are good, you just try to hit something hard. If I try to hit a home run, I tense up. If I had tried to hit a home run to right field my first time up, I'd probably have hit a line drive off my ankle."

Brett said that over the course of a 162-game season he has days when his mind wanders and his hitting suffers, but big games sharpen his concentration.

"You don't hear anything when you're hitting good," Brett said. "You don't see anything but the ball. It's like a twilight zone. You hit it and run to first base.

"On the home runs I hit, I was halfway to first base before I heard the crowd. You don't feel nothing, you don't hear nothing. You're in a no-man's land. It's a good feeling."

Although Brett virtually is certain to be in that special group of players who are voted into the Hall of Fame in their first year of eligibility, honors and statistics never have been a matter of great concern to him.

"If he gets 3,000 hits, I don't think it would mean much to him," Quirk said. "He knows he's good, but he doesn't perceive himself as a Hall of Famer. I don't think he knows how many lifetime hits he has. But the one thing he has is an unbelievable memory for people's names and for what pitchers throw him. You talk with him about the game in the 1978 playoffs when he hit the three home runs off Catfish Hunter and he can remember every single pitch."

Howser describes Brett not only as a great situation hitter, but an ideal player to manage.

"I haven't seen anybody any better because he can use the whole field, he knows pitchers and he knows himself," Howser said.

"He doesn't have any ego at all. He knows he's the leader on the club, but he doesn't have any ego. His best friends on the club are the rookies and Al Zych (the equipment manager). He doesn't big time anybody.

"Rarely does he not come by here after we've won and say 'Nice managing, Skip.' He's something special to me. He's also something special because of what he means to a manager. A manager needs a lot of help when things go bad."

Brett has a wry sense of humor that he often turns on himself.

He is an avid card player in the clubhouse, but when asked about his pinochle skills he replied, "I'm always in a slump. I'm the worst in the league."

When a reporter noted some books in his locker Friday night, Brett said, "People send them to me because they think I'm a genius. I look at the covers and check to see if there are any pictures."

Regarding his lack of interest in statistics and his status in baseball, Brett said, "The past is past. I don't care what I did in 1980. That's over and done with. You can't change it. I can't live on what I did tonight. If I don't go out there and play well tomorrow, they'll boo me to death. I take it one day at a time.

"When I'm finished, I'll sit back and say this is what I did. I don't want to get too satisfied."

The most poignant moment Friday night came when Brett was asked about the time earlier in the season when he came out of a slump after reviewing a video tape he made with the late Charley Lau, who was the Royals' hitting instructor in the early years of Brett's career.

"I knew what was on the tape," Brett said, "but I wanted to see his smiling face and remind myself of all the time we spent together. The good times and the bad. Today I hope there's a smile on his face if they have color television in heaven."

As Brett left the clubhouse Friday night he paused at the door of Howser's office and said:

"Nice managing, Skip."

The Royals'
Big Comeback

TORONTO—Gentlemen, start your engines. The I-70 World Series is about to begin.

Even now that the Royals have won the championship of the American League it is hard to understand how they have done what they have done.

They are a team that has lived all season on pitching and guts and a minimum of offense. They ranked 13th in hitting in the American League this season and have been involved in more death scenes than Agatha Christie. But whatever the situation, they keep coming back.

Wednesday night they completed their biggest comeback of all when they defeated Toronto 6-2 in the seventh game of the American League Championship Series and qualified to meet the Cardinals for the championship of Missouri. Other parts of the world that come under the jurisdiction of Peter Ueberroth also will be included.

"The thing we've had going for us is that when things look bad, we're always cool and confident," Hal McRae said. "We always seem to do what we have to do. Maybe we're a little crazy."

Maybe they are. Maybe the whole season is a little crazy. And even though the Cardinals will be overwhelming favorites in the World Series, maybe there is more craziness yet to come.

Things looked bad when the Royals fell 7 ½ games behind the Angels in July. Things looked bad late in the season when the Royals were swept at various times by Texas, Seattle and Minnesota. Things looked bad when Toronto took leads of 2-0 and 3-1 in the American League Championship Series.

In falling behind Toronto, it seemed the Royals finally had gone too far. Winning three straight games against the champions of the American League East, generally regarded as baseball's best division, was the craziest thing the Royals had attempted all season.

But Sunday in Kansas City Danny Jackson pitched a shutout, putting the champagne and the first Canadian World Series on hold. Tuesday night in Exhibition Stadium the Royals scored a 5-3 victory. Now it was the Blue Jays who were getting sweaty palms and a feeling of apprehension.

How could the champions of the American League East possibly lose three straight to the light-hitting Royals? And if they did, wouldn't they be accused of, well, you know, choking?

Wednesday night the Blue Jays were worried about stopping George Brett and McRae. They held both of them hitless, but the Royals turned their offense over to a fellow named Sunny. Sunny is not an intimidating sort of name and normally Jim Sundberg is not an intimidating hitter, but on this occasion he drove in four runs with a single in the second and a bases-loaded triple that landed on top of the right-field fence in the sixth.

Toronto Manager Bobby Cox called it a wind-blown pop fly, but the three runs counted just the same.

The Blue Jays left nine men on base and surrendered meekly after Sundberg's triple, going hitless in the sixth, seventh and eighth.

The biggest threat to the Royals came when a fan fell over a railing into their bullpen.

"He was trying to catch a ball and did a Greg Louganis," Dan Quisenberry said.

This was a night when even an injury to Bret Saberhagen couldn't bother the Royals. Saberhagen started, but had to leave the game after three innings because of a bruised pitching hand suffered when he tried to grab a batted ball. Charlie Leibrandt, a left-hander, followed him and pitched into the ninth, giving up two runs and five hits. When Leibrandt came in, he forced Rance Mulliniks and Al Oliver, both left-handed hitters, out of the lineup, thus limiting the Blue Jays' maneuverability in the late innings.

Dave Stieb started for Toronto, pitching on three days of rest for the second time in the series. He lost his control as well as his stuff in the sixth inning, but Cox stayed with him until he surrendered Sundberg's decisive triple.

Stieb walked Brett and hit McRae. Pat Sheridan, who homered in the fourth, drove a ground ball into the hole, but shortstop Tony Fernandez made a great stop and threw to third, forcing Brett.

Stieb then walked Steve Balboni. Cox had a relief pitcher ready, but he elected to stay with Stieb and Sundberg hit his triple, which was carried along by a brisk wind.

Cox claimed Stieb still had good stuff, but was done in by the elements.

"The ball Sundberg hit was a legitimate pop-up, but the wind took it," Cox said. "That was a lot of runs for one pop-up. Sheridan's home run was wind blown, too. Stieb hadn't lost his stuff. He made a good pitch on Sundberg and it just got up in the wind.

"I'm disappointed and frustrated. You hate to get beat on a pop-up. We had opportunities to win the game. We just didn't do it."

Like so many teams that have lost to the Royals this season, the Blue Jays couldn't convince themselves that the best team had won.

"I feel we're a better club," catcher Ernie Whitt said. "But give them a lot of credit. They definitely had some good pitching."

Third baseman Garth Iorg said the Blue Jays simply left too many men in scoring position.

"I definitely feel that we're the better team," he said. "I think we're in a tougher division, and we won 99 games. I feel we're the best team in the league. And I'm taking nothing away from Kansas City. As they say, in a short series anything can happen and anything did happen."

Second baseman Damaso Garcia, commenting on the merits of the teams, said, "I still believe we're the better team. Definitely."

Cox declined to comment.

"I don't know about that," he said. "I wouldn't want to compare teams."

Even though the Royals had a winning record against the American League East this season, and even though they made a spectacular comeback against the Blue Jays, they are likely to get little respect in the World Series, especially a Series in which the designated hitter will not be used.

The Royals are probably the weakest offensive team to appear in the Series since the Mets of 1969 and 1973. The 1966 Dodgers also were a marginal offensive team, but overall they had a little more offense than the Royals.

"I think our players feel we can win it," Manager Dick Howser said. "We beat some awfully good clubs this year. If our pitching is good, we can shut down anyone."

For confirmation, call the Toronto Blue Jays, who scored five runs in the last three games and had two home runs in the entire series.

The
St. Louis Blues

Maestro, play the "St. Louis Blues" please. Make it mean and low down, just the way Charlie Leibrandt was treated by the Cardinals on Sunday night.

And bartender, another drink. Just a little something to soothe the spirit and drive away the memories.

Remember those happy days leading up to the World Series? Remember the fountains at Royals Stadium spouting blue water? Sunday night things changed. The Cardinals scored four runs in the ninth inning and won the second game of the World Series 4-2. It was an experience that turned the entire city blue.

Leibrandt pitched the game of his life for eight innings. He held the Cardinals scoreless on two hits. Jack Clark, who destroyed the Dodgers, described the experience this way: "He breezed through us like we didn't exist."

Then came the mean, low-down ninth when the Cardinals scored four runs after two were out, three of them on a double by Terry Pendleton.

The hit wasn't much to look at, but in terms of its impact on the World Series, it registered an 8 on the Ueberroth scale.

It gave the Cardinals a sweep of the two games in Royals Stadium, and never in history has a team lost the first two games of the World Series at home and come back to win.

It was a hit that set off wails of anguish and turned every man, woman and child in the city into a second guesser.

How could Dick Howser have left Leibrandt in there to lose the game? Why didn't he bring in Dan Quisenberry? Why? Why? Why?

Wasn't his failure to make a pitching change a vote of no confidence in Quisenberry? What could the man have been thinking of?

Get a rope. Write to your congressman. Call Tom Lasorda and see what he would have done.

Did Howser truly make a colossal blunder?

That is the question everybody is asking today, so let's try to arrive at an answer. A reasonable answer. One based on reality, not emotion.

To arrive at a conclusion it is necessary to take two antacids, a headache powder and replay the ninth.

Leibrandt came into the inning with a 2-0 lead and had pitched a relatively easy game. He had thrown only 108 pitches and had retired 14 men in order.

He gave up a double to Willie McGee on a sharply hit ball down the third-base line.

However, Leibrandt showed no signs of weakening as he retired Ozzie Smith on a bounce to George Brett and made Tommy Herr the second out on a fly.

Some people are saying Howser should have brought in Quisenberry to pitch to Clark. That is nonsense. The way Leibrandt was pitching, if Howser had made that move, the fans would have come down on the field after him.

Leibrandt fell behind Clark 3-0, and then Clark singled to left, scoring McGee.

"I didn't hit it real well," Clark said. "The ball just found the hole. I was looking for a fastball and got a change. I was just lucky to hit it in the right spot."

There was still no reason to make a change at this point. If Quisenberry were the Dan Quisenberry of 1983 and 1984, that would have been different, but Quisenberry has been erratic, and Leibrandt still appeared to have good stuff.

Tito Landrum, the next hitter, slapped a 2-2 pitch into right field for a double, Clark stopping at third.

"I just tried to make contact," Landrum said.

Cesar Cedeno was the next hitter, and now it was decision time for Howser. He could bring in Quisenberry, in which case Cardinal Manager Whitey Herzog said he would have used the left-handed-hitting Andy Van Slyke. The Royals then would have had the option of pitching to Van Slyke or giving him an intentional walk to bring up Pendleton.

Herzog said that in the event of an intentional walk, Steve Braun, a left-handed hitter, would have batted for Pendleton.

Quisenberry has had trouble with left-handers. In the fourth game of the playoff with Toronto, Quisenberry gave up a game-winning double in the ninth to pinch hitter Al Oliver. In that game Leibrandt had shut out the Blue Jays for eight innings and was replaced by Quisenberry after giving up a walk and a game-tying double.

Quisenberry also gave up a game-winning hit to Oliver in the second playoff game.

An alternative to bringing in Quisenberry was to stay with Leibrandt and let him face Cedeno or Pendleton.

"If he was struggling and they had some hard-hit balls, I would have made the move," Howser said. "Just the way he was throwing the ball, I felt good about it."

Howser said he conferred with his pitching coach, Gary Blaylock, and they both felt that Leibrandt still had good stuff.

"It was my decision, but Gary agreed that it was Charlie's game to win or lose," Howser said. "The way Quiz has pitched or hasn't pitched had nothing to do with that decision. It just didn't work out, that's all."

Pendleton doubled on a 2-1 count, and the Royals lost the game.

Because his decision didn't work out, Howser will have to live with a winter of criticism, but he made a reasonable decision in electing to stay with Liebrandt. The fans who are berating him now are the same ones who criticized him this season whenever he brought in Quisenberry and Quisenberry had a bad game.

Quisenberry led the American League in saves, but he has not worked a lot and his effectiveness, especially against left-handers, has declined late in the season. This is not the dominant Dan Quisenberry that so many people remember.

Leibrandt pitching to Pendleton, or Quisenberry pitching to Van Slyke or Braun. That is the bottom line, and a reasonable case can be made for either decision.

"People are going to get on Howser for not bringing in Quiz," Herzog said, "but Clark didn't hit the ball hard. It just found the hole. Even on the game-winning hit I thought Leibrandt made a heck of a pitch. We didn't hit the ball hard all night.

"I don't think anybody pitched better against us all season than Leibrandt did for eight innings."

Would Herzog have made the pitching change had he been managing the Royals?

"I'll never answer that," Herzog said. "I've got enough trouble managing my own club."

He paused a moment and then thought better of what he had said.

"If they had hit two line drives I probably would have, but we didn't hit a ball good," Herzog said.

After the game Quisenberry was surrounded by reporters wanting to know if he felt that Howser had lost confidence in him because of the decision to stay with Leibrandt.

"He's had people on base all year and gotten out of it," Quisenberry said of Leibrandt. "He's great at getting out of jams. He had a better year than I did. He can have men on second and third in every inning and not give up any runs."

Quisenberry said he thought he might have come in when Clark came to the plate and again when Cedeno came up, but he refused to second-guess Howser, saying his role is not to manage the club but to be ready to pitch.

Was he insulted?

"No," Quisenberry said. "I'm not the kind of player who says I should come in this situation or not come in."

Did he feel Howser has lost confidence in him?

"If he has, I wouldn't have been up throwing in the ninth," Quisenberry said. "It doesn't matter what I think. Charlie is a great pitcher, and he has pitched great in jams all year. I think Dick just had a lot of faith in Charlie. He wasn't getting launched a lot.

"This team has hurt together and poured champagne together. Win or lose, we'll go on living together."

Howser said he never had seen Leibrandt so disconsolate after a loss.

"I went into the trainer's room and told him he'd get another shot at them, but he didn't even answer me," Howser said.

Leibrandt stayed in the trainer's room for 30 or 40 minutes and then came to his locker.

"I don't have anything to say tonight, gentlemen," he told reporters.

He dressed quickly while staring into his locker and then left.

The loss has put the Royals in an almost impossible position. They are two games down, they have scored a total of three runs, and they have wasted two great pitching performances.

The Royals also lost the first two games of their playoff with the Blue Jays, but those defeats came on the road. In the Cardinals, the Royals are facing a different sort of opponent. To put it another way, the Blue Jays and Cardinals are not birds of a feather.

A Team
That Won't Die

ST. LOUIS—Maybe E.T. really does exist in some distant galaxy. Maybe leprechauns really can be found cavorting in the mists of Ireland. And maybe the Royals are going to make one last enchanted comeback in a season where the improbable has become commonplace.

By pitching the Royals to a 6-1 victory Thursday night over the Cardinals, Danny Jackson not only kept the Royals alive in the World Series, he gave Kansas City fans a license to believe that this team with the funny looking offense and the solid gold pitching staff just might bring Kansas City its first world championship.

The odds still are heavily against the Royals. They trail the Cardinals three games to two, and no team has ever come back to win a World Series after losing the first two games at home as the Royals did.

And yet the odds were not good when the Royals trailed the Angels by 7 ½ games in the American League West. They were not good when the Royals were swept late in the season by the Rangers and then later by Seattle and Minnesota.

They were not good when the Royals trailed Toronto three games to one in the American League Championship Series. They were not good when the World Series opened and the Cardinals went ahead three games to one.

But by now it is evident that the Royals are not a conventional team, and this is not a conventional season. Many years ago there was a book written entitled "Been Down So Long It Looks Like Up To Me." It is a pity the title is taken. It would be perfect for the story of the Royals' season.

"We're in good shape," Hal McRae said after the victory Thursday night. "We're going to win. We're right where we want to be with our backs against the wall. We fight good off the ropes."

Rope-a-doping the Cardinals will take some doing, however. Saturday night Danny Cox will start against Charlie Liebrandt, who pitched a shutout for eight innings in the second game, only to lose in the ninth. Cox gave up only two runs through seven innings.

If the Royals live through Saturday, they will send Bret Saberhagen, a 6-1 winner in the third game, against John Tudor on Sunday night. Tudor was the winning pitcher in the Series opener and pitched a shutout in the fourth game.

This is a Series that has been dominated by pitching, and there is no reason to think that pattern will change. The Cardinals have a nifty team batting average of .196 and have scored 12 runs. They are known as a running team, but with their lead rabbit, Vince Coleman, injured, the other rabbits have scarcely gotten out of the hutch. They have stolen two bases, have been caught stealing once, and have been picked off twice, including Thursday night when Willie McGee was picked off first.

The Royals are batting .262 and have scored 15 runs, a meek average of three a game. Not only are the Royals outhitting the Cardinals, they are also outrunning them, having stolen four bases.

"Our ball club is not hitting," Cardinal Manager Whitey Herzog said. "They've got great pitching, but once in a while you'd think we'd hit a little better."

Herzog said the Royals' staff compares favorably with the best in the National League.

"You talk about the Mets and Dodgers, but they're right there with them," Herzog said. "With the kind of arms they've got, I don't see why they can't dominate that division for a long time. We're lucky to be where we are."

Jackson saved the Royals in game five of the AL Championship Series by pitching a shutout at a time when the Royals were trailing Toronto three games to one.

He found himself in a similar situation Thursday night and held the Cardinals to one run on five hits. He has made four post-season appearances and has a 1.04 earned run average.

Jackson's career has made a remarkable turnaround in the last 16 months. Today he is a playoff and World Series hero. Last season he was baseball's only over-the-road pitcher.

He was optioned to Omaha in mid-June, but he and his wife, Jody, were expecting their first child and did not want to move from Kansas City. When the Omaha club was at home, Jackson left Kansas City every day at 1 p.m., drove to work in Omaha and returned after the game. He stayed in Omaha only on the nights he pitched.

As the I-29 pitcher he drove an estimated 16,000 miles in 10 weeks.

Despite dominating the Cardinals Thursday night, Jackson struggled in the first three innings. After the first inning, catcher Jim Sundberg was so concerned about Jackson's control and his lack of velocity that he debated about conferring with Manager Dick Howser.

Jackson said he finally settled into a groove in the fourth and got his rhythm. From that point on the Cardinals got two hits, both of them singles, and in one stretch Jackson retired 11 straight batters.

The offensive star of the game was Willie Wilson, who singled in the first and tripled home two runs in the second. Wilson is batting .364 in the Series. Buddy Biancalana also singled in a run in the second, had two hits for the night and walked.

Biancalana has an on-base percentage of .500, with four hits and four walks. "He looks like Baby Ruth and we're pitching him like Baby Ruth," Herzog lamented.

In keeping with the distinctive nature of this Series, the game Thursday night produced some unusual developments.

The Cardinals used five pitchers. They recorded 15 strikeouts, with Todd Worrell fanning six straight batters, tying the World Series record. Yet the Cardinals gave up 11 hits and four walks.

There was a controversial play at the plate in the second when Sundberg doubled on a ball that Tito Landrum reached but couldn't hold and then scored on a single to right by Biancalana.

Sundberg came in head first, slid wide of the plate and touched it with his left hand as catcher Tom Nieto dove to tag him. Sundberg was called safe by umpire John Shulock. The Cardinals protested vigorously. Television replays were inconclusive.

"I felt I got my hand in before he could get me," Sundberg said. "The only place I felt anything was on my foot. If he got me higher up, he must have just grazed me."

The most dramatic moment of the game came in the seventh when George Brett slid into the Royals' dugout trying to catch a foul pop off the bat of Terry Pendleton. Like a wide receiver running a crossing pattern, Brett ignored the danger and kept his eye on the ball, although he was unable to make the catch.

He was caught by Coach Lee May in what seems likely to go down as the defensive gem of the Series.

Brett was poked in the eye while falling and developed what he described as a little haze.

"Every time I looked at something, it was like there was a little outline around it," Brett said.

Brett remained in the game, but he was replaced in the last of the ninth by Greg Pryor.

With the Series moving back to Kansas City, the Royals were in an upbeat mood.

"Wouldn't that be something," Brett said when asked about the possibility of the Royals coming back to win. "As a team, it would be great not just to win the Series but to defy the odds. It would definitely be very rewarding."

Frank White said the Royals found some added incentive when they got to their dressing room Thursday afternoon.

"We got here about 3:30, and guys were in putting up lights, platforms and TV monitors," White said. "A lot of guys got irritated. We said we were not going to let them celebrate here.

"This is the most exciting year of my life. We've struggled all the way, but the guys have rooted for each other. You saw George slide into the dugout and Balboni run into a wall. That's the way this team is."

A Series dominated by pitching does not make for great theater, but with the Royals returning home in a challenging position the quality of the drama should improve.

The Miracle Royals

For better or worse, there is a time in human affairs when events assume a momentum of their own and overwhelm any attempt to control them. Perhaps that is the only rational way to explain the team that took its place in history Sunday night as the Miracle Royals.

No matter how long baseball is played in Kansas City, there never will be another season like the season of '85.

Those who were eyewitnesses to it will tell their children and their grandchildren about the light-hitting team that kept making comeback after comeback and then won the seventh game of the World Series with an 11-0 rout of the Cardinals, who came into the Series as 2-1 favorites.

The Cardinals led the National League in hitting, but they were limited to 13 runs by the Royals and batted only .185, the lowest average ever for a seven-game Series. The team known as the running Redbirds stole only two bases while the Royals were stealing nine.

"It's amazing," Cardinal Manager Whitey Herzog said. "I know they've got good pitching, but if they were that good, they would have 130 games in a weak division."

There is reason to wonder if any team ever again will win a World Series the way the Royals did. To say they won the hard way is to hopelessly understate the case. What the Royals did was the equivalent of winning the Tour de France without touching the handlebars, or climbing Mount Everest without a rope.

The Royal's success can be explained in part by their superb pitching, but pitching alone cannot account for a team coming back from 3-1 deficits and winning both the American League Championship Series and the World Series. Pitching alone does not explain how the Royals became the first team in history to win the World Series after losing the first two games at home.

"You have to throw intangibles in," Manager Dick Howser said Sunday night. "You can't deny that now. If we got beat tonight, intangibles wouldn't have meant a hill of beans, but now that we've won, you can talk about it.

"How can you explain the look in a player's eyes? I can't explain it. I call it a fighter pilot's look. It's not in awe. It's not saying, 'Oh, gee, we're in the World Series.' I've seen it for a long time on this team."

Anyone who has followed sports is aware that real-life fairy stories sometimes have unhappy endings, but from the time Darryl Motley drove a two-run homer deep into the left-field seats in the second inning, the blue-clad fans in Royals Stadium became true believers. This was the Royals' year, and nothing was going to stop them.

John Tudor, who had won two Series games for the Cardinals and shut out the Royals in game four, struggled from the outset in his matchup with Bret Saberhagen. This pairing of 20-game winners was expected to produce a great pitching duel, but the the fastball, the changeup, and the surgical control Tudor exhibited in pitching his shutout were missing.

Tudor was a man trying to survive on guts and instinct.

"I felt good before the game, but I didn't make the pitches I had to make," Tudor said. "There's no way to change it unless you've got some kind of time machine."

Sometimes pitchers will be off early in a game and then find themselves, but things grew worse for Tudor when the Royals scored three runs in the third. A walk, a checked-swing single by Brett, a double steal and a walk to Frank White filled the bases. Tudor walked Jim Sundberg and was gone.

Bill Campbell relieved him and gave up a two-run single to Steve Balboni.

The Royals scored six runs in a tumultuous fifth, and with Saberhagen methodically cutting down the Cardinals, it was obvious that the Royals had only to run four more innings off the scoreboard and Kansas City could start celebrating its first World Series championship.

The World Series was not the only thing that got away from the Cardinals in the fifth. The Cardinals also lost their composure, and both Herzog and pitcher Joaquin Andujar were ejected by plate umpire Don Denkinger even though the score was 10-0 at the time.

When Denkinger called a 2-and-2 pitch to Sundberg a ball, Andujar argued vigorously. Herzog came out to save his pitcher and wound up getting ejected himself after arguing with Denkinger. Andujar had to be restrained by his teammates and was partly carried from the field.

The Cardinals' frustration with Denkinger was principally a carry-over from Saturday night when he called Jorge Orta safe on a play at first at the beginning of the Royals' half of the ninth. They went on to score twice and defeated St. Louis 2-1.

"I'm not ashamed of what happened," Herzog said. "The umpiring had nothing to do with us getting kicked 11-0, but it did have something to do with us losing Saturday night.

"I did say to Denkinger I didn't think we should be out there tonight, that we should be at home. While the inning turned around when he blew that play, he didn't miss the foul pop or the passed ball. But if (Todd) Worrell gets that out, he blows 'em away.

"He's not a bad umpire, but the human element comes in, and he blew the play. It's just one of those things, but when somebody takes something away from you, it bothers you."

Ozzie Smith also said he did not think the incident reflected badly on the Cardinals.

"When you're being cheated, how else are you supposed to react?" Smith said.

Andy Van Slyke took a different view.

"I feel sorry for the kids around the country more than anyone else," Van Slyke said. "Now they think this is the way a major-league ball player acts. In a 11-0 game there are not questionable calls. You just shut your mouth and play the game. You swallow your pride, tip your hat and come back to spring training next year."

With an 11-0 lead to work on, Saberhagen disposed of the Cardinals on three hits over the final four innings. On Saturday he became a new father. On Sunday he became the Series Most Valuable Player.

"When you get in a batting slump, there's nothing you can do about it," Herzog said. "If you don't have two hot hitters, there's nothing you can do.

"They hit the ball good tonight. Call it laser beams, star wars or whatever it was, they were lighting us up pretty good."

Like the Blue Jays before him, Herzog was not convinced the Cardinals had lost to a superior team.

"In a five-game or a seven-game series, pitching dominates, and they just dominated us," Herzog said. "I don't think the Royals could win our division. I don't think they could win the American League East. But they're World Champions, and I'll tip my hat to them."

While Herzog was puzzling over the Cardinals' loss, the Royals were bathing in champagne to celebrate their first-ever World Series championship.

"This is a special club, and these are special players," Howser said. "We've had one game we've had to win so long I can't remember when we had a luxury game. If we hadn't won three of four from California at the end of the season, we wouldn't be here.

"I can't explain it. A lot of people say voodoo is involved. It's amazing to me. You walk that tightrope so long, and if you lose one game, you're finished. The guillotine has been there for a long time.

"It was a struggle, but we had good pitching. In 14 playoff and World Series games, we didn't have a poorly pitched game. We played 14 pressure games in a row, and our pitching was good."

Frank White stood out of range of his champagne-spraying teammates and smiled in wonderment at what he has described as the greatest season of his life.

"When we were down 3-1 to Toronto, I had four playoff tickets, and I couldn't sell them for $10," he laughed.

Dan Quisenberry, soaked in champagne, said, "It's glorious. What else can you say. It's glorious."

Glorious, improbable, crazy, wonderful unbelievable—the season of '85 was all of those things and much more.

Herzog
Wins a Series

ST. LOUIS—Whitey Herzog has been a patient suitor in his love affair with baseball. Someone less ardent might have been turned away by the disappointments he has experienced, but he always proceeded on the assumption that this would be a love affair with a happy ending.

As a high school senior, Herzog lost a fly ball in the lights, a misplay that cost the New Athens Yellowjackets the Illinois state championship. As a fringe major-league player, he spent eight seasons sweating out roster cuts and trading deadlines. A call to the manager's office invariably brought bad news.

As a manager, he won three division championships in Kansas City but lost three times to the Yankees in the playoffs. After a second-place finish in 1979 he was fired.

But Wednesday night the disappointments were washed away in a tide of champagne. The Cardinals defeated the Brewers 6-3 in the seventh and deciding game of the World Series, catcher Darrell Porter was named the World Series Most Valuable Player, Herzog received a visit from his employer, August Busch Jr., and a telephone call from President Ronald Reagan. Herzog took the phone call in his office.

"Mr. President? Yes. I can hear him," Herzog said. "Yes, sir. I certainly want to thank you for calling."

There was a pause.

"I know you're a great baseball fan and I appreciate it."

There was another pause.

"Thank you very much. I sure appreciate this. Thank you very much, Mr. President."

Herzog said the president had been watching the Series aboard Air Force One and thought it was very exciting. Reagan also mentioned the rivalry between the Cards and the Chicago Cubs in the days when he was a baseball broadcaster.

Shortly after Reagan's call, Busch arrived to congratulate Herzog and share a victory drink.

"I'll drink this and you drink champagne," Busch said, holding up a bottle of Budweiser Light. "Here's to you. God, it was a marvelous thing. You deserve more credit than anyone I know."

The last visitor was Brewer Manager Harvey Kuenn. They shook hands and Kuenn offered his congratulations. As he started to leave, Herzog said, "It's a long way from Davenport."

Herzog played for Quincy, Ill., in the old Three-I League at the same time Kuenn played for Davenport, Iowa.

Despite the fact that he personally rebuilt the Cardinals and managed them to a World Series Championship, Herzog's reaction was much more subdued than that of his players. He had a few drinks of champagne, just as he did when the Cardinals won the National League Championship Series, but he showed little emotion.

"I don't think I get excited any more," Herzog said. "I don't want to act like I don't appreciate what's happened, but that's just the way I feel.

"Baseball has been good to me since I quit playing. As a player I was intelligent enough that I never went to a manager and told him to play me or trade me. I spent eight years in the majors and I was fortunate to be there that long. I hustled and managers liked me. If I was getting out of high school and I scouted me, I wouldn't have signed me."

Appropriately, the Cardinals' final victory came in a game typical of their season. They scored three runs in the sixth inning, taking a 4-3 lead. Joaquin Andujar pitched through the seventh and Bruce Sutter was brought in to finish.

"I felt no one in the world could second-guess me if we got beat with him," Herzog said. "He can get six outs pretty good."

Sutter, who had given up four runs to the Brewers in his last four appearances, retired the Brewers in order in the eighth. The Cardinals added two runs in their half of the inning, and Sutter faced only three batters in the ninth.

Andujar, who was hit on the right leg just below the knee in the seventh inning of the third game, gave up three runs and seven hits in seven innings. Herzog said he was starting to get the ball up and with a one-run lead he preferred to win or lose with Sutter.

"If Andujar had not gotten hurt, we would never have come back to St. Louis," Herzog said. "I'll tell you why we won. We have better defense all around, we have more speed and our pitching was good.

"We played Montreal, and people said Montreal was better. We played Philadelphia, and people said they were better than us. They kept saying that, but we kept beating them. If we keep the ball in the park, we've got a chance to win. I think we'll get more credit now."

Porter said that Sutter's stuff was no better or worse than it was in the two games in which he was hit hard, but the situation worked to his advantage.

"He needed six outs and they were down," Porter said. "They had to try and get some hits. You want aggressive hitters up there against Bruce."

Keith Hernandez also said that Sutter is a situation pitcher.

"You put Bruce in a game where we're winning by five or six runs or losing by two or three and he's not the same Bruce Sutter." Hernandez said. "You bring him in where the score is tied or we have a one-run lead and the game's booked."

Porter finished the Series with five runs-batted-in and one homer, and he did an excellent defensive job. Even so, he expressed surprise at being named the Series MVP.

Porter also was named the MVP in the National League Championship Series.

"I still can't believe I've won these two awards," he said. "It's really neat, but I really think there wasn't one standout. It's a high point. I didn't have any idea I'd ever be in this position. I learned a whole lot about playing this year. The Lord humbled me. The award surprised me, but I'm glad to accept it. It's an awful good feeling."

Porter said it was also a good feeling when the Cardinals scored two insurance runs in the eighth, one coming home when he lined a single to right.

"I was so glad when we got those two runs in the eighth," Porter said. "I didn't want to have to face Simmons, Oglivie and Thomas with a one-run lead."

Unlike his teammates, Porter celebrated with a bottle of sparkling grape juice. He underwent drug-and-alcohol rehabilitation when he was with the Royals in 1980 and no longer drinks alcoholic beverages.

"I'm not breaking my sobriety for this," Porter said.

Among the Brewers who came to the Cardinal clubhouse was Bud Selig, the club president, and he sought out Porter.

"I appreciate everything you guys did for me," Porter told Selig.

Later he expanded on the point, saying, "I started to have my problems over there. Selig was one of the first people who came to me and said, 'What can I do?' I wasn't ready for help then, but I appreciated it."

Herzog signed Porter as a free agent after Porter played out his contract with the Royals and could not reach agreement on a new one. Porter had trouble hitting and catching through the last half of the 1980 season, but Herzog said he thought Porter was simply out of shape and decided to gamble on him.

Among the players who celebrated quietly was Gene Tenace.

"This one means a lot to me because I'm on my way out the door," said Tenace, 36. "This team knows how to play the game of baseball. We don't have the power of some other clubs, but we know how to win."

CHAPTER 3

PRO FOOTBALL

The First
Super Bowl

LOS ANGELES—In the days leading up to the Super Bowl, Vince Lombardi said that if the Packers lost to the Chiefs it would not be the end of the world. Expanding on this wisdom from the oracle of Green Bay, it stands to reason that the sun, the moon and the stars will not come crashing down around the Chiefs as a result of their 35-10 loss to the Packers Sunday.

There will be other games and other seasons and hopefully other opportunities to win championships.

Nonetheless, the decisiveness of the Chiefs' loss is disappointing and they will have to live a little longer with the taunts of being a Mickey Mouse team in a Mickey Mouse league.

The Chiefs could have scored a moral victory for themselves and the American Football League simply by playing the Packers close. They did just that for a half. Then they were overwhelmed.

Fred (The Hammer) Williamson, who had promised to inflict unbearable pain on the Green Bay receivers, was himself knocked out and carried off the field. Late in the game the Chiefs suffered a final embarrassment when the Packers substituted freely.

"The most important thing about the Super Bowl was being here," commented Jack Steadman, the Chiefs' general manager.

Lamar Hunt said he saw several NFL people after the game and they were gracious.

"One of them was Art Modell of Cleveland," Hunt said. "He could see I was down, I guess. He said, 'Welcome to the club. Now you know how the other 13 teams in this league feel. It's been happening to us for years.'"

It is perhaps of some consolation that the Chiefs played the Packers on almost even terms for a half and forced the Packers to start blitzing in the second half, a tactic Lombardi uses reluctantly.

The Packers scored first but the Chiefs drove 66 yards in six plays early in the second quarter to tie the score. A play-action pass to Otis Taylor was good for 31 yards and then Len Dawson passed seven yards to Curtis McClinton who was open in the end zone.

The Packers struck back with a 73-yard drive in 13 plays but the Chiefs took the kickoff and moved from their 18 to the Green Bay 24 in seven plays. Mike Mercer kicked a field goal and the score was 14-10 at halftime.

Buddy Young, a former NFL star who is a special scout for the league, said he thought the Chiefs would have an advantage coming out for the second half.

"They've found out the Packers are human," Young observed.

The Chiefs took the kickoff and gained 20 yards in three plays. Then Willie Wood intercepted a pass intended for Fred Arbanas and returned it 50 yards to the Kansas City five. Elijah Pitts burst over left tackle and scored.

Neither the Chiefs nor the Packers could make a significant advance on their next possessions. With the ball on the Chiefs' 27, Dawson threw an incomplete pass and then was hit for losses of 14 and 11 yards, with the Packers blitzing on both plays.

The Packers scored on their next possession to increase their lead to 28-10. For the Chiefs, the rest of the game was an eternity.

The Packers, although they are an older team, got stronger as the game progressed. The Chiefs' offensive line, which played a strong first half, faltered in the last half. The pressure on Bart Starr, the Packer quarterback, was spotty and the Chiefs were unable to contain Max McGee, the verteran end who caught seven passes for 138 yards.

Coming into the game Hank Stram expected the Chiefs to have trouble stopping the Packers but he hoped to win by outscoring them. It was a plan that worked only for a half.

In his post-game appearance Lombardi said the Chiefs did not compare with the best teams in the NFL.

"That's what you wanted me to say—now I've said it."

Commenting on the Chiefs' stack defense, Lombardi said it was effective against the running game but vulnerable to passing and the Packers had been able to take advantage of it.

The crowd of 63,086 was a disappointment. Many people in Los Angeles blamed the lower than expected attendance on the local television blackout, saying people boycotted the game in protest.

As a concluding thought, it should be noted that the Chiefs' loss was far from the most one-sided ever suffered in a championship game. As recently as 1964 the Browns defeated the Colts, 27-0. In 1961 the Packers defeated the Giants 37-0. In 1957, Detroit defeated Cleveland 59-14. The most one-sided game of all was the Bears' 73-0 victory over the Redskins in 1940.

The Chiefs made a poor showing but they are a young, improving team and they will be back.

Winning It All

When the Jets upset Baltimore 16-7 last year in the third Super Bowl, NFL partisans dismissed it as an aberration, taking refuge in the cliché that anything can happen on a given day. They will have to be much more resourceful if they are to explain away the 23-7 drubbing the Chiefs inflicted on the Minnesota Vikings Sunday.

The Vikings were 14-point favorites. They were expected to leave the Chiefs bruised and bleeding and re-establish the superiority of the National Football League. The Chiefs and their fancy formations would be no match for Bud Grant's Purple Gang.

Instead the Chiefs, playing the last game ever under the banner of the American Football League, took the Vikings, disassembled them piece by piece and left the parts scattered over the surface of the Sugar Bowl.

The Vikings are described as a basic team that likes to punish their opponents with the running of Dave Osborn and Bill Brown. Sunday Osborn gained 15 yards and Brown 26.

The Vikings like to use quarterback Joe Kapp on what they call the short roll. Normally he passes but he also runs for key yardage when his receivers are covered. Sunday Kapp gained nine yards rushing. He threw for 183 yards but was intercepted twice.

Gene Washington is the Vikings' leading receiver. He caught one pass for nine yards and was covered so well by Emmitt Thomas and Jim Marsalis that he was thrown to only three times.

With their running game taken away and and Washington little more than a bystander, the Purple Gang was almost helpless offensively. John Henderson wound up being the main target. He had 111 yards of receptions but his longest gain was for 28 yards.

Kapp, known as a tough man in a saloon fight, has a reputation for occasionally running over linebackers. Sunday it was Kapp who was run over. Aaron Brown, the defensive end who disabled Oakland's Darryl Lamonica a week ago, smashed Kapp to the ground with about six minutes left in the fourth quarter. Kapp was a folorn figure as he left the game with his right shoulder drooping.

Defensively the Vikings were unable to exert the type of pressure that they thought would reduce Len Dawson's effectiveness. The Minnesota ends were double teamed and the tackles were seldom able to penetrate. The Chiefs' running game produced 151 yards.

The Vikings were convinced they could line up and whip the Chiefs physically just as they whipped the Rams, the Browns and other NFL clubs. It was a major miscalculation.

Minnesota's deepest penetration in the first half was to the Chiefs' 38. The Vikings attempted one field goal but it was from 56 yards.

The Chiefs held a 16-0 lead at halftime on a five-yard touchdown run by Mike Garrett and three field goals by Jan Stenerud.

Minnesota had one chance to get back in the game. The Vikings scored the first time they had the ball in the second half, driving 59 yards to a touchdown that made the score 16-7. Now the Vikings had to hold the Chiefs and score again. Instead they gave up a touchdown drive that sealed the outcome.

There were two big plays on the Chiefs' drive. Facing a third-and-7 at their 32, the Chiefs sent Frank Pitts around left end on a reverse. He was run out of bounds but made the first down.

The Vikings drew a personal foul penalty and then Dawson passed to Otis Taylor on the Viking 41. Earsell Mackbee came up to meet him but Taylor broke the tackle and raced down the sideline. He eluded Karl Kassulke at the 8 and scored.

The Chiefs' victory confirmed that the AFL had achieved parity with the NFL. The two leagues have broken even in the first four Super Bowls and now the AFL will pass from existence as it is absorbed into the NFL.

The game was especially meaningful for Dawson who achieved a life-long ambition at a time when he does not have too many years left in his career.

Dawson decided to forgo an operation on his injured left knee early in the season because it would have kept him out the rest of the year. He played in pain but Sunday made the pain worthwhile.

In the week leading up to the game a story broke that Dawson might be called to testify before a grand jury investigating gambling in Detroit. Nothing came of the report and Dawson has received support from many people, including President Nixon.

It was an important victory for Hank Stram who has had a surprising number of critics even though the Chiefs have won league titles in two of the last four seasons and have a 26-6 record for the last two years. Some of Stram's critics have complained that he doesn't win the big ones. Now he has won the biggest game of all.

This was also a memorable victory for Lamar Hunt, the founder of the AFL.

"I'm happy for our team and I'm happy for Kansas City," Hunt said. "This is my greatest thrill. I'm also happy for Len Dawson. For seven years he was a great quarterback and received no recognition. He had game after outstanding game but when they wrote about great quarterbacks they never mentioned him. I said it would take a Super Bowl for him to get proper recognition and now he has it."

The final scene of this Super Bowl victory took place in a hotel in the French Quarter where the Chiefs held their victory party. As the celebration reached its climax, several of the Chiefs put Stram on their shoulders and carried him around the room while the onlookers raised their glasses as he passed.

Hunt Enters
Hall of Fame

Lamar Hunt, the founder of the American Football League, will be inducted into the Professional Football Hall of Fame tomorrow in Canton, O. The timing is unusually appropriate because 13 years ago the formation of the A.F.L. was announced to an unsuspecting world.

The announcement was made by the late Bert Bell, who was commissioner of the National Football League. In light of what was to come, it may seem strange that the commissioner of the N.F.L. was involved but then Bell was not acting entirely from humanitarian motives.

Hunt, who was only 26 in the summer of 1959, had conceived the idea of a new league following an unsuccessful effort to purchase the Chicago Cardinals and move them to Dallas. The thought came to him on a flight from Chicago to Dallas. Hunt describes the experience by saying, "It was sort of like a light bulb coming on."

Hunt first obtained a commitment from Bud Adams in Houston to enter the new league. He also received positive responses in Denver and Minneapolis-St. Paul. Hunt's next challenge was to line up franchises in New York and Los Angeles.

In June of 1959 Hunt decided to ask for a meeting with Bell. His purpose was to see if there still might be a chance of getting an N.F.L. expansion team in Dallas. Bell ruled out any possibility of such a development. When Hunt returned to Dallas he met with Davey O'Brien, a former college and pro star who was held in high regard by Bell.

Hunt asked O'Brien to go to Philadelphia and discuss the idea of a new league with Bell. Hunt even held out the hope that Bell would become the commissioner of the new league as well as the N.F.L.

"It was a very naive thought," Hunt later confessed, "but I wanted to get into this thing peacefully. I was at least intelligent enough to know that I did not want to start a war."

Bell met with O'Brien and turned down the proposal that he become the commissioner of the new league. However, he did tell O'Brien that Hunt was free to come to him for advice. Hunt interpreted this as an encouraging development and moved ahead with plans for his new league.

On July 26, 1959 he received a call from O'Brien who said Bell was going to testify before the Senate Antimonopoly Subcommittee, which was investigating monopolistic practices in professional sports. Bell wanted Hunt's permission to announce the formation of the A.F.L. at that time.

"I was only 26 at the time and this sounded like a pretty good idea," Hunt recalls. "I remember thinking to myself that nothing could give us a bigger story."

Hunt gave Bell permission to announce the formation of a 6-team league. In truth Hunt had only four teams but he covered up this little problem by telling Bell that the names of the cities and the owners were not to be announced until later.

Hunt flew back to Washington for the hearing and sat in the back of the committee room listening to Bell's testimony. Bell told the committee that he was making the rounds of the pro camps and was to visit the Baltimore Colts that afternoon. He said he was anxious to have enough time to tell the committee about the formation of a new league.

Bell declared that there was no monopoly in professional football and that the N.F.L. would foster and nourish the new league. The words "foster" and "nourish" seemed especially significant to Hunt.

The Associated Press story from Washington that day contained a sentence that read: "The commissioner said he had checked with the owners of all 12 teams in his league and the idea hadn't met with a single objection."

Thus the A.F.L. was born in a spirit of harmony and co-operation. Hunt was soon to learn that while the owners of the 12 N.F.L. teams had no objection to the "idea" of a new league they had entirely different feelings about the possibility of it becoming a reality.

The only man who disturbed Hunt's sense of euphoria was Jack Corbett, who had founded the International Football League three years earlier. Corbett declared, "The N.F.L. is not serious about supporting any new league, mine, Hunt's or anyone else's. This is strictly a maneuver to get Congress off its back."

It soon became apparent that Corbett was a man who knew the facts of life.

Hunt continued to receive encouragement from the N.F.L. until Aug. 29. On that date a reporter called Hunt at home and asked him if he had heard the news from Houston. Hunt said he had not. The reporter told him that George Halas and Dan Rooney had announced that the N.F.L. was expanding into Dallas and Houston. Only 30 days earlier Bell had promised that the N.F.L. would "foster" and "nourish" the new league.

It developed that the N.F.L. was unable to put a team in Houston because Adams had contracted for the only available stadium, but the N.F.L. did establish itself in Dallas and also persuaded the owners of the Minneapolis-St. Paul franchise to switch from the A.F.L. to the N.F.L.

Later the N.F.L. offered Hunt and Adams franchises if they would disband the new league, but Hunt and Adams refused to make any sort of a deal in which the other owners would be left out.

The A.F.L. began its first season of play in 1960. The war between the A.F.L. and the N.F.L. lasted for six seasons. It was not until the spring of 1966 that negotiations leading to a settlement were begun. In the end the A.F.L. forced the N.F.L. to accept all of its members, although it made indemnity payments to the N.F.L. teams in New York and San Francisco.

Not only did Hunt found the A.F.L. but his wealth and his integrity held it together. He also played a leading role in bringing about the merger with the N.F.L. Hunt once said that had he been aware of all the problems that were to develop he would never have started the A.F.L. At the time he undoubtedly meant what he said but tomorrow in Canton he will come before his peers with great pride and no regrets.

A Christmas Day Classic

The 50,374 spectators who saw yesterday's playoff game between the Chiefs and the Miami Dolphins left Municipal Stadium knowing they had seen one of the greatest games in the history of professional football. It will be remembered as a Christmas day classic, but for the Chiefs it had a bah-humbug ending.

It was a game that produced two predominant emotions, numbness and disbelief.

On a playing field littered with missed opportunities, the Chiefs lost to Miami 27-24 in the second quarter of sudden-death overtime. The game consumed 82 minutes and 40 seconds, making it the longest in pro football history.

The Chiefs were in position to win the game with 35 seconds remaining in regulation playing time. Miami had tied the score, 24-24, with 1:35 left but Ed Podolak returned the ensuing kick-off deep into Miami territory. After three running plays, the Chiefs called on Jan Stenerud to attempt a field goal from the 31.

In other years a 31-yarder would have been a "gimme" for Stenerud, but through much of this season he has approached field goal kicking with all the uncertainty of Sam Snead hanging over a long, downhill putt.

This time Stenerud swung his foot into the ball and in the hushed stadium the distinct sound of leather hitting leather could be heard. The sound, however, was not reassuring and neither was the flight of the ball. The kick angled off to the right and the official signaled that it was no good.

Dave Hill stood straight up in disbelief. For a moment all of the players seemed immobilized. Then Stenerud ducked his head and trotted slowly to the bench. Hank Stram tapped him lightly on the seat of the pants.

Stenerud's miss sent the game into a sudden death overtime, the first such game in pro football since the Packers defeated the Colts in 1965.

The Chiefs won the toss at midfield and elected to receive to start the overtime period. The kick-off was returned to the 46 and the Chiefs drove to the Miami 35 before running out of downs. Stenerud attempted a field goal from the 42 but it was blocked by Nick Buoniconti.

From that point on the Chiefs slowly lost field position and momentum. Two possessions later they moved the ball from their 20 to the 50 but gave it up on an interception. With 11:13 left in the second quarter of overtime play Miami started a drive that led to a game winning field goal by Garo Yepremian, a native of Cyprus who has known good times and bad in the kicking business.

Jim Kiick gained five yards on a sweep and then Larry Csonka broke over left tackle for 29 yards to the Kansas City 36. Three plays moved the ball to the 30 and then Yepremian brought the game to a close with a 37-yard field goal.

Csonka's big gain came on what is called a misdirection play. The Dolphins had achieved only limited success running straight ahead so this time Bob Griese and Kiick started a play to the right. Csonka cut back between them to the left side and there was no one there to stop him.

The call turned out to be especially effective because the Chiefs were using double coverage on both wide receivers and once Csonka got into the secondary there was no one close to him. Csonka, in explaining how the play came about, expressed great admiration for Willie Lanier, the Chiefs middle linebacker.

"It's tough running against a grizzly bear and it's worse if he's a smart one," Csonka said. "Lanier against power football is what defense is all about.

"We had been going straight ahead and having trouble. The misdirection play was a great call by Griese. He really knows how to hurt a defense. Bob Kuechenberg got the defensive end. Larry Little (right guard) was in front of me. I took hold of his pants and off we went."

Little said he was unaware that Csonka had hold of him.

"I didn't feel it," Little said, "but since I wasn't sure of where he was I guess that's why I ran so fast. I was kind of surprised the play went the way it did. I'm supposed to block Lynch but he had moved the other way with the flow so I just blocked straight ahead."

Yepremian said he was aware of little that was going on around him when he kicked his game-winning field goal.

"If the Chiefs said anything to me I wasn't aware of it," Yepremian said. "I didn't hear anything but the crowd and usually I'm not aware of that. I wanted to concentrate and make sure I kept my eye on the ball and followed through. If I don't follow through I don't get enough height."

In regard to the pressure, Yepremian laughed and said, "I just closed it out of my mind—but I knew this kick would make or break me."

Buck Buchanan called yesterday's loss the most disappointing of his career and it was apparent that many of his teammates agreed. The most frustrating aspect of the loss was the large number of missed opportunities.

In the second quarter an interception broke up a drive in Miami territory. Just before halftime Podolak fumbled and Miami recovered on the Kansas City 12. The Chiefs held but Yepremian kicked a field goal to tie the score, 10-10. There were the two missed field goals by Stenerud, one from the 29 and one from the 31 along with the one that was blocked from the 42.

Long after the game was over Hank Stram sat in a nearly-deserted dressing room. Normally he is stoic in the face of defeat but this time it appeared his emotions were close to overcoming him.

"To go so far..." he said, his voice trailing away.

"It's tough to take, to lose this way. It has to be the toughest loss we've ever had. It's just incredible."

As the last visitors departed Stram sat motionless in his chair staring into space.

Strange Man That George Allen

NEWPORT BEACH, CALIF.—For a man who does not swear, over-indulges only in ice cream and preaches the Christian work ethic, George Allen is a remarkably controversial football coach. He has been praised by the president and eulogized by his players. He has been called a liar and a conniver by an employer. He has been fined and censured by Pete Rozelle.

The members of the Redskins speak of Allen with great emotion. "George Allen is an amazing man," commented Cornerback Pat Fischer after the Redskins' play-off victory over Dallas. "This is an amazing team. I would do anything for either of them."

Before the game Herb Mulkey, a young running back, told a reporter, "I don't know what will happen, but I tell you this, the team will be together around George Allen no matter what happens."

After Allen left the Los Angeles Rams to join the Redskins, quarterback Roman Gabriel observed, "I have a lot of respect for Allen as a coach. I used to as a man. Personally, he and I don't see eye to eye the way we used to. He's so tied up in football he's not aware he hurts people sometimes. Like maybe telling two players each of them will start."

Merlin Olsen, Rams' tackle, said, "George is a player's coach. He makes you feel like he's doing it for you. His strength is in organizing and unifying a team in its defensive strategy. He works hard to establish trust between himself and the players.

"Then after a while you find George doesn't tell the straight story. He's always got some gimmick. After a while you just sigh and say, 'Well, George wants to get us up for another game.'"

The late Dan Reeves, who twice fired Allen as a coach of the Rams, gave a deathbed interview in which he accused Allen of lying, cheating and disloyalty.

In an earlier interview Allen had berated Reeves, saying, "I operated in an atmosphere of hatred. Our whole team did. Reeves hated me. He hated the team. He sought to split us so we'd come apart. Somehow I held the pieces together."

Allen is famed for his policy of trading draft choices to obtain established players. He has been eminently successful, but on several occasions he became overzealous and obtained players by trading draft choices he already had given up.

Following the 1971 season San Diego and Buffalo charged he had traded the same draft choices to each of them. Allen had given his No. 3 and 4 choices in the 1973 draft to the Chargers for Speedy Duncan and the same picks to Buffalo for Ron McDole.

In addition he had swapped his No. 2 choice to the Rams for Rich Petibon and to the Jets for Verlon Biggs. The issue was appealed to Rozelle, who gave the Redskins' No. 1 choice for 1974 to the Rams to satisfy their debt.

A short time later Allen made a trade with San Francisco in which he gave up high 1974 and 1975 draft choices to get the 1973 picks he owed San Diego. The commissioner stepped in again and fined Allen $5,000 and censured him before an unprecedented executive session of club owners.

Rozelle disclosed that Allen had made similar deals when he was with the Rams but added that no fines were assessed because Allen had quickly worked out an agreement with the teams involved.

Numerous spying accusations have been made against Allen. The Lions claimed they once devised a new goal-line offense for the Rams and when they lined up in it Maxie Baughan of the Rams yelled, "Here it is, here it is."

Allen was once accused of hiring a woman to push a baby carriage past an open practice field where the Colts' were working out in Hollywood. The carriage supposedly contained a midget taking films of the Colts' plays.

The most famous spying incident took place before a game with Dallas in 1967. The Cowboys were working out in an open field at the time. There was a parking lot near the field. The Cowboys chased the fans away. A custodian happened to notice a car parked for the second day near the parking lot. He copied the license number and traced it to a rental firm.

The car had been rented to Johnny Sanders, the Rams' player personnel director, who was found to be staying in a nearby motel with a Rams' scout. The Cowboys protested to the league office. Allen dismissed the charges lightly by saying, "We think it's pretty funny."

While Allen has been devious in trying to get an edge on his opponents, his success has come about in large measure because of his fanatical dedication to work and detail. Allen has his 10 commandments of football which read:

"1. Football comes first. 2. The greatest feeling in life is to take an ordinary job and accomplish something with it. 3. If you can accept defeat and open your pay envelope without feeling guilty then you're stealing. 4. Everyone, the head coach especially, must give 110 per cent. 5. Leisure time is that five or six hours when you sleep at night. 6. No detail is too small. No task is too small or too big. 7. You must accomplish things in life, otherwise you are like the paper on the wall. 8. A person without a problem is dead. 9. We win and lose as a team. 10. My prayer is that each man will be allowed to play to the best of his ability.

In an interview Allen once said, "I don't want to do anything but football. I don't want to talk about anything but football."

His wife, Etty, made the following observation about her husband's fondness for ice cream: "I think he likes it because he doesn't have to chew it. It doesn't take any time. Chewing would take his mind away from football."

Allen has been called a genius. He has also been called the flim-flam man. Whatever his true personality and whatever his methods they have carried him to a 71-24-5 career record and a berth in the Super Bowl.

Adversity Molds a Hero

It was a scene that left its imprint on the mind just as a flash of white light burns itself into the eye.

The Super Bowl game between Kansas City and Minnesota had been over for 30 minutes or so. Len Dawson stood on a rubbing table in the trainer's room with reporters around him. His son, Len Dawson, Jr., 11, was at his side.

A reporter asked Len, Jr., what he thought of his dad.

"He's good" the boy replied with that great gift of candor that only the young possess.

This was the moment that Len Dawson, Sr., had lived and worked for since he was a scrawny high school quarterback in Alliance, O. He was the quarterback of a world championship professional football team. Only he, the members of his family and a few close friends could be fully aware of the disappointments, sufferings and personal slights he endured to achieve his goal.

"He may not look like it," one of his friends observed earlier in the week, "but lord he is tough inside."

Were it not for that quiet inner toughness Dawson would never have been standing on that rubbing table explaining how the Chiefs won the Super Bowl. He is a man to whom nothing has come easily.

In high school he had to overcome the handicap of size. After he was graduated from Purdue University he spent two seasons with the Pittsburgh Steelers and three with the Cleveland Browns. In those five seasons he started only two games, including exhibitions. Never did he start and finish a game.

At this point it appeared he might be finished as a professional football player but his career was rescued when he got an opportunity to go with the Dallas Texans, who were later to become the Chiefs.

He soon developed into an outstanding pro quarterback but he was unable to achieve the recognition to which he was entitled. His critics called him an N.F.L. castoff. Even within the A.F.L. he suffered slights. A year ago just ahead of the A.F.L. All-Star game Joe Namath made some comments about the outstanding quarterbacks in the A.F.L. He mentioned Daryle Lamonica, John Hadl and by implication himself. He ignored Dawson.

At the start of the 1969 season Dawson was third on the all-time A.F.L.-N.F.L. list in percentage of completions. He led all quarterbacks in touchdowns per passing attempt. He also led in most touchdowns per completion. He was tied for third place with Bart Starr and Johnny Unitas in the category of average gain per attempt. He ranked seventh in career touchdown passes and 18th in all-time passing yardage despite sitting on the bench for five years at Pittsburgh and Cleveland.

Regardless of his accomplishments Dawson's image was still that of an N.F.L. castoff. His only chance of changing it was to play on a Super Bowl champion.

When the Chiefs reported for the start of practice at William Jewell College in July Dawson and most of his teammates had a feeling that this was going to be their year. Athletic teams seem to have sixth sense about such things. Sometimes it comes early in the season and sometimes it comes late. With the Chiefs it was there all season.

In the end the Chiefs' premonition was right but little did Dawson realize how difficult his year of vindication was going to be. Seldom if ever has an athlete had to endure what Dawson did.

In the Chiefs' final exhibition game, Dawson injured his right hand diving for a fumble. The injury was painful and made it difficult for Dawson to grip the ball but even so he started the season opener against San Diego and led the Chiefs to victory.

The hand slowly improved but against Boston in the second game of the season Dawson was hit while throwing a pass and suffered a knee injury. The knee did not appear to be unusually sore at the time and Dawson did not think too much about it.

The team flew back to Kansas City immediately after the game and it was during the plane trip that the knee began to swell. The pain became severe after Dawson arrived home and he slept fitfully that night.

He was examined the following morning by Dr. Joseph Lichtor, the team orthopedist, who said it appeared Dawson had suffered damage to a tendon. Dr. Lichtor recommended that another opinion be obtained before a decision was made regarding surgery.

Dawson and his wife, Jackie, flew to Oklahoma City where he was examined by Dr. Don O'Donoghue, one of the nation's foremost orthopedic surgeons. Dr. O'Donoghue said the medical collateral ligament was partly torn and recommended immediate surgery.

A third examination was performed in Kansas City by Dr. Fred Reynolds of St. Louis, another noted orthopedist. Dr. Reynolds said in his opinion the knee did not require surgery, at least for the time being. He said that if all went well Dawson would be able to play again in five to six weeks.

That was what Dawson wanted to hear.

"I wanted to play," Dawson explained near the end of the season. "I had never been out before except for a game or two and I couldn't believe the injury was that bad.

"When you play football you have to live with injuries. I've had a lot of things wrong with me and they have always responded. I felt this injury would react the same way. I've had several injuries that were more painful. I got kicked in the calf of my leg once. It hemorrhaged and I couldn't walk for five days.

"Last season I bruised my thigh when I was thrown into a goal post. It hemorrhaged, too, and I had a lot of pain with it. I've played with broken ribs and my hands so jammed that I couldn't take the snap from center.

"Since the knee wasn't as painful as those injuries I couldn't register in my mind that it wasn't going to respond. Besides, I don't think anybody likes to be operated on. Football players are no tougher than anyone else when it comes to going under the knife."

Dawson also was influenced by the Chiefs' chances for a winning season.

"I had worked awfully hard this year and things were going well," Dawson said. "I had a jammed hand earlier but the pain was clearing up. We were going so well as a football team that I couldn't stand the thought of being out an entire season.

"In making my decision I thought it would be better to be out five or six weeks rather than an entire season. I asked myself, 'If I take five weeks and the knee doesn't respond how much worse was I going to be? Medically, I knew it was best to have surgery immediately, but I wasn't 24—I was 34—and I knew I wouldn't be playing this game much longer. If I laid out an entire season I would be a 35-year-old quarterback with a knee operation and that's not a very good position to be in.

"In the end I guess my strongest motivation was the possibility of us winning and going to the Super Bowl."

Dawson missed five games. He returned to action November 2 against Buffalo, entering the game just before halftime. He played the entire second half and led the Chiefs to a 29-7 victory. Dawson went on to start against San Diego, New York, Oakland and Denver.

Dawson suffered a personal tragedy two days before the Jets game when his father passed away. Dawson played one of his greatest games against the Jets and then flew to Alliance, O., for the funeral.

He reinjured his knee in the Denver game and was held out of a December 7 game with Buffalo. The Chiefs ended the season against Oakland in the now famous three-yards-and-a-cloud-of-controversy game. Dawson went all the way but threw only six times. He went into the game with his knee aching.

The Chiefs met the New York Jets in the first round of the A.F.L. playoffs. The game was played in New York on a cold windy afternoon. Dawson took one of his worst physical beatings, but he outpassed Joe Namath in the churning winds and the Chiefs played brilliant defense to win, 13-6.

Asked afterward if his knee ached Dawson said, "my whole body aches."

Then it was back to Oakland for the A.F.L. Championship. By this time Dawson's knee was improved. Oakland scored first but the Chiefs won, 17-7, and were back in the Super Bowl.

Just as Dawson was beginning preparations for what was to be the most important game of his life NBC news carried an unsubstantiated story that he and four other professional football players would be called to testify before a Detroit grand jury that was conducting a gambling investigation.

"I was shocked," Dawson said later when asked to give his reaction. "I didn't know what it was all about. I'll bet 90 percent of the people don't know what it means to be subpoenaed. I wasn't sure myself. As I understand it anyone who has information of any type can be called before a grand jury. The names of most people who are to appear before a grand jury are never made public."

Dawson issued a statement in which he said he was innocent of any wrongdoing. Commissioner Pete Rozelle came to his defense. The public lined up solidly behind him. Before the Super Bowl game President Nixon called Hank Stram to say that he knew the rumors involving Dawson were unfounded.

The night before the Super Bowl Dawson came down with a 24-hour virus. He had little or no sleep. Prior to the game he was able to eat a bowl of milk with crackers and a candy bar.

Despite the illness, his lack of sleep and the intense pressure he played one of his finest games, leading the Chiefs to a 23-7 victory over the Vikings. Dawson completed 12 of 17 passes for 172 yards, threw for one touchdown and had only one interception.

Dawson was named the game's most valuable player and was awarded a car by *Sport Magazine.*

This was the same Len Dawson who was so light his sophomore year in high school he wanted to give up football.

"I didn't even want to go out but all my brothers played football so I did," Dawson recalls. "I was nothing more than a dummy. I held the bag and I was so light they knocked me down and the bag too. The line averaged 200 pounds. I weighed 125. I didn't feel like going on."

This was the same Len Dawson who seldom got off the bench in Pittsburgh and Cleveland.

"I blame myself more than Buddy Parker or Paul Brown for not getting a chance to play with the Steelers and Browns," Dawson explains. "It was a matter of not being aggressive enough. Bobby Layne was at Pittsburgh when I first went there. He had won a championship for Parker. Brown had Milt Plum and he was successful. Both Parker and Brown are one-quarterback coaches. How could I expect them to start me over Layne or Plum."

This was the same Len Dawson who, after establishing himself in the A.F.L., answered N.F.L. people who criticized him by saying, "How can they tell. They haven't seen my play."

The kid from Alliance who got knocked over with the blocking dummies has come a long way.

Thank You,
Hank Stram

By now all of the reasons behind the dismissal of Hank Stram have been analyzed and reanalyzed and the public response has shown the fans welcomed a change. But before Stram's departure becomes a closed subject there are some things that need to be said about the man and his accomplishments.

Stram has known good times and bad in his 15 years as a pro coach, but winning has been a consuming passion with him whether the Chiefs were playing a rookie game, an exhibition or appearing in the Super Bowl. The late Paul Christman once remarked to me that he couldn't stand to lose even if he were playing a game of checkers with his kids. Stram approached winning with a similar intensity.

His overall record clearly reflects his ability as a coach. In regular-season competition he won 124 games, lost 76 and had 10 ties. He won three American Football League championships and is one of only six coaches who has recorded one or more Super Bowl victories. The others are the late Vince Lombardi, Weeb Ewbank, the late Don McCafferty, Tom Landry and Don Shula.

Because of our jobs Stram and I were brought into close association.

There were times when he was irritated by the things I wrote, and there were times when I was irritated by things he said and did, but he accepted the fact that I had a responsibility to my paper and I understood that he had a responsibility to the Chiefs.

On Monday following the close of the regular season I wrote a column sharply critical of Stram, not from a coaching standpoint, but in regard to the decline of the team and his loss of credibility with the public. At the time I had no idea that his job was in jeopardy, but in the aftermath of his firing I assumed that he felt my column was a factor. I have been through a great many hirings and firings in my years as a newspaperman, but it is a disturbing feeling to think you have played a part in causing a man to lose his job.

Yesterday I received a call from Stram. He said he had been think-ing that I might be worried that my column had led to his dismissal and he just wanted me to know that this was not the case.

Unfortunately, this was the side of Hank Stram that the public did not get to see. This is the Hank Stram who kept his veterans on after they had outlived their usefulness and who came to the assistance of his friends when they needed help.

There are many memories from my years with Stram but two stand out above the others. One goes back to the time of the 1970 Super Bowl when the Chiefs had defeated the Vikings, 23-7, and removed the stigma of their humiliating loss to Green Bay. The Kansas City writers were invited to a team party at the Royal Sonesta Hotel. Supposedly it was a private party, but seemingly everybody in New Orleans except the Vikings showed up. When I arrived Stram was being carried around the room on the shoulders of his players. As he passed glasses were raised in salute.

It was the triumphant end to a remarkable season. In the last game of the regular season the Chiefs lost to Oakland, 10-6, and threw only six passes. Had they won they would have captured the division title and the playoff games would have been played in Kansas City. In los-ing they qualified as a wild card team but they had to play on the road. The fans were angry and the players were questioning Stram's strategy.

The Chiefs defeated the Jets, the defending Super Bowl champions, in the first round of the playoffs and then upset the Raiders, 17-7, in Oakland. The Vikings were 14-point favorites in the Super Bowl, but they were never in the game.

The other memory of Stram that remains indelible is his reaction to the Chiefs' 27-24 playoff to Miami in 1971 in the longest game ever played. I had gone to the Miami dressing room first and by the time I reached the Chiefs' dressing room on the other side of the field at old Municipal Stadium, Stram was alone in his office. He was sitting in a chair with his back against a wall and for a minute or two he said nothing.

Finally he shook his head almost imperceptibly and said in a whis-per, "to go so far..." Seemingly he was going to say more, but he lapsed into silence. After another minute or so he made one more ef-fort to talk. "It's tough to take losing this way. It has to be the toughest loss we've ever had. It's just incredible." He fell silent again, his body caught up in a zombie-like trance. I excused myself and left, although I'm not sure he even knew I was there.

I remember the dressing room celebration in Buffalo after the Chiefs defeated the Bills, 31-7, to qualify for the first Super Bowl. The players threw Stram in the shower and then poured champagne over his head. Later E.J. Holub cut off the tie of Milt Woodward, who was then the commissioner of the A.F.L.

After the first Super Bowl Stram stood in the dressing room at the Memorial Coliseum in Los Angeles patiently answering reporters' questions. "They just beat us, that's all," he said. In the Packer dressing room Lombardi was declaring, "The Chiefs don't rate with the top teams in the N.F.L."

There are many other memories—plane trips, hotel room conversations, golf games, 101 dinners. But now an era has come to an end. Stram is leaving by public demand, but with the passing of time his accomplishments will be viewed with greater appreciation.

The Remarkable
Emmitt Thomas

One of the defensive mechanisms that nature provides for us is a reduced mental awareness of the aging process.

Time passes, gray hairs appear and facial lines deepen, but we tell ourselves that we don't feel older and for the most part we visualize ourselves as being younger than we are. Then, on rare occasions, something happens that forces us to accept the reality of our years.

It could be a casual occurrence such as looking at an old photograph or trying on an old suit. It could be a son or daughter going off to college or the assumption of a new role in business.

For Emmitt Thomas it is becoming the senior member of the Chiefs in years of service.

In some ways it seems only a few years ago that Thomas walked into the Chiefs' camp at William Jewell College, a slender, somewhat bewildered young man fresh from Bishop College. He was not taken in the draft, but he could run the 100-yard dash in 9.5 seconds and Hank Stram projected him as a flanker or a defensive back.

"One of the things I remember about that first camp is how hot it was," Thomas laughed. "Fletcher Smith had been taken in the eighth round that year and we came up a week early so we'd be ready. The first thing I remember about Hank is that he told me I'd have to get a haircut.

"Because I was a free agent I was willing to play any place, but I kind of figured I'd wind up being a defensive back. They already had receivers like Otis Taylor, Chris Burford, Gloster Richardson and Frank Pitts, so I didn't see much chance for me breaking in there.

"I look back now and I can remember when I used to tease Buck (Buchanan) and Len (Dawson) about being the senior members of the team. Buck used to tell me that some day it would happen to me and I'd laugh at him. Now I look around at all the new faces and see Otis working with management and you wonder where the time went.

"I was fortunate. I played with some great players and they made the job easier."

This will be Thomas' 13th season with the Chiefs and his reputation as one of pro football's all-time great cornerbacks is secure. Whether he starts or not is no longer a matter of great importance to him, but he is certain to be used extensively because for the most part the defensive unit will be young and inexperienced.

The Chiefs have two outstanding young cornerbacks in Tim Collier and Gary Green, but Collier will be starting only his third season in the NFL and Green his second.

"Playing behind Collier or Green wouldn't be a disgrace," Thomas said. "Both of them have outstanding ability. I think they are comparable to what Jim Marsalis and I were at the same stage of our careers.

"But if they're going to start I'm going to make them earn it. With the change to the three-man front we'll probably be using five backs quite a bit. The way I understand it, if they think I deserve to start I'll start, but it's no problem if Collier and Green start. I'll just do whatever I can to help."

A major change will take place in pass defense this season because of the new rule designed to virtually eliminate harassment of the receiver. Under the rule a receiver can be bumped only once and cannot be bumped at all once he is five yards beyond the line of scrimmage.

In effect, the change will eliminate the bump and run, a technique that was developed by the Oakland Raiders and was being picked up by other teams at the time Thomas broke in.

"The new rule will affect me the most because I've played under the old system so long," Thomas said. "But if you've got speed and quickness you can adjust.

"Kent McCloughan and Willie Brown started the bump and run at Oakland. Tom Bettis came to the Chiefs as an assistant the same year I was signed and Bettis loved the bump and run. We went at it full blast.

"The way I see it, you're going to have to give the receiver a little bit more room and make sure he is in his last route before you react. The receivers will use a lot of double moves and you're going to have to be real patient."

Even though the defensive backs will be under greater pressure, it can be assumed that Thomas will adapt. He enters this season hoping to equal the Chiefs' record for career interceptions held by Johnny Robinson. The all-time record for interceptions is 79, held by Emlen Tunnel.

After Thomas started his first game for the Chiefs in 1966 Stram observed, "You have to be open minded about free agents. You can't go on reputation."

Emmitt may not have had much of a reputation when he arrived, but now he is the standard by which other defensive backs are judged.

The Ideal
Middle Linebacker

If a panel of football coaches were to gather in front of a computer and feed in all of their requisites for the ultimate middle linebacker, the creation that emerged almost certainly would bear a close resemblance to Willie Lanier, who today became the second member of the Chiefs to enter the Professional Football Hall of Fame.

Linebacker Bobby Bell was named three years ago.

Lanier stood 6 feet, 1 inch, weighed 245, had great natural strength, played his position with what might best be described as controlled fury and had such quickness and agility that he made 27 career interceptions.

More than any other single player he was the person who solidified the Chiefs' defense in the period between the first Super Bowl, when they lost to the Packers 35-10, and the fourth Super Bowl, when they defeated Minnesota 23-7.

The loss to the Packers exposed problems in the defensive line, at linebacker and in the secondary, but with the key additions of Lanier, linebacker Jim Lynch, tackle Curly Culp and cornerback Emmitt Thomas, the 1969 Chiefs were the best defensive unit in professional football.

Not only was Lanier a great player, he was a pioneer at his position.

Lanier and Lynch both joined the Chiefs in 1967 and both went to camp competing for the middle linebacker job. One was black, one was white. One was from obscure Morgan State. The other was from Notre Dame and had won the Maxwell Trophy.

At that time no black player ever had become a regular at middle linebacker and no black player ever had called defensive signals. Lanier not only broke both of those barriers, but he and Lunch became good friends and were roommates on the road.

Lynch was the 47th player taken in the draft that year, and Lanier was the 49th. Lynch was considered a sure thing. Lanier was regarded as something of a gamble. But Lanier was bigger than Lynch, hit harder and eventually won the job.

"When I first came to camp I didn't know Willie Lanier other than as a name," Lynch said. "I came into camp from the All-Star game and when I saw the way Willie was playing, there was no question in my mind that unless there was a lot more to the game than I thought there was they had a middle linebacker and it wasn't me. He hit so hard it was unbelievable."

The 1967 season began with Lanier backing up Sherril Headrick at middle linebacker and Lynch being used as a swing man at middle and outside linebacker. When the 1968 season began, Lanier was starting in the middle, Lynch was at right linebacker and Bell on the left side. It was to become one of pro football's all-time great linebacking units.

Lanier's aggressiveness and his willingness to stick his head into opposing runners resulted in physical problems that cut short his rookie season. He began to suffer double vision and in a game Oct. 30, 1967, he collapsed in the huddle.

Lanier said later that when he woke up in the hospital the first thing he could remember thinking was, "Am I dying?" His next reaction was concern for his pregnant wife.

He returned to the lineup in 1968 with a specially padded helmet and a different style of tackling. He lost none of his aggressiveness, but he no longer attempted to spear running backs.

"I hit as hard as I ever did," Lanier said, "but I used my shoulders instead of my head. I think it made me a better tackler."

At the time of his retirement, Lanier looked back on the early years of his career and said, "In the beginning, it was important for me to be the best because I was the first black middle linebacker in the league. It was a challenge. Because it was a situation a black had not come into before, a lot of people didn't think I would make it.

"I had to play well enough to knock down the myth that a black couldn't play middle linebacker. I look around now and I see a lot of other black middle linebackers in the league and I feel good about it."

Much of Lanier's career paralleled that of Dick Butkus, the great Chicago Bears linebacker who played from 1965 through 1973 and is a member of the Hall of Fame. Butkus and Lanier were regarded as the best middle linebackers of their era, and by 1972 Lanier had surpassed Butkus.

"Butkus always went out to overpower people," Lanier said near the end of his career. "The longer I played the more I realized that quickness and being in the right place could keep me out of a lot of trouble. You can't constantly try to overpower people when most of them are as big or bigger than you are.

"Butkus always tried to project the animal image. I never believed in that. I'm not trying to destroy people. After a while that sort of comes back on you. I think Butkus became a victim of his own image."

Lynch describes Lanier as a highly intelligent player who reacted quickly to changing situations.

"He could be such a dominant player. I used to marvel at his reserves of ability," Lynch said. "You can't appreciate that unless you played with the guy. All of the great players have that quality. There was never a relaxing time for me in a game. I could never let down. Lanier was very disciplined. He also had the ability to get into a play, know where he was supposed to be, realize as the play developed that he would be wasted and then adjust to make a big play.

"We were playing a game against Denver and we had not played well in the first half. Denver had the ball on its 2 or 3 and all of a sudden Willie blitzed and got a safety. There was no way in the world he was supposed to do that, but he just reacted to a situation he saw developing."

Lanier, speaking from his home in Richmond, Va., said one of his first reactions to being named to the Hall of Fame was to find himself reflecting on his years as a high-school and college player and what his years with the Chiefs meant to him.

"Sunday I was watching television when they showed the segment about the first Super Bowl," Lanier said. "The part about the Chiefs brought into focus how much it meant to have a chance to play with such quality people. To forever be a part of that kind of relationship and have those ties—it's hard to explain how much that means.

"There are very few things you put yourself into where other people are so closely involved. As individuals, I think we tend to be closed to others, but because of the nature of the sport you let your teammates see inside you.

"Being named to the Hall of Fame takes you back to your true beginnings."

The Chiefs
at 20

BUFFALO, N.Y.—Lamar Hunt was regarded as a "boy owner," Len Dawson was playing quarterback. Ed Budde, Bobby Bell and Buck Buchanan were rookies. Hank Stram had his own hair. And Kansas City, ready or not, had a new professional football team in a struggling organization known as the American Football League.

The year was 1963 and the Dallas Texans had become the Kansas City Chiefs, to the dismay of their players and the indifference of Kansas Citians, who would have preferred a National Football League team.

Today the Chiefs begin their 20th anniversary season as a Kansas City entity. It is an occasion for replaying old Super Bowls, recalling the howls of the Wolfpack and the games at Municipal Stadium and and reliving an era when professional football was poorer, simpler and, in many respects, more fun.

How much different was professional football in those days? Well, an owner once sabotaged an A.F.L. meeting by having the commissioner's papers taken from his hotel room and shipped out of town. When the Texans played their final regular-season game in Dallas in 1962, Hunt and Barron Hilton, then the owner of the Chargers, considered closing the Cotton Bowl to the public and watching the game by themselves. When Hunt met Charles O. Finley for the first time after relocating his team in Kansas City, Finley, then operating the A's in Kansas City, proposed they move their teams to Atlanta.

The sabotaged meeting was the handiwork of Harry Wismer, the glib but bankrupt owner of the New York Titans, the team that later became the New York Jets. Although on one occasion the Titans didn't have enough money to get their uniforms back from the cleaners, Wismer balked at giving up the franchise. Joe Foss, then commissioner of the AFL, called a meeting in New York to challenge Wismer to show why his franchise should not be revoked.

Foss and his assistant, Milt Woodard, were staying at the Waldorf. While they were out of their suite, Wismer called the bell captain, identified himself as Foss and said an emergency had developed in Dallas. He did not have time to return to the hotel, but his bags just needed closing, and if the bell captain would see they were put on a flight to Dallas he would be well rewarded.

The meeting had to be postponed, but a short time later an agreement was reached in which Sonny Werblin purchased the rights to the franchise for $1 million.

The idea of closing the Cotton Bowl to the public developed at a party in Dallas the night before the game between the Texans and Chargers. Hunt told a story of two N.F.L. owners who, in the early years of the league, considered locking the gates, sitting on opposite sides of the field and cheering their teams in solitary splendor.

The story intrigued Hilton, who later said to Hunt, "Why not do it tomorrow?"

Relating the story later, Hunt said, "I guarantee you we came within an inch of doing it."

Hunt's first encounter with Finley took place in the spring of 1963. Hunt and Stram had come to Kansas City for a speaking engagement. Stram, out for a morning walk, happened across Finley, whom he knew slightly. Stram invited Finley to his room to meet Hunt.

Finley and Hunt talked for a while, then Finley said he had a proposition. He explained that Atlanta was building a stadium and he had helped start the project. His approach to helping was letting it be known that he was looking for a place to move his club, and Atlanta might have a chance to get it if the city built a stadium.

With the stadium under construction, Finley said he and Hunt could create the biggest story in sports by moving their franchises to Atlanta and leaving Kansas City without professional athletics.

"This is a lousy town and no one will ever do any good here," Finley told Hunt.

Hunt, who was trying to sell 25,000 season tickets, quickly excused himself.

In 19 years the Chiefs have won two league championships, one Super Bowl and have established themselves as an exciting element of life in Kansas City. They have provided us with triumphs, disappointments and some wonderful memories.

CHAPTER 4

OLYMPICS

Double-teamed
in Mexico

MEXICO CITY—Anne Snider, a pretty blond from Bay Village, Ohio, stood outside the Olympic stadium yesterday. The afternoon was sunny and pleasant. The flags that ring the stadium rose and fell in a light breeze. From time to time the stadium reverberated with cheers.

Anne stood and stared at the elevated ramp that leads from the stadium to the athletes' practice field and dressing room. Spectators walked under the ramp laughing and chatting. On occasion, Anne gulped hard to keep from crying. Once she ran a finger across the bridge of her nose and under one eye.

In January, Anne will become Mrs. Jim Ryun. She had come to Mexico City hoping to share the joy of an Olympic 1,500-meter victory with her future husband. Now she was waiting to extend some sign of consolation to him. He had run second to Kenya's Kip Keino. After years of punishing work and self sacrifice, Ryun had been denied his most cherished goal through a series of circumstances involving injury, ailments, the Kenya cabal and Mexico City's 7,300-foot altitude.

When Ryun appeared on the ramp he and Anne exchanged glances. He continued to jog as he cooled down, his eyes staring at the ground. Occasionally, he ran both hands along his temples and then clasped them over his head. Living with defeat is a part of competing, but an Olympic defeat has an element of finality to it. A baseball player can think of tomorrow. A football player can think of next week. It takes four years to try again in the Olympics, and no one can be sure if another chance will come.

It was a bitter moment in the life of the greatest middle distance man the United States has produced. He had run better than anyone had reason to expect. He had overcome physical handicaps including a bout with mononucleosis. Yet he had come in second, losing to a man who had the advantage of living at an altitude that is approximately the same as Mexico City's.

The pattern of the race was relatively simple. Ben Jipcho, Keino's teammate, assumed the role of the rabbit. He took the lead at the outset and ran the first lap in the unusually fast time of 56 seconds. Keino stayed close to the lead. Ryun had no choice but to lay back.

Keino took the lead after a lap and a half. Jipcho had set the pace that Keino wanted and now Jipcho's job was over. Ryun could not afford to lose contact with Keino but neither could he make his move too soon. With two laps remaining, Ryun decided he could wait no longer. He made his move and for a time he began to close the gap but Keino was uncatchable, winning by about 25 yards. His time was 3:34.9, breaking Herb Elliott's Olympic record of 3:35.6. Ryun ran a respectable 3:37.8.

Following the awards ceremony, Ryun sat down on a grassy slope outside the stadium to talk about the race and the problems he faced preparing for it.

He disclosed that in addition to his widely publicized attack of mononucleosis, his preparations were hampered by a kidney ailment and a pulled muscle. In mid-summer he became so discouraged he almost quit.

He voiced objections to holding the Olympics at a high altitude site. Dr. Roger Bannister, the first man to run the 4-minute mile, shares Ryun's feelings as do many other runners.

"I ran the best race I could possibly run," Ryun said. "I've run against Keino four times and beaten him three times. This is the first time I've run against him at altitude. It is the last time.

"Two years ago I ran at altitude and went out in :61 and I couldn't finish. I rested and then came back and ran a 4:30. By the end of the summer I was down to 4:15, but every time I ran I nearly died.

"I knew then that adjusting to altitude was a very big problem.

"This year it seemed like everything went wrong. It got so bad I almost gave up. I hurt myself and I had sickness. I knew I had to be at my best at sea level to have a chance in the Olympics, so I ran in the Eugene (Ore.) meet. That was when I nearly gave up. I ran 3:59.5 and was nearly beaten by Liquori. Marty is a good runner, but I knew I had to do better than that. I can't tell you how discouraged I was.

"I started training hard, harder than I should have right after getting over the mono, but I had come too far and I decided to give it a try in the trials and see what happened.

"I wanted to make it in the 800, but people didn't understand that I had been set so far back in my training I could not do the necessary speed work. I decided to give the 800 a try anyway. I wanted to satisfy my own curiosity. It couldn't hurt me and it could help tone up my muscles.

"I had to pull out of the 800, but I got through the Tahoe trials in the 1,500 and I still had hope. Then the night after the trials I started passing blood in my urine. I had been to Wichita to see Anne. I went on to Topeka and I went to a doctor there. I didn't know what to expect. He said I had a kidney infection. This caused me to lose additional training time.

"By then it seemed that every time I got over one thing something else happened.

"I went back to Alamosa. I trained for one day and pulled a muscle. I couldn't do any serious training for four days. Then I started doing cross-country with George Young, but I couldn't do speed work.

"I didn't feel good when I first arrived here," Ryun continued, "but I felt more confident after running the first and second heats Friday and Saturday. Four days before the heats I couldn't break 70 seconds for a quarter. I felt tired, and I was afraid the mono was coming back on me.

"They ran some tests here. Nothing showed up and they said I was just tired. I tried extra rest, but it didn't seem to do any good. Last Tuesday I still wasn't running well. I was really down. I felt I would be lucky to make it in the first heat.

"You may laugh at me about this, but Anne was the one who got me straightened out. She got me off in the corner and chewed me out. I can't remember exactly what she said, but it came at exactly the right time. It got me going again. She deserves a great deal of credit for snapping me out of it.

"As it turned out the first heat was easy. I felt good, but considering how much my training had been interrupted I was concerned whether I could go three days at this pace.

"The second day went fairly easy too, but I reinjured the pulled muscle in my right leg. When I warmed up for the finals I wasn't sure whether I could run. I stayed off the pace hoping I could catch Keino in the last half. I knew if I stayed with him my leg might give out. I ran as well as I could.

"I know people will say it's disappointing not to get the gold medal. It is, but really, I'm pleased to have come this far at a time when everything went wrong.

"'The biggest thing I had to do was remove the doubts I had. Fear of failure was the thing that bothered me most. Fortunately, I couldn't have run better than I did here. Should I go on and run to 1972 I would no longer have a fear of failure.

Jim Ryun has lost few races in the course of his career. Yesterday he was only second best, but considering what he endured to gain his silver medal it was an impressive accomplishment.

A Tragic Scene
in Munich

MUNICH—The bridge leading from the press center to the Olympic village was thronged with people.

Youngsters clung to the hands of their parents. A man stopped to photograph the vista of buildings and playing fields. A bus honked for pedestrians to move over.

There was a disturbing air of normality to the scene considering that two men lay dead in the Olympic village and the XX Olympiad was slowing to a halt. But a few hundred yards down the road the scene began to change.

Two soldiers wearing side arms stood together on a small hill overlooking the field hockey area. An armored police truck had been pulled across the walk in front of a concession stand. Police lines were up and passage was difficult to obtain. Fifteen armored trucks stood side by side in nearby parking lots.

A few hundred yards beyond was a hill that overlooked part of the village. To the left of the hill were a cluster of flags and a recreation area where 200 or so athletes were gathered. To the right was a series of 4-story apartment buildings. No more than 200 yards away was building No. 31, where the most tragic drama in Olympic history had its beginning.

Two Israeli athletes had been killed and nine others were being held hostage by members of a Palestinian guerrilla group known as "Black September." The terrorists had demanded the release of 200 Palestinian prisoners by the Israeli government under threat of killing the hostages.

Several deadlines had been set. The most recent was 5 o'clock, but it had come and gone. A German sniper dressed in a red and white track warmup suit was on the roof of building 31. He was flattened against a wall of the building's penthouse, a machinegun dangling from his left hand.

The apartment on the two floors immediately beneath him was occupied by the terrorists and their captives. Occasionally one of the terrorists stuck his head from a door on the upper level apartment area. At his appearance movie cameras began to whir.

"We have enough of that shot," one cameraman said to another. "We're getting low on film."

"He doesn't look very happy," observed his colleague, who had been looking at the terrorist through a long lens. "It looks like he has a stocking of some kind over his head, with the eyes cut out. There's a guy in the apartment below who looks like he's wearing a cowboy hat."

In a taller housing unit across the street athletes stood on their balconies and observed the scene, apparently oblivious to the possibility that shooting could start at any time.

The sniper tiptoed away from his position for a few minutes, then returned. More men in warmup suits began appearing on the roof of one of the connecting buildings.

"They're all snipers," observed a young Swedish track athlete, who identified himself as Kenth Ohman. "I was in the village when they put him on (the roof)."

Ohman, who attends New Mexico University, said the shootings and the seizure of the Israelis had not had an immediate impact on the athletes.

"The word spread kind of slowly," Ohman said. "This afternoon people in the village were still playing table tennis and miniature golf."

A sniper dressed in a blue suit ran across the roof and one of the terrorists again appeared at the door. The terrorist then pulled back and a few minutes later the blue-clad sniper left the roof, descending down a protected stairway. The sniper in the red suit followed. Six or seven snipers and several officials then gathered on the balcony of an adjacent building.

On several occasions one of the terrorists appeared on a third floor balcony and looked down. As time passed rumors spread that negotiations were progressing and the terrorists would leave the building by busses and would be taken to helicopters.

Darkness began to settle over the village. Lights flicked on in the apartments that housed the athletes and officials. With the sunlight gone, all the photographers began dismantling their equipment and prepared to leave. Only the television cameramen remained.

Suddenly a squad of men carrying machine guns appeared in a lower-level garage that runs under several of the buildings. They took up positions behind concrete posts, heightening speculation that the terrorists were getting ready to leave. Time dragged by, but nothing happened.

About 10:30 p.m. (Munich time) the long vigil came to an end. A bus pulled up in front of building 31. The Israelis boarded first. The guerrillas were behind them. The group was driven to an improvised heliport where three helicopters were waiting.

One after another the helicopters took off, skimming across the edge of the Olympic Village, their blinking red lights quickly fading in the night sky as they made a 20-mile flight to Fuerstenfeldbruck Air Base.

There the ordeal came to an end in a bloody shootout.

Fall Ends
Ryun's
Hopes

MUNICH—~~Jim Ryun came limping along the balcony that leads to~~ his room in building No. 14 of the Olympic complex. He was wearing his blue track uniform and the top to his warmup suit. His right knee and right ankle were wrapped in gauze and tape. He had a pressure bandage on his left ankle. His left knee had a knot on it.

With Ryun were two friends, Mr. and Mrs. John Byron. Ryun hobbled to the door of his room, opened it and motioned for everybody to come in. As he did he managed a funny little smile of resignation. It was a surprising gesture because it seemed he should have been weeping.

His last hope of winning an Olympic gold medal had been shattered a little more than an hour earlier when he was tripped from behind and fell in what was supposed to be a routine 1,500-meter qualifying heat.

Ryun and Billy Forjour of Ghana had tangled their feet as the two trailed the pack in the last 500 meters. Kip Keino of Kenya, who defeated Ryun in Mexico City, won the heat.

At the time Ryun returned to his room he was still hopeful that a special appeal on his behalf might be successful, but later it was turned down. Even if his appeal had been upheld his injuries almost certainly would have prevented him from running.

"I've just finished talking to the doctor," Byron said as Ryun sat down on his cot in the cluttered room he has been sharing with three other athletes. "Jim has severe abrasions of the right knee, and I mean they're severe. He has a deep spike wound in his right ankle, a sprained left ankle and a pulled kneecap in his left knee.

"He also has contusions of the throat where he hit himself with his knee."

Ryun pushed the small ice bag on his left ankle, trying to get it into the right position.

"I'm going on the assumption that the appeal will be successful until I hear otherwise," Ryun said, "but even if I win the appeal I don't know whether I will be able to run.

"It's strange. I was at the top of the turn and I really felt confident. The pace was great. I was running a good race and I felt strong. I was starting to break out of traffic and all of a sudden I found myself on the track.

"I honestly can't tell you what happened. I think my knee hit my jaw as I was going down. I could have been unconscious for a little while because the first thing I can remember is trying to get to my feet. As I was getting up I remember thinking I might have a chance to catch up to the field. In a heat you're not running against one man. All you have to do is finish fourth."

"I was thinking that I had made up 100 yards at Drake one year and I was hoping I could do it again, but this field was too strong. I finally saw that I couldn't catch up. All I can remember thinking through the last lap is that this couldn't possibly be happening.

"I've never fallen before. I thought I was being so wise staying out of traffic. Keino went into the lead on the far side and I let him go because that's what I was hoping he would do. I thought if he picked up the pace the others would drop off."

The door to Ryun's room opened and his coach, Bob Timmons, came in. He walked up to Ryun, shook his hand and said affectionately, "You old moose, I just couldn't believe it."

Timmons sat down on the cot to examine Ryun's left ankle and foot.

"The arch is sore," Ryun said. "I can feel the ligament, too. It hurts where it comes around behind the ankle.

"I'm having trouble straightening my left knee, too.

"When I started to get up after the fall I looked down and there wasn't any shoe there. Actually the shoe was still on my foot but it was all torn up."

Asked how his wife, Anne, was reacting, Ryun replied, "She's holding up very well. She's been through this all before."

Lake Placid's Heavenly Fuzz

LAKE PLACID, N.Y.—The 1976 Winter Olympics in Innsbruck, Austria, are strongly identified with Franz Klammer's wild plunge down a mountainside that enabled him to win a gold medal in downhill skiing. His performance is viewed as something of a memorial to the heroic nature of man.

With four days of competition remaining at the Lake Placid Olympics, the possibility exists that the XIII Winter Games will become a memorial to the frailties of mankind and his machines. Even so, not all of the memories of these Games will have to do with bus problems, the Olympic crisis, tearful figure skaters and surly bobsledders.

The Lake Placid Olympics are presided over by the Rev. Bernard J. Fell, a policeman turned Methodist minister. He is president of the Lake Placid Olympic Organizing Committee, and in these precincts he is known as the Heavenly Fuzz. A few days ago, Fell proposed that the bus crisis be solved by invoking an Olympic spectator ban. He was threatened with excommunication from the Olympic movement and was made to see the heretical nature of his ways.

Business has been disappointing in Lake Placid. Normally the Chamber of Commerce can be counted on as a font of optimism, but Edward Wybrick, president of the Lake Placid Chamber of Commerce, concedes that business "isn't meeting anybody's great expectations."

That does not mean, however, that there is no fun to be found in Lake Placid.

Main Street is the Olympic shopping mall, and in the course of a day a fascinating variety of people can be seen there. They are wearing parkas, fur coats, capes, hats of dyed beaver and chinchilla, Levis, moon boots and shoe packs.

Snow bunnies abound, but the Lake Placid Volunteer Fire Department has been ordered to suspend the "10" contest it was conducting in searching for a girl measuring up to the rating of Bo Derek. The mayor said the contest was clogging the street in front of the firehouse and creating hazardous congestion.

On Main Street it is said that a "10" is a girl with an automobile sticker who normally would be a 4. Cars are not permitted past outlying police checkpoints without permits, which are the most hard-to-get items at the Olympics.

One of the signs displayed in several areas of downtown reads, "Welcome World—We're Ready." The Church of the Nazarene on Main Street has a sign that reads, "Welcome World—The Lord is Ready." There is no price gouging at the Church of the Nazarene, which advertises free soup and coffee.

Price gouging is abating in Lake Placid. An Olympic buffet at the Holiday Inn which once cost $15 has been reduced to $6.95. Other restaurants also have lowered prices. Humor is even found in areas where price gouging takes place.

Concession stands at Olympic events charge $4 for a glass of wine and $2 for an Olympic hot dog. When a hot dog buyer complained that his purchase was cold, the man behind the counter suggested that for $2 he should keep it as an Olympic souvenir.

Although the transportation problems have been so acute that Gov. Hugh Carey of New York has called a limited emergency, people manage to laugh at some, although not all, of their problems.

When an Italian delegate to the International Olympic Committee found himself assigned to attend two meetings scheduled at the same time, he was heard to observe, "It is impossible to be at two meetings at the same time. Of course, with the bus situation here, it is impossible to be any place at any time."

A West German writer lamented, "How come you Americans can put a man on the moon and you can't put a bus in downtown Lake Placid?"

Overhead on a crowded bus going to a ski area, a man turned to his wife and said, "I wish we had our piano here."

"Why would you want our piano here?" his wife said.

"Because our tickets are on it," he replied.

There are numerous horror stories about the housing accommodations, especially from the foreign press. A large number of British writers have been housed at the Hillside Hotel, which is a former tuberculosis sanitarium.

"We're hearing phantom coughs in the night," one British writer grumbled.

126

John Hennessey of the *London Times* was assigned a $55-a-night room that he found to be lacking in certain amenities, including a window. His room was also without a bath, running water, a closet, hooks and a dresser. He recently moved to the Lake Placid Club, where he is paying $155 a night.

Dudley Doust, a former reporter for *The Star* who now works for the *London Times*, is among those staying at the Hillside.

"As far as this place is concerned, the Olympics are the greatest thing since TB," Doust complained.

Although eating and drinking is becoming a bit cheaper in Lake Placid, being an Olympic spectator is expensive. Figure skating is the most expensive ticket, commanding a price of $67.55. Ski jumping is $28 and the luge is $22. For $28 you also can see downhill or slalom skiing. The price of admission includes an opportunity to suffer frostbite and fall on the ice. Dan Lauck, sports writer for *Newsday*, a Long Island, N.Y., paper, fell and dislocated his right shoulder covering the downhill.

Olympic press headquarters is located at Lake Placid Central High School. There are two bars in the building. One is located in Mrs. Whalley's home-economics room. The other is in Mrs. Thayer's room. Her class is not identified. The smell of beer, booze and sandwiches is likely to be with Mrs. Whalley and Mrs. Thayer for some time after the Olympics are over.

The only free Olympic event is the awards ceremony on Mirror Lake near downtown. Mirror Lake is one site where there is only the thrill of victory.

The weather is moderating in Lake Placid, the bus service is improving and if Eric Heiden wins five gold medals in speed skating, perhaps he will replace Klammer in the affections of Olympic fans.

The Lake Placid Olympics are not necessarily a memorable event, but at the same time they will not be forgotten soon by those who have been exposed to this bumbling yet sometimes charming experience.

Hockey Team Saves the Olympics

LAKE PLACID, N.Y.—The elders who control the Olympic Games piously decry the intrusion of nationalism into their festival, but privately they recognize that nationalism is as essential to the Olympics as heroes and villains are to a professional wrestling match. Sports fans respond only to emotional involvement or parimutuel machines.

On Sunday night the Olympic flame was extinguished in this Adirondack Mountain hamlet to the accompaniment of music and pageantry. Through last Thursday these XIII Winter Games were so burdened with problems that they were being called the Apocolympics. Then on Friday night a hockey game changed the face of the Olympics and lighted bonfires of nationalism across a nation depressed by Iran, Afghanistan, inflation and fears of recession.

The Russian Olympic hockey team is widely acknowledged to be the best in the world. The U.S. was seeded seventh in the Olympic tournament. On Friday night the Russians played the U.S. and the unthinkable came to pass. The U.S. won 4-3.

Jim McKay, the ABC Olympic anchorman, called it the greatest upset in the history of sports. In the passion of the moment, there were those who said that McKay understated the nature of the upheaval. They saw it as the equivalent of the Afghanistan rebels driving the Soviets back across the border and advancing on Moscow.

Americans were standing and cheering in their living rooms. The crowds in Lake Placid waved American flags and chanted, "U.S.A., U.S.A., U.S.A." The celebration ended just in time for the nation to return to its TV sets Sunday and watch the U.S. clinch the gold medal by defeating Finland 4-2.

Before the Olympics began, some misgivings were expressed about the structural integrity of the fieldhouse roof. After the events of Friday and Sunday, the natives have proof that reverberation will not bring it down.

All sports fans love a winner, but judging from the reaction of the public, a case can be made that the Olympic hockey team has been sent to minister to the American spirit. For purposes of symbolism, the hockey stick has taken its place alongside the fife and the drum.

This is a team that sings "God Bless America" and "America the Beautiful" in the dressing room. These players hug each other, roll on the ice and slap hands with the crowd. On Sunday they were holding on to this great, glorious moment in their lives as though they were determined not to let time wrest it from their grasp.

Rarely has the nation had such unspoiled, delightful heroes.

When Eric Heiden won his fifth gold medal in speed skating Saturday to become the greatest individual performer in Winter Olympic history, he spoke a bit cynically for one so young, saying that there was not much you could do with gold medals. He suggested a warmup suit would be better because it would be more useful.

When Mike Eruzione, the captain of the U.S. team, received his gold medal Sunday from Lord Killanin, president of the International Olympic Committee, his expression was ecstatic. It was also evident that anyone who attempted to mess with Mike Eruzione's medal would get busted in the mouth.

Eruzione is the symbol of this team and the essence of its appeal to the American public. He is an underdog who played for two seasons with the Toledo Goal Diggers of the International Hockey League because the National Hockey League was not interested in him. The IHL is loosely described as a non-professional league. Eruzione struggled to make the Olympic team. Fortunately he was successful, because he scored the winning goal against the Russians.

Before the game with the Soviets, Eruzione was asked how he liked being in the Olympics.

"Great," he replied. "Where else can you go to the movies free, eat free and play 20 games of Space Invaders (an electronic game) for nothing."

Was the U.S. victory over the Russians a fluke? The answer is yes and no. The Russians are a much more talented team, but on Friday night the U.S. outplayed them. Part of the credit has to go to the head coach, Herb Brooks, who devised a strategy combining elements of the

Russian game and the National Hockey League game with some strategy of his own.

The Soviets pass more and their wings and center exchange positions. The U.S. did this, but Brooks also had his team using more of the ice to pass the puck and had them body checking as the NHL teams do.

The U.S. hockey victory somewhat obscured Heiden's achievement of winning more individual gold medals than anyone else in the history of the Winter Olympics. Until Heiden came along, no one had even competed in all five skating events. As the emotionalism of the hockey victory subsides, the magnitude of Heiden's accomplishment will grow.

Heiden's victories at 500, 1,000, 1,500, 5,000 and 10,000 meters are comparable to a runner winning in both sprint and distance events. Heiden broke every Olympic record and holds three world's records or pending world's records.

There were many other great performances, but perhaps closest to Heiden in the super hero category was Ingemar Stenmark, the Swedish skier who won both the giant slalom and slalom. His grace, as well as his times, set him apart from other skiers.

There were many things wrong with the organization of the Lake Placid Olympics. The lack of adequate bus transportation through much of the Games for fans, workers and the press was by far the most disruptive.

The cost of staging the Games, now estimated at $200 million, is also distressing, and the financial condition of the Lake Placid Olympic Organizing Committee has been called into question. Most of the cost of the Games is being assumed by the federal government and the State of New York.

The last of the medals has been presented, the athletes are heading home and the U.S. team is responding to an invitation to visit the White House. Only one last presentation remains to be made in Lake Placid—a whopping bill to the American taxpayer.

When a Shooter Needs Her Accountant

MONTREAL—Some unusual happenings took place yesterday at L'Acadie, the pastoral site where the Olympic shooting events are being held. They involved Margaret Murdock of Topeka who won a gold medal and then lost it an hour and a half later because of a clerical error.

Murdock is a friendly woman of 33 who goes to college, looks after a small son and could teach Annie Oakley a few things about handling a gun. Her talents are such that she does what women are not supposed to be able to do: She shoots on equal terms with the best male marksmen in the world. To put her ability in perspective, if she were a golfer she would be competing with Jack Nicklaus and Johnny Miller for the major championships.

In a way the male shooters have adjusted to her and in a way they haven't. Because she served in the Army, Margaret is known as Wac. One man familiar with the shooting scene observed yesterday that when Margaret wins an event the men make it a point to congratulate her warmly and even put an arm around her shoulders.

"But you should hear them when they walk away," he laughed. "She has them talking to themselves. She's the only woman in the world who is on a par with men."

Yesterday Murdock wasn't on a par with the male shooters, she was better than all of them except Lanny Bassham, an Army captain. And if she had brought her accountant along, she might have beaten him.

Murdock and Bassham tied in the smallbore rifle from three positions, prone, standing and kneeling. Even though both finished with scores of 1,162, Bassham won the gold medal with the help of a scoring mistake and a tie-breaking system of debatable merit.

The smallbore event goes on for 5 ½ hours or so. If two shooters tie, the winner is the one with the most points for the last 10 shots.

The shooting started yesterday under good conditions. The weather was pleasant, the wind of previous days had moderated and white clouds hung in fluffy clusters. According to the insiders, Bassham was supposed to win, although the Russians were a threat.

And Margaret Murdock? Well, supposedly she hadn't been shooting too well in practice. Joe Berry, the team manager, said Margaret was a little heavy and not in top shooting condition. Berry apparently has tough standards considering that Maragret was able to practice for only two weeks before the Olympic Trials and still beat out two gold medalists and 80 or so other males.

But then she wasn't shooting against the Soviets or Lanny Bassham. And besides, she's a woman.

When the shooting started it quickly became apparent that neither gender, weight nor lack of practice was going to stop Margaret Murdock. But in the end she lost out to someone with a pencil.

Following are the events that transpired as Murdock won and lost her gold medal:

The first event of the day is from a prone position. Murdock shoots rounds of 100, 99, 99 and 100, two points short of a perfect score. Interest in Margaret is picking up. The next round of 40 shots is from a standing position. This should be the most difficult of all for a woman, but someone recalls that Murdock holds the world's record of 385, which she set in the Pan-American Games. This time she has a 376.

With only the kneeling event left she is four points ahead of Bassham and tied with Werner Siebold, a bearded German shooting two positions to her left. An Israeli is between them and not doing well. After 30 shots Murdock is two points ahead, but she takes an eight on her first shot in the final series of 10. The German finishes the round while she is waiting to take her eighth shot.

She fires and gets a 9, cutting her lead to one point. She finishes with two 10s and a gasp goes up from the crowd. The officials call for silence.

Outside, Bassham is saying that he should have two more points than he is credited with according to observers who checked the targets through telescopes. The unofficial total at this juncture is Murdock 1,161 and Bassham 1,160. If Bassham gets even one of the two points he claims, he will win because of the tie-breaking system.

Murdock leaves the shooting area and he calls, "Wac, what did you get?"

"I had problems out there," she replies.

"You had to do better kneeling," Bassham says. "Well, however it turns out, good shooting."

An autograph seeker wants to know if he can impose. "Sure, sure," Margaret says pleasantly. Talking with a friend she observes, "On that last shot kneeling I knew I would be in for a medal."

Murdock's mother, Mrs. Robert Thompson, greets her. Mr. Thompson is trying to find Murdock's son, Brett, who is 5 and has been out running with the abandon of an excited 5-year-old. Mrs. Thompson says that she did not watch her daughter shoot.

"I never have been able to watch Margaret, not even in college," she explains. "When she was at Kansas State they offered to give me a special seat, but I'd just wait until it was over. I stay away because I get nervous when she's in competition."

Mrs. Thompson recalls that her daughter won a letter shooting on the men's team at Kansas State, but wasn't allowed to wear it on campus.

Perhaps an hour or so after the competition Margaret's father tells her that the official score has been posted on the board and it is 1,162, a point higher than the unofficial score. For the first time she has reason to think she might win a gold medal.

More time passes and Bassham's score from the kneeling position has not been posted. A 391 has been tentatively entered in crayon, but if his claim for two additional points is upheld he will get a 393. It is after 5 o'clock when an attendant begins to put up the numbers. Mrs. Murdock watches along with the spectators. With agonizing deliberation the attendant puts up a 3, then a 9 and finally a 1. Margaret shouts and is embraced by the members of her family.

Having done what a woman is not supposed to do, she now does a very womanly thing and begins to cry. Bassham comes over to congratulate her, but he looks grim.

A few minutes later, standing in front of the scoreboard, he observes, "I don't feel I got outshot. I wish she had beaten me by 10 points. Margaret hasn't beaten me this year. I know I'm a better shooter. The only time she has beaten me in the last two years was at the Pan-Am Games, and I hadn't practiced for two months.

"I'm not saying she doesn't deserve a medal. She does." Bassham paused and then added, "I'd like to see her targets."

An hour and a half later Margaret Murdock lost her gold medal. A clerical error was discovered that gave Bassham a tie. Since he had 98 points to Mrs. Murdock's 96 for the final 10 shots he was the winner.

No one, let alone a woman as nice as Margaret Murdock, should have to go through the agony of winning and then losing a gold medal. But what should be remembered about the day at L'Acadie is that no one outshot her.

U.S. Skier Wins,
Rivals Grumble

SARAJEVO, YUGOSLAVIA—When first sighted from the finish line of the men's downhill course, Bill Johnson was only a streaky brush stroke of color on the snow white canvas of Mount Bjelasnica.

The crouched figure grew rapidly in size until first his black helmet became visible and then the peppermint stripes on his uniform. With each hundredth of a second he grew bigger and bigger until he hurtled under the orange and white banner at the finish line and emerged as America's giant of the Sarajevo Winter Olympics.

The scoreboard, which had blinked off the progress of his runaway plunge down the mountain, had stopped at 1 minute, 45.59 seconds, the fastest run of the race. Americans cheered. The Austrians and Swiss gulped.

Johnson watched as the next seven skiers completed their runs. None of them was able to overtake him and at that point there were no legitimate challengers left on the mountain. The kid from California with beach-boy nonchalance and a love of speed not only had won a gold medal but had become the first American man to win a medal of any description in Olympic downhill racing.

To the Austrians and the Swiss, an American winning the men's downhill is an almost unbearable effrontery. If the downhill goes, will the Alps be next?

This was an especially bleak day for the Austrians, who had won 10 medals in the downhill since it was first held in 1948, including four golds.

It is unlikely that Johnson believes in predestination, assuming he has even heard of it. His tastes run more to Pac-Man and fast cars than esoteric matters. But in the Olympics there are occasions when a team or an individual appear preordained to win. At Lake Placid, N.Y., in 1980 the U.S. hockey team played in an atmosphere of enchantment.

Here the spell was passed to Johnson, who only a year ago was competing in the Europa Cup, skiing's version of Triple A baseball.

From the beginning, everyone agreed that the course at Mount Bjelasnica suited Johnson. The flat areas on the course favor a glider and Johnson is the best glider in the world. When gliding, a skier goes into a crouch that is called a tuck. The aerodynamics of the position allow for maximum speed.

Johnson is not a technically accomplished skier, but Mount Bjelasnica is not a technically demanding course. In addition, the snowy conditions here have helped Johnson. The men's downhill was postponed twice and the Austrians and Swiss were hoping that the delays would spook Johnson. Instead, it was his rivals who became morose as they watched Johnson make a succession of impressive practice runs.

In four of his practice trips Johnson finished first twice and second twice. On Wednesday he was the first to go down the slope and had the best time of the day. The next six skiers had poor times, an indication of Johnson's ability to handle the snow and the course.

After his last run the confident Johnson said that going down Mount Bjelasnica was "like riding a bike."

Karl Schranz, the great Austrian skier, had said on Tuesday that Johnson would be in a perfect position on the start list if he were between fifth and 10th. Johnson drew the No. 6 slot.

Johnson was so confident that he predicted he "definitely" would win the race. Like Joe Namath, who guaranteed a victory for the New York Jets in Super Bowl III, he delivered.

He had a little trouble with an icy gate early in his run, but thereafter his performance was almost flawless. He scarcely came out of his tuck in taking the last two bumps, a remarkable feat of skill and strength.

The bottom part of the course is flat and Johnson made the most of it.

"When I came down to the bottom part I was really going fast," Johnson said. "I took quite a bit of air on the last two bumps. I was probably close at the second midway timing. I smoked 'em all on the second part."

Smoke them he did because the second, third and fourth-place finishers all had better times than Johnson going into the final third of the course.

The Austrians and the Swiss were critical of the course in practice, saying it was too easy and did not place enough technical demands on the skier. Their attempts to belittle the course left Johnson unfazed.

"If it was so easy, why didn't they win?" he asked with a smile. Temperamentally, Johnson has the perfect makeup for downhill racing. He is a free spirit who likes the fast lane on the course and off.

"I go out and chase girls," Johnson said, explaining his recreational preferences. "I party three or four times a week."

Johnson, 23, has a reputation as a drinker, but he said, "I don't go out and get drunk much now. In the winter I try to concentrate on skiing."

In addition to girls and partying, Johnson enjoys getting in his Pinto runabout or his Malibu and going for the sound barrier. How fast does Johnson drive?

"Over 100 miles an hour," he said. "I like to go off jumps in my car and get airborne."

Johnson's absorption with having a good time was costly two years ago when he was dropped from the World Cup team.

Johnson claims he had been suffering from the flu and had not been training. When he showed up at training camp he had problems with some required subjects such as the five-mile run.

Bill Marolt, the U.S. Alpine director, has a slightly different version of the incident.

"We established some physical standards," Marolt said. "He didn't meet those standards. I think you have to have a certain amount of discipline. If someone comes to a camp they know is physical and they are not prepared, they can't possibly be concerned about what they are doing."

Having said that, Marolt concedes that a coach has to make allowances for downhill skiers.

"I don't think Bill is one of our most disciplined skiers," Marolt said, "but you want free spirits. You don't see a lot of athletes who aren't free spirits."

Marolt speaks of Johnson's ability to glide in the same way that football coaches talk about great running backs.

"Basically his ability is innate," Marolt said. "You watch him head on and his skis go back and forth."

Johnson amplified the point by making a wobbling motion with his right hand.

"He can do that because he is able to keep his skis flat. His weight distribution over his skis is very good. We've taken guys in a wind tunnel the last three years and worked on tucking. You have to be stronger than hell to take the bumps and come right back into the tuck."

Johnson's talent became apparent at the outset of his career. He won his first race in his second year of skiing and began skiing full time seven years ago when he got out of high school.

"When you do something that much you're bound to get good at it," Johnson said.

Skiing is an expensive sport, and money was a problem for Johnson from the time he began. His brothers and sisters gave up skiing because of the cost, and Johnson had trouble finding a program after he got out of high school.

"I looked for the cheapest program I could find," Johnson said. "That was Mission Ridge. I paid $400, which was pretty cheap. I washed dishes and did other things to pay for a house to live in.

"I won the Northwest Cup my second year, but there was no recognition so the next year I went to White Face in New York. It was kind of a power play. The winter Olympics were in Lake Placid and I wanted to get close to the ski team.

"I got some recognition after they watched me ski there, and I got to be a forerunner at Lake Placid. Several guys from the team wanted to be forerunners but my coach, Chris Jones, recommended me. I kind of scammed them."

Last season Johnson was sent from the World Cup team to the Europa Cup team, but the demotion was a break for him, a point Marolt emphasizes.

"I think a bell went off in Bill's head a year ago when he won three of four European downhills," Marolt said. "That's when he found out how exciting skiing can be."

Reflecting on his predictions of victory, Johnson conceded that what he did was risky.

"I did put a little pressure on myself," he said. "If I had come in second, I'd be a real bum."

Instead he did what he said and he has become America's hero of this winter festival.

Hollywood
Comes to the
Olympics

LOS ANGELES—Take New Year's Eve on Times Square, the Mardi Gras and the Fourth of July celebration on the Charles River Esplanade in Boston. Combine them with Hollywood's most spectacular musicals, balloons, a cast of 18,000, 2,500 pigeons, 92,000 spectators, the Olympic torch and the President of the United States and you have some idea of what the opening ceremonies were like for the 23rd Olympiad in Los Angeles.

It was an all-American celebration of the world's biggest athletic show that filled the eyes and pounded against the eardrums. Never mind that the Olympic movement has enough problems to fill Malibu Canyon. Never mind that the Russians and their closest friends didn't come. There never has been an Olympic show to equal the one staged Saturday in the Los Angeles Memorial Coliseum.

If you saw it and your heart didn't beat a little faster, you should consult your nearest physician.

It was a celebration of American music, American dancing, Hollywood pizzaz and Olympic pageantry. It was almost worth the $200 price of admission just to watch 84 baby-grand pianos slide through the columns of the peristyle at the Coliseum and hear a once-in-a-lifetime rendering of "Rhapsody in Blue."

There was the massive visual impact of spectators holding up colored plastic cards and the Coliseum coming alive with the flags of the 140 competing nations. There was the moving sight of the athletes crowding on the track to see Jesse Owens' granddaughter, Gina Hemphill, as she carried the Olympic torch around the stadium.

Even the temperamental Los Angeles weather behaved, showing its best profile as the Olympics began on a sunny almost smogless afternoon. A cooperative sun hung just above the rim of the Coliseum as the Olympic flame was lighted.

This was an afternoon for the Olympic nations to pass in colorful review and flaunt their feelings of nationalism, for young men and women to celebrate being alive. This was a time to revel in the vigor of youth and anticipate the excitement of Olympic competition.

They came from every nook and cranny of the world—Antigua, Bhutan, Bangladesh, Djibouti, Fiji, Gabon, Grenada, Lesotho, Mozambique, Nepal, Rwanda, Seychelles, Togo, Swaziland and Zimbabwe. It was the Rand McNally world gazette come alive. They marched through the warm afternoon smiling, waving and undismayed by the certain knowledge that the United States will take home more medals in women's gymnastics than they will win collectively.

A total of roughly 8,000 massed athletes and officials heard President Reagan open the Games with a 16-word proclamation, one of his few recent utterances that even the Democrats could applaud. His words were followed by the lighting of the Olympic flame that will burn through 15 days of competition.

Today the athletes go their own ways in competition, but for one sunny afternoon they stood together, united in their youth, their humanity and their commitment to sports.

The opening ceremonies are rigidly ritualistic in many respects but they also provide an opportunity for the host country to express its individualism.

In Mexico City mariachi musicians played while members of the Ballet Folklorico danced around the track. Young Germans did Bavarian dance numbers at the Munich Olympics, 5,000 doves of peace were released and cannons boomed from an adjacent hill built from the rubble that was hauled to the site when the reconstruction of Munich began after World War II.

Queen Elizabeth opened the Games in Montreal. During the parade of nations she shuffled from one foot to another as if her shoes were hurting. Gymnasts circled the track waving colorful ribbons, and the crowd cheered Mayor Jean Drapeau, though the city ran up $1 billion in debts preparing for the Olympics.

In Moscow, 16,000 performers took part and Red Army soldiers carried in the Olympic flag. Thousands of gymnasts performed and young people dressed in the costume of Mischa, the Soviet brown bear mascot, paraded around the stadium to the music of Russian composers.

Other than winning a medal, Olympic champions remember the opening ceremonies as their most emotional experience of the Games.

John Naber, the swimming star of the Montreal Games, was one of 10 U.S. Olympic gold medalists who carried in the Olympic flag Saturday, and he became emotional just practicing his role.

"It's a gift wrapping, a fabulous gift wrapping," Naber said of the opening ceremonies. "I'm kind of an emotional guy and even during rehearsal I had tears in my eyes."

Al Oerter, a former University of Kansas athlete who won four gold medals in the discus, recalls his first opening ceremony in 1956 as an almost overwhelming experience.

"It was so draining emotionally that if the track and field competition had been held the following day, I don't think I could have competed," Oerter said. "They asked me to carry the flag in Mexico, but we were competing early and I had to defer."

Billy Mills, the Kansas athlete who won the 10,000-meter run at Tokyo in one of the great Olympic upsets, recalls the flood of emotions that swept through him that day. He remembers feeling that he was representing two entities, the Sioux Indian nation and the United States. And yet he felt he was not fully a part of either because his white friends called him Indian and his Indian friends called him by a nickname that meant half breed.

Mills said he had to fight back tears at Tokyo and found tears in his eyes again as he practiced carrying in the Olympic flag Thursday.

"The difference was that this time no one saw me," he said.

The opening ceremonies at the first modern Olympic Games in 1896 in Athens were brief and to the point. Crown Prince Constantine of Greece gave a speech, King George I read an opening declaration consisting of one sentence, trumpets sounded, a choir sang the Olympic Hymn and then the dignitaries got out of the way while the field was cleared for the first heat of the 100-yard dash.

Saturday, the Olympics met Hollywood, and they soared off together into the stratosphere of the grandiose.

The First
Women's Marathon

LOS ANGELES—It may be fact or it may be nothing more than froth concocted by a teller of tales, but a story has been passed down through the years that the first woman to run in an Olympic marathon was a Greek named Melpomene who slipped into the 1896 Games by changing her name and convincing the officials she was a man.

Melpomene may be no more authentic than the Greek muse of the same name, but even if she did beat Joan Benoit getting into the marathon, she sure didn't run like Benoit did Sunday when Benoit became the first certified female winner of an event that makes equal demands on a runner's lungs and soul.

Not only was this a historic marathon, but it brought together Benoit and Grete Waitz, the world's two leading women marathoners, for only the second time in their careers. They both ran in Boston in 1981, but Waitz did not finish.

The race itself turned out to be a disappointment. After the first 40 minutes the only people on the course close to Benoit were wearing uniforms and riding motorcycles. Even so, the spectators who lined the route saw Olympic history in the making and had a chance to marvel at Benoit, who looked as if she could go on running forever, or at least until some maintenance man appeared to flip the off switch.

The other members of the field were reluctant to challenge her early in the marathon because of the warm temperatures and the length of the race. Later, their only hope of finding her would have been to send out a missing person's report.

"I was never sure what she would do," said Jacqueline Gareau, a Canadian runner. "She went out so fast. She's kind of incredible."

This not only was a momentous day for Benoit, but for women's track.

As recently as the early 1970s, track buffs smiled condescendingly when the women's marathon was mentioned, just as baseball fans smile when someone brings up the American League West. In those not-too-distant days any time under three hours was considered world class for a woman.

In 1973 a time of 2 hours, 55 minutes was considered good and in 1975 Jacquie Hansen made history by going under 2:40. Waitz broke the 2:30 barrier in 1979, and Benoit now holds the world record of 2:22.43.

Benoit's winning time of 2:24.52 on Sunday is 13 minutes, 49 seconds slower than the winning time for the men's marathon four years ago in Moscow, but it's comparable to the winning time of 2:23.03 run in 1952 by the great Emil Zatopek of Czechoslovakia.

From 1932-60, the Olympic fathers viewed women as too delicate to run farther than even 200 meters. The women pushed hard for the marathon and finally were given approval to test their lungs in the smog of Los Angeles.

The historic nature of this occasion was reflected in the attitude of the spectators who lined the route. One group was composed of members of the Seroptimist Club. They left Valencia at 6 a.m. and arrived about an hour before the race started. Jan Heidt, who runs a bookstore, explained the women in her group had come only because this was the first women's marathon.

The first footfalls in this event came as the field circled the track at Santa Monica College two times and then set off on an athletic and sociological adventure through the streets of Greater Los Angeles.

From Santa Monica College they went down 17th Street past the Omega Cleaners and the Greater Morning Star Baptist Church which is housed in a modest yellow stucco building. They turned right on Olympic Avenue and passed the Jalisco Cafe, which advertised food, beer and pool, as well as dancing Wednesday through Saturday.

From this depressed area they went to Wilshire Boulevard and eventually to San Vicente, a tree-lined street where the costly homes have iron gates and Spanish tile roofs.

Benoit had a lead of about 50 yards when she reached San Vicente and Waitz needed to begin to move with her, but she hung back.

"I wasn't sure I wanted to go out so fast and take a chance," she said.

The race moved down Ocean Avenue past expensive condominiums and hotels and then into another depressed area where apartments advertised units by the day, week or month.

Waitz's position was becoming hopeless. Apparently she had hoped to run a tactical race, but it is difficult to run tactically when you can't see your opponent.

The race wound through Marina Del Ray and the yacht basin.

"At the marina we made a U-turn and I kept waiting for the pack," Benoit said, "but I didn't see them."

When Benoit came off the Artesia freeway she looked again. No one was there. On she went, a solitary, methodical figure. Her triumphal tour took her down Jefferson to Rodeo Road, where life is a lot different than it is on Rodeo Drive. She ran past the House of Refuge, reached Exposition Avenue, made another turn at Benjie's Liquors and headed to the Coliseum, where she crossed the finish line running just as smoothly as she had when she passed the Jalisco Cafe.

She made one of her victory laps in the Coliseum carrying an American flag, hugged her parents and tried in vain to find her fiancé.

Benoit said she was reluctant to take the early lead because someone might think she was showing off in the Olympics and she might falter later on. As her lead grew, she kept expecting someone to challenge, but no one did.

"Nobody came and I didn't complain," she said.

Waitz, who is 30, was considered the favorite, but her attitude toward running is changing.

"It is different now than when I was younger," she said in an interview a year ago. "It was harder to lose when I was younger. Running is the big thing in my life now, but you do discover there is a world outside the running world. It's not the end of the world when I lose a race."

Benoit is a relentless trainer who runs more than 100 miles every week. She runs 20-plus miles once a week and 12 to 16 miles several times a week. She has had surgery on both of her Achilles' tendons and had arthroscopic knee surgery shortly before the Olympic trials.

"I don't know where my competitiveness comes from," she said. "I keep asking myself about it, and I get no answer. I plan to keep competing. I think I have another personal record in me."

Benoit says she is oblivious to almost everything when she runs.

"I basically space out," she said. "I just kind of follow the yellow brick road."

Except that Sunday the road she followed was gold.

CHAPTER 5

BASEBALL

Memories of
Municipal Stadium

The light towers and the high-pitched upper deck of the old stadium at Twenty-second and Brooklyn are visible from Interstate 70, rising massively above the smaller buildings around them. The architecture is of another generation, conveying the impression that Babe Ruth and Jimmy Foxx would have felt at home here.

From a distance the stadium is still somewhat imposing but up close there are signs of decay—peeling paint, rust stains, cracked cement. Even so there is a graceful sweep to the stands and the lush green of the playing field is inviting. Despite its defects, the stadium has a charm and dignity that only the passing of time can bestow.

Ted Williams played here. So did Bob Feller, Willie Mays, Stan Musial, Enos Slaughter and Yogi Berra. Mickey Mantle brought fans shouting to their feet with his awesome home runs. Early Wynn won his 300th game here. Back in the Triple A era, when the Blues were Kansas City's team, the stadium was the scene of Carl DeRose's perfect game.

In 1958 the Yankees clinched the pennant here. In 1967 the White Sox lost the pennant here. It was on June 16, 1961 that Lew Krausse made baseball history by shutting out the Angels in his first professional start. He was 18 and had just been graduated from high school.

The memories go on and on.

Tomorrow night the Royals will play the Minnesota Twins in what probably will be the last opening game in the old stadium before the team moves to the Truman Sports Complex.

Because this probably is the last opener at Twenty-second and Brooklyn tomorrow night's game will be a nostalgic and a historical event. Almost half a century of baseball history has been made at this site. Even though the Royals' new stadium will be nicer, brighter, larger and more comfortable, there will be just a touch of sadness to this season for those of us who are baseball sentimentalists.

The present stadium is the sixth used by professional baseball teams in Kansas City. A search of *The Star's* files indicates that the first was Athletic Park, located at Southwest Boulevard and Summit Street. The Kansas City Union Baseball team played there in 1884 and 1885.

In 1886 Kansas City was a member of the National League and games were played in League Ball Park, which was located at Independence Avenue and Lydia. The stadium sat in a hollow, which was later filled in for construction of a Billy Sunday tabernacle. Other members of the league were Chicago, Detroit, New York, Philadelphia, Boston, St. Louis and Washington. Kansas City finished seventh, thereby establishing a standard of performance that the city's major league teams would follow closely in later years.

Pink lemonade and something called Hokey-Pokeys, a 5-cent cake of ice cream, were the big concession items. And just to show that there is nothing new, they were having ladies' days back in 1886 and on one occasion pictures of the players were given away to the ladies.

Kansas City's third professional park was located at what is now Truman and Montgall. It was opened in 1889. The American Association, the triple A league of which Kansas City was a member for 54 years, was organized in 1901. Kansas City played its games in Association Park at Twentieth Street and Prospect Avenue. The Federal League, which had a Kansas City franchise, played in a park at Forty-ninth and Tracy.

Professional baseball moved to its present location in 1923 when George Muehlebach built what was then described as the finest park in the minor leagues. It was called Muehlebach Field but in later years the park was known as Ruppert Stadium, Blues Stadium and finally Municipal Stadium.

Muehlebach Field was opened on July 3, 1923, with Kansas City defeating the Milwaukee Home Brews, 10-7. A story in *The Times* of the following day read:

"George Muehlebach, proud and smiling, moved to the front of the platform before the huge grandstand of Muehlebach Field yesterday to acknowledge the cheers of 14,000 fans, proud and grateful for the finest ball park in the minor leagues. George Muehlebach's dream—yet, the same dream the fandom of Kansas City has been dreaming for two decades—has come true."

The park served Kansas City's minor league teams through the 1954 season with virtually no changes. In November of 1954 Arnold Johnson purchased the Philadelphia Athletics' franchise and moved it to Kansas City. Blues Stadium was purchased by the city and rebuilt.

On April 12, 1955, major league baseball came to Kansas City. The Athletics opened against Detroit and defeated the Tigers, 6-2. Mrs. Carrie Sloan was the first person through the gate. Former President Harry S. Truman threw out the first ball.

The Athletics won the game in the sixth inning when they scored three runs to break a 2-2 tie.

It was a day of pride, excitement and unrestrained joy for Kansas Citians. It was the finest day in the history of the old stadium.

In the years that followed Kansas City baseball fans suffered with losing teams and unpopular ownerships, but even though Kansas City has never had a winning major league season in the stadium there have been many memorable events.

One of the most exciting was Krausse's 4-0 victory over the Angels. The A's signed Krausse for $125,000 and a crowd of 30,505 filled the stadium to see him make his professional debut. He had turned 18 less than two months earlier.

Krausse limited the Angels to three hits. In the ninth they put two men on base after two were out but Krausse preserved his shutout by retiring Lee Thomas on a popup.

Wynn won his 300th game here while sitting in a radio booth. Wynn was released by the White Sox and was picked up by the Indians for the express purpose of giving him a chance to gain his 300th victory. He was 43 at the time.

Wynn pitched five innings in the second game of a double-header on July 13, 1963. Jerry Walker, his roommate, replaced him. Wynn showered and watched the rest of the game from a radio booth as Walker preserved a 7-4 victory.

The Yankees clinched the pennant here on September 14, 1958 in the first game of a double-header. The White Sox blew their chances to win the pennant in 1967 when they lost a double-header to the A's on September 27. Had they won they would have gone into first place with three games to play, all of them against Washington. Chuck Dobson defeated the Sox, 5-2, in the opener and Catfish Hunter won the nightcap, 4-0.

Two years ago the stadium was the scene of a new start in Kansas City baseball. The Royals, under the ownership of Ewing Kauffman, played their first game and defeated Minnesota, 4-3, in 12 innings.

Now the old stadium will be dying a day at a time.

The A's First Game

A throng of 32,844 came to Municipal Stadium yesterday to celebrate Kansas City's entry into the American League. It was a happy, noisy crowd when it arrived. By the end of the afternoon it was a jubilant crowd that cheered the Athletics' suspenseful 6-2 victory over the Detroit Tigers and then went off to continue the celebration long into the night.

This was, without question, the greatest sporting event in Kansas City's history and the Athletics responded with a performance befitting the occasion.

There was fine pitching by Alex Kellner and Ewell Blackwell. There was brilliant fielding that produced three double plays and one outstanding catch by Bill Renna. There was solid hitting, notably by Bill Wilson who led Kansas City's 9-hit attack with a home run, a double and a single in three official trips.

The crowd, which spilled over onto the embankments in left and right field, came to the stadium prepared to cheer and responded enthusiastically when the Athletics took a 2-0 lead in the first three innings. Then an air of tenseness developed as the Tigers rallied for a run in the fourth and another in the fifth to tie the score.

The Athletics didn't keep their followers in a state of suspense for long, coming back to score three runs in the sixth inning. Wilson added a final run in the eighth with his homer.

Ned Garver, the Detroit starter, donated what proved to be the winning run when he walked Elmer Valo with the bases loaded in the sixth. It was Don Bollweg who provided the knockout punch by lining a 2-run single to right following the walk to Valo.

The Tigers threatened in the late innings but successive double plays in the seventh, eighth and ninth left them with nothing to show for their efforts.

Detroit collected eight hits for the day, six of them coming against Kellner, who started and worked the first six innings.

149

The husky left-hander was tough in the early innings when his control was good but he faltered in the fourth and fifth. Then he recovered to retire the Tigers in order in the sixth.

With the score tied, Kellner was removed for a pinch hitter in the last of the sixth, but picked up credit for the victory since he still was the pitcher of record when the Athletics went ahead to stay in that inning.

Blackwell was a surprise choice as his successor. The sidearming right-hander had pitched only one inning for Kansas City in spring training and was considered an unknown quantity.

The pitcher who was once known as The Whip has lost the snap in his fastball but with a little cunning and some good defense he survived, although his pitching injected a high level of suspense into the closing innings.

In the seventh he gave up a single and a walk with one away and got out of the jam by getting Harvey Kuenn to hit into a double-play. The eighth was a repetition of the seventh, with J.W. Porter hitting into the inning-ending double play.

In the ninth Blackwell walked Jim Delsing with one out. Bob Wilson popped to Pete Suder who doubled Delsing off first base to end the game. Blackwell was mobbed by his teammates as he walked quickly to the dugout.

As late as noon there was some doubt that the game would be played. The field was thoroughly soaked by Monday night's heavy rain and there was more rain forecast yesterday afternoon.

As a result the tarpaulin was kept on the infield until just before game time. There was no infield or batting practice and the opening ceremonies were cut to a minimum.

The rain failed to materialize, however, and this seemed to be a good omen for the Athletics who took the field to the accompaniment of a thunderous cheer and got away to an early lead.

The crowd cheered Kellner's first strike, which came on the second pitch of the game. They cheered Bill Renna's routine catch of Harvey Kuenn's fly in the first. Then they really opened up when the Athletics scored their first run against Garver in the second inning.

There were two out when Wilson doubled to center. Joe DeMaestri followed with a single to center and the A's were off.

In the third inning the Athletics struck again after two were out. This time Jim Finigan doubled and it was Gus Zernial who brought him around with a single to short right field.

The Tigers managed only two hits off Kellner in the first three innings but in the fourth Ray Boone scored from third on a long fly by Bill Tuttle. The ball carried 380 feet into right-center but Renna made a fine running catch.

The Tigers tied the score at 2-2 in the fifth when Bob Wilson, their catcher, hit a towering home run over the left-field fence.

The Athletics in the meantime were doing little with Garver but they finally steered him down the road to defeat in the sixth.

Renna opened the inning with a double off the left-field fence. Wilson walked and DeMaestri, after missing connections on two attempted bunts, moved the runners up on a ground ball to Boone at third. Actually this was a double play bounce but Boone juggled the ball and finally had to settle for retiring DeMaestri.

Joe Astroth was walked intentionally to fill the bases and Boudreau sent Valo to the plate to bat for Kellner.

The first pitch was a ball and on the second Valo swung so hard his cap flew off. Garver got two strikes as Valo fouled off the next pitch but two balls followed for a full count. Valo fouled the next pitch and then Garver threw inside for ball four. Renna was forced home and the A's were on top, 3-2.

Boudreau then called for Bollweg, a left-hander, to bat in place of Vic Power against the right-handed Garver. Again the count went to 3 and 2. This time Bollweg lined the payoff pitch sharply into right field. Fred Hatfield lunged for the ball but it sailed by the second baseman just out of reach. Wilson and Astroth scored on the hit and Valo was thrown out trying to reach third. Pete Suder flied out but the A's already had enough runs.

Wilson's home run completed the scoring.

When the A's third double play ended the game the fans came to their feet to let out one last roar.

Maybe the A's are an eighth-place club as the experts have predicted but at the moment they are tied for first place in the American League and Kansas City is ecstatic.

No Ego Trips
for Howser

Before the Royals and Detroit Tigers are loosed upon each other to determine the championship of the American League, a few words are in order regarding the man who was the dominant force behind the 41-day stretch drive that enabled the Royals to come from 11 games under .500 and win the West.

Managers often are blamed for things over which they have little or no control and sometimes are given credit for things that are not really of their doing, but the Royals of 1984, the funny-looking team with the kid pitchers and the interchangeable parts, are Dick Howser's creation.

He has nurtured his young players and his rookie pitchers, imparted confidence to a doubting Steve Balboni, has shown compassion for his veterans who are in diminished roles and he has juggled. My lord, how he has juggled!

Regardless of what happens in the playoffs, Howser's performance has confirmed his position as a member of baseball's managerial elite.

Unlike some of his peers, Howser never has deluded himself into thinking winning is a function of the cerebral cortex. He has too much respect for playing talent to believe in geniuses. In Howser's view, turning frogs into princes is a matter best left to the Brothers Grimm. Or, as he likes to say, "It's no fun playing with a short stick."

When he became manager of the Royals in August of 1981, Howser made the point that he would have remained a baseball coach at Florida State rather than manage a major-league club that was facing a massive rebuilding program.

And yet it seemed the stick Howser was holding at the start of this season was at best nubby. The Royals had gone through a drug scandal. They were rebuilding their pitching staff. The outfield was in a state of flux. Balboni had been declared surplus by the Yankees and was not in great demand.

The Royals could have tried to do a patch job with older players as the Phillies did last season. Instead, Howser and General Manager John Schuerholz decided to go with young players and assume the risk of having an embarrassing season. Even the veteran members of the club thought it was unlikely the team would be able to reach .500.

As the season progressed Howser had to make some difficult decisions. Hal McRae, long the league's best designated hitter, was told he would have to platoon with Jorge Orta. Paul Splittorff, with some gentle urging, retired. Larry Gura was removed from the starting rotation and sent to the bullpen.

"It's always tougher when you're dealing with established players," Howser said. "I wanted Mac to be our DH. He's had a great career. But you have to do what you think is best to win. I called him in and talked with him when I decided to make the move. It was not a long discussion.

"Mac said, 'Do what you have do do.' You look Mac in the eye, he looks you in the eye and you get it worked out. I know how he feels, but he's accepted it and hasn't complained. I appreciate that.

"With Gura, I just told him he was going to the bullpen. I had done that last year, too, so it wasn't like we were doing it for the first time. Split and I just sat down and talked. I think he sensed he couldn't go on too much longer. It makes it tougher when you're dealing with good guys."

George Brett, who has played under four managers here, marvels at Howser's unflappability.

"He was exactly the same way when we were behind as he was when we were winning," Brett said. "He looks like he's been managing for 40 years. He doesn't get excited, win or lose. But you have to be that way with young players or you put added pressure on them.

"In some respects he's not much different from Jim Frey or Whitey (Herzog). They sat back and let you play. But Whitey could really air it out when you messed up. If you did something Whitey didn't like, you'd get it then and again in the clubhouse in front of the team. Dick sort of looks at you out of the corner of his eye with that bewildered look and you know you've messed up.

"I'm sure you could talk to some of the guys who aren't playing and they'd be hacked off, but you wouldn't want them on the team if they didn't want to play. I think Dick has done a tremendous job. He rarely gets mad, but I know I wouldn't want to test him to see how far he bends before he breaks."

Balboni said that when he was not hitting well and Howser platooned him for a while, Howser called him into his office and explained that he still thought of him as an everyday player.

"When I didn't do well he encouraged me," Balboni said. "He's great in giving you confidence. You always know where you stand with him. At New York, it was a matter of guessing. Then all of a sudden, I'd stop playing and I'd be gone."

Mike Ferraro, Howser's third-base coach, also was his third-base coach with the New York Yankees. Ferraro incurred the wrath of Yankee owner George Steinbrenner in the second game of the 1980 playoff with the Royals when he sent Willie Randolph home and Randolph was thrown out. Steinbrenner demanded Ferraro be moved to first base. Howser said that if Ferraro was moved, someone else would be managing the club.

"What's funny is that stuff like that had been going on all year and Dick didn't even make me aware of it," Ferraro said. "I didn't know what was going on until the end of the season. It was not just me he was protecting, but the pitching coach and everyone else George was upset with.

"Dick knows how to win. He is patient and intelligent. He doesn't miss many things and he doesn't overmanage. He does the right things at the right time. He understands that errors and mistakes are part of the game. But if you want to be tough, Dick can be tough."

One of Howser's admirers is Bill Rigney, a long-time major-league manager who is assistant to the president of the Oakland A's. In Rigney's view, managing is intuitive and he likes how Howser goes about it. He also thinks that at 48 and with four full seasons of managerial experience, Howser is entering the peak years of his career.

"You have to manage from here," Rigney said, pointing to his heart, "and from the seat of your pants. And there's one other thing. Never turn your back on the utility players when they're warming up."

McRae Expounds on Hitting

FORT MYERS, FLA.—In the opinion of George Brett, there is no better student of hitting in the major leagues today than Hal McRae.

"Hal likes to take things apart and put them back together," Brett said. "I'm not that way. It's like dissecting a frog in your high-school biology class. I couldn't even stand to look at it. Once Mac dissected it, he'd know everything there was to know about the frog and how to do it all over again."

Last spring McRae dissected his batting swing, moved a few parts around and then put it all back together. At the time many people were saying McRae was through.

The word was out that if you wanted to get McRae out, all you had to do was jam him with a fastball. If you made a mistake you didn't have to worry because he couldn't drive the ball anyway. Good guy. Too bad. But baseball is a young man's game.

McRae insisted his problems were mechanical. He said that once he improved his rhythm at the start of his swing he would be able to get the bat head to the ball quicker and his problem would be solved.

People in baseball shrugged. Washed-up hitters always have an explanation that has nothing to do with the fact that they are aging.

McRae's project took a few more months to complete, but on July 22 he reclaimed his role as the club's everyday designated hitter. From that point on he batted .291 and drove in 46 runs in 203 at-bats.

McRae will be 40 July 10, but this spring he is driving the ball with authority in batting practice, and Manager Dick Howser is counting on him to be his cleanup hitter again.

"I knew with my rhythm deal, if I kept applying it in games, it would fall into place," McRae said. "Things don't leave you that fast. I felt it would work if I perfected it. I know how it feels when you make a good pass at the ball. I know what it's like to see the ball. I just wasn't doing it consistently."

McRae acknowledges that his reflexes are slowing, but he argues that the thinking hitter can compensate by adjusting his swing. Those who fail to adjust must find another line of work.

"My reflexes can't be as good as they were five years ago so I have to look for a way out, a solution" McRae said. "Your ability to drive the ball goes first, but if you can make adjustments, you can find a way to get the bat into a good hitting position. There's no reason for me not to be able to hit the ball hard. If I get the bat head in a good position, there's no way I won't hit. But I may have to find a way to get it to that position quicker. You slow down, but you find ways to compensate."

McRae attributes 75 percent of his hitting knowledge to what he learned from the late Charlie Lau, who was the Royals' batting coach when he joined the club.

"Charlie would talk with me about something, I would apply it in a game and then we'd talk about it again," McRae said. "He was a good communicator."

McRae acknowledges Brett's assessment that he is the type of hitter who isn't satisfied unless he understands every aspect of his swing.

"Sometimes people say I think too much, but that's my nature," McRae said. "I get more satisfaction that way. You learn through trial and error. Hitting instruction has always lagged behind pitching instruction. It still does. What you have mostly are a lot of clichés. Nobody breaks things down."

McRae believes the mental as well as the mechanical aspects of hitting are neglected.

"When I was going good, I was real good. When I was bad, I was real bad. If you can cut that bad period down, you can add 20 points to your average over a season.

"A hitter has to know how to think at the plate, how a guy is going to pitch you. You've got to have a game plan every time you go up. You have to do what you want to do, not what the pitcher wants you to do. You've got to dictate. If you do what the pitcher wants, you have much less chance to be successful.

"The more hits you get the more predictable pitching becomes because you know they're going to try to go back to ways they've gotten you out. If I'm successful, the pitcher is reacting to me.

"When you get hot, the first thing that happens is that you get very relaxed and confident. You pick the ball up from the pitcher extremely well. You can visualize him throwing something before he actually throws it. You slow the ball down.

"Everything is in sync. Your body and mind are working as one unit. You can hold it maybe eight to 10 days and you've got to take advantage of the situation when you've got it.

"They talk about picking up the rotation on the ball and seeing the ball hit the bat. I don't know if that's possible, but you get the feeling you can do almost anything.

"I'll tell you what I've done that's almost scary. I've gone from the on-deck circle to the plate without knowing how I got there. I've been on deck and visualized a guy throwing me a breaking ball and hitting it out of the park and had it happen. When you're going bad, you can visualize yourself striking out and do it.

"As a hitter, all kinds of crazy things happen.

"One time they were getting me out on sliders and I was walking around the clubhouse with my hand held out saying to myself, 'You've got to be out there. That's what they're doing to you. They're getting you out with sliders.' Tom Poquette was swinging a bat. I saw him. I knew what he was doing and I walked right into him. He hit me on the arm with the bat. They thought my arm would be broken, but it wasn't too bad. A short time after that I got hot."

It's too bad Charlie Lau wasn't around last year to watch his old pupil's splendid comeback. It would have been one of his proudest moments.

Finley
Comes to Kansas City

For better or worse, Charles O. Finley and Kansas City have been joined together in the bonds of major league baseball. It is a tenuous union, but there is a possibility that in time it will grow stronger.

Kansas City earnestly wanted home ownership of the Athletics. Finley prevented the city from achieving its goal. In view of this fact, he can scarcely expect a hero's welcome here even though he rides into town with a satchel of money and statements of good intent.

At the same time, Finley is not entirely to blame for the failure of the home ownership drive. With adequate financing, home ownership could have been achieved, but no one here came forward with enough money to ensure the success of the campaign.

The sad facts of the case are that in seven months of intensive campaigning Kansas City was able to raise only $2.6 million toward the purchase price of the franchise. Undoubtedly additional money could have been raised through a public stock sale, but the American League does not regard this as a desirable form of financing.

At the time the Kansas City group appeared before the American League in St. Louis for conditional approval, its financing was considered so marginal that strong opposition developed. It took an all-out effort by officials of the Athletics to win the endorsement of the A.L.

The largest amount invested by an individual toward purchase of the A's was $50,000. The largest amount invested by a corporation was $100,00, with the exception of the Schlitz Brewing Company, which put up $200,000. Schlitz is a Milwaukee corporation, although it does have a branch brewery here.

Many individuals, most notably Byron Spencer, did heroic work on behalf of the home ownership project and contributed heavily of their time and money. But help from the top was not there.

The Kansas City group could still exercise its option to buy the 48 per cent minority stock; if it did, this could prove to be an important factor in keeping the club in Kansas City permanently. It has become known, however, that some influential members of the group are opposed to buying the minority holding.

Even with its financial problems, the Kansas City group might have succeeded in getting the franchise had it not been for legal entanglements and a feud between Mrs. Carmen Humes, widow of Arnold Johnson, and the Chicago stockholders.

From the beginning it seemed that nothing worked quite right for the Kansas City group.

Now Finley is in control, and there appears to be a good chance that he will wind up with 100 per cent of the A's stock, although he has expressed an eagerness to take some Kansas Citians into the corporation.

Tomorrow Finley will appear in the Cook County Probate Court to formally submit his bid of $1,975,000 for the stock held by the Johnson estate. Next he will seek approval from the American League.

Then will come the matter of the minority stock. Finley says he is willing operate with only 52 percent, but he has already made various efforts to obtain the minority stock, and he apparently believes that he will be able to acquire at least 80 percent of the stock. He must have this amount to obtain important tax advantages.

So far Finley has done everything possible to assure the Athletics' fans of his good intentions, and it must be admitted that there are certain advantages to having him in the picture.

He is a man of wealth and if he is so inclined he has the resources to run a first-class operation. In addition, he is certain to provide strong leadership since he will be the sole owner of his stock.

Among the important promises made by Finley are: (1) That he has no intention of moving the club; (2) that he will put all profits plus money of his own into a rebuilding program; (3) he will not sell out to make a capital gains profit; (4) he will come to Kansas City and work actively in the season ticket sale; (5) he will consider moving here after his oldest son graduates from high school in 1962.

These are excellent points. If Finley lives up to them then Kansas City will be as well or perhaps better off under his ownership.

It is likely, however, that more than words will be needed to convince the fans of Finley's intentions. The bitter taste left by the Johnson operation still lingers, and the public is justifiably suspicious of absentee ownership.

Rich Gale's
Night of Horror

The horror ended quickly for most of those killed in the Hyatt Regency hotel tragedy. For the survivors, the nightmare lives on.

It manifests itself in images that well up from the subconscious, in sleep that won't come, in minds that won't focus, in efforts to make sense out of the senseless.

In the everyday world, there are bills to be paid, groceries to be purchased, children to be scolded and parties to be given, but catastrophe leaves us disoriented. What was important before no longer is important. The mental blocks we erect against death and the fragile nature of our existence are torn down. The imperfections we so carefully camouflage suddenly are laid bare.

Rich Gale is one of the survivors of the Hyatt disaster. He also is a pitcher for the Royals, but at the moment baseball and the financial hardships imposed by the strike don't seem quite as important to him.

Gale was tending bar in the lobby when the two skywalks fell. He was lucky. He walked away unharmed physically. But like the other survivors, he is wondering how long it will be before he can laugh again or enjoy such simple pleasures as a steak or a game of racquetball.

In time, the memories of Friday night will recede, but Gale and others like him are going through a difficult readjustment.

"When it happened, I kept thinking, 'This is something you see in the movies. It doesn't happen to real people,'" Gale said. "I couldn't fathom it. I kept waiting for someone to stop it and say everyone was all right."

The scene that followed was both vivid and unreal. The rescue efforts, the blood, the horror, the fruitless attempts to call his wife, Susan. Finally, on the way home, he passed her and waved frantically.

"I stuck my arm about four feet out of the Jeep and she saw me," Gale said.

When Gale arrived home there were phone calls from relatives, friends and the media. He told himself he felt all right. He proved it by fixing himself a sandwich. Then he attempted to pour some lemonade—and dropped the pitcher. He tried to catch it, but it broke and he suffered a severe cut on one finger that required stitches.

"It just hit me right about then," Gale said. "I was wondering if I should have stayed. I was asking myself if I could have done more. Normally my pulse rate is abnormally low, about 48. When I had the stitches taken, it was about 100.

"I didn't sleep hardly at all Friday night. I kept seeing a couple of sights I don't even want to talk about. I remembered two fellows who had played golf in the muscular dystrophy tournament at Blue Springs. They had been at my bar that night. They didn't survive.

"Saturday, I had to get out of the house. We went to see a movie, 'Arthur.' It's a comedy, but I didn't want to laugh. I just wanted to get my mind off things. We came back home, ate, watched the news update and finally went to bed. Sunday we went to church. When I prayed for the people involved, I felt it was one time God was listening to me."

A degree of normalcy is beginning to return to Gale's life, but he struggles with the philosophical question of why such a tragedy happened.

"People will tell you God has reasons for all of these things," Gale said. "We've all heard the statement that God works in mysterious ways, and I suppose it's never more appropriate than it is now.

"I feel frustrated I couldn't have done more, but I didn't have medical disaster-type training. I've been thinking recently about going into medicine. The fact we're not playing baseball doesn't seem as important as it did Friday afternoon. The financial straits we're in because we're not playing aren't as important.

"I'm just glad I'm alive and my wife wasn't there. Some of the people who didn't survive were at my bar....

"If any good came out of it, I guess it was in the way the people of Kansas City responded. The people who came out to give blood did as much as a lot of us who were there."

In October, Gale was part of the joyous celebration that took place when the Royals brought the World Series to Kansas City for the first time. Today, he is a grieving survivor of Kansas City's greatest tragedy.

Finley a Titan
of Turmoil

In his 16 tyrannical seasons as owner of the A'S, Charles O. Finley has done such interesting things as move his team, albeit abortively, from Kansas City to Louisville, fire a utility infielder in the middle of a World Series and lead a drive to unseat the commissioner.

Season after season it is assumed that Charles O. can't possibly top what he did the year before, but as Sal Bando was saying Friday night, "This is the most hectic year we've had. I've never seen anything like it." When you've worked for Finley at the major league level for most of 10 seasons, as Bando has, that's saying quite a bit.

Charles O. tuned up for the bicentennial season by firing his manager, Alvin Dark. Some years back he fired Alvin twice in one night so this was fairly routine stuff, but the reason for this dismissal was unusual. Dark, who Finley called "the preacher man," was addressing a church group and said that unless Charlie changed his ways he might not be on the right side for the great game in the sky.

Finley has never been one to endure criticism patiently, especially from a manager who lost three straight games in the playoffs. Dark was fired and Finley hired Chuck Tanner, the former manager of the White Sox. Tanner had a contract with the Sox for a salary of $60,000 a year. Finley decided he would pay $25,000 or so and let Bill Veeck pick up the rest of it. Veeck declined and the dispute over Tanner's salary has yet to be resolved.

Moving right along, Charles O. was now ready for the great spring salary confrontation. Salary battles have long been one of his favorite pastimes, but this year the ground rules were different because the players could elect to play out their options and become free agents. Even so, Finley negotiated as if he thought the Messersmith case had something to do with World War I and open-cockpit airplanes.

Joe Rudi, one of baseball's best hitters, asked for a salary of $125,000. Charlie said no. Rudi offered to sign for three years at

$115,000, $135,000 and $150,000. Charlie said no. Rollie Fingers, probably the best relief pitcher in baseball, asked for $140,000. Charlie said no. Fingers proposed a 2-year contract calling for $130,000 and $180,000, which would put him on the same level with Mike Marshall. Charlie said no.

Finley did offer Reggie Jackson a 3-year contract calling for $150,000, $175,000 and $200,000, but when Jackson's agent asked for an additional $75,000 a year to be deferred over a 10-year period Finley told him he had an hour and a half to change his mind or he would trade Jackson.

"I don't run away from a fight," Finley declared.

Having proved again what a reasonable man he is, Finley traded Jackson and Ken Holtzman to Baltimore. They would not be the last to go. Just before the trading deadline Finley sold three unsigned players, Rudi, Fingers and Vida Blue, touching off the following series of events:

Commissioner Bowie Kuhn held a hearing and nullified the sale. Finley filed a $10 million damage suit against the commissioner and refused to use the players. The commissioner said that unless the players were used in a normal manner there would be grave consequences. Finley said, "I'm not concerned about the grave consequences." Finley's players threatened to strike. Finley said he would bring up 25 players from the minors. Later Finley changed his mind and after his players took a strike vote and were ready to walk out Finley agreed to use Rudi, Fingers and Blue.

There were more complications. Blue was signed to a 3-year contract before the sale was announced, presumably at the request of the Yankees. According to Blue, he was told he would not be sold or traded. Paul Corvino, identified as a business consultant for Blue, met with the commissioner and threatened to file a suit over Blue's contract. Blue in turn said he had given Corvino no power of attorney and raised the possibility that he might sue Corvino.

Still to be resolved are the dispute about Tanner's salary, Finley's damage suit against the commissioner, the legality of Blue's contract and the question of where Blue, Rudi and Fingers will finish the season. And, if Finley wins his suit, there is the little problem of where baseball will get the $10 million to pay him.

"It's amazing," Bando says. "We've had a lot of things happen before, but nothing like this. I do feel, though, that taking the strike vote brought us together. I think now we have more respect for each other."

"This has been a nightmare for me," Rudi declares. "I got off to my best start in the majors, but then I hurt my knee sliding. I got back in the line-up and then we had the sale. The next thing the deal is called off, but then Charlie won't play us. My average went from .300 to .259."

Rudi is appreciative of the stand his teammates took in voting to strike, but he says the players were not looking for a chance to challenge Finley.

"I don't know that you'd call our strike vote a victory over Charlie," he said. "It's just that neither Kuhn nor McPhail (Lee McPhail, president of the American League) would take a stand. Kuhn said we were supposed to play and there would be a penalty if we didn't, but then he didn't do anything. I'm just proud my teammates were willing to stand behind me."

Fingers professes to be unconcerned about all of the unresolved problems.

"By the time they get it all settled in court I'll probably be retired and have 15 kids playing in the majors," he laughed. "I'm just happy the guys were behind us. It wasn't fair for Charlie to make this team play with 22 players."

Tanner, who points out that the A's have not been at full strength physically since the start of the season, believes his club is ready to make a move. "We're in the best health we've been in all year," he said. "We've been through all these situations and we've hung tough. That's what impresses me about this club."

For the last few days the A's have been going through a tranquil period in which they have been able to concentrate on baseball, but of course that won't last long. Charles O. can't abide big salaries, Bowie Kuhn or tranquillity.

Saberhagen
Moves In

FORT MYERS, FLA.—Rookies are supposed to speak softly and blend in with the clubhouse walls, but Bret Saberhagen arrived in camp last spring at the age of 19 wearing pastel-striped shorts and a white, narrow-brimmed hat that looked as if it had come from a Miami mafioso boutique.

Dan Quisenberry calls him a "natural flake." George Brett describes him as "goofy." Saberhagen explains himself more circumspectly by saying, "I kind of keep everybody loose."

Not only did he keep everybody loose last season, but he emerged as the youthful prodigy of the staff—the kid who broke Detroit's opening eight-game winning streak, pitched a shutout against the Angels in a big late-season game and turned in a solid starting performance against the Tigers in the playoffs.

Manager Dick Howser equates him to a young Catfish Hunter in terms of his poise and his ability to throw his fastball to spots at such an early age.

"Whatever maturity is, he's got it," Howser said.

And along with pitching maturity, Saberhagen has a youthful non-chalance and a sublime sense of confidence that amazes and delights his elders.

"He's such a likable guy you can't get mad at him," said Brett, who put up Saberhagen at his home in Kansas City and watched in fascination as Saberhagen causally helped himself to Brett's clothes, his car and his Dom Perignon champagne.

Saberhagen's confidence first became evident to the public when he broke the Tigers' winning streak in his first major-league start. Going into that game he said, "I'll beat them. I feel I'm pitching good. Nobody told me they were unbeatable."

Pete Rose, a man famed for his bubbling confidence, scarcely could have spoken more fearlessly.

After the game Saberhagen said, "I had a good feeling we were going to win. The percentages were with us. Eventually you knew they were going to lose."

Royals pitching Coach Gary Blaylock has a vivid recollection of his first encounter with Saberhagen, as does Brett.

"He's the most unusual kid I've ever seen," Blaylock said. "The first time I ever saw him he was pitching in the instructional league. Mike Jones was there, too. Jones was coming back from his neck injury and it took him a lot of time to warm up.

"Bret was going to pitch first and Jones was going second. Bret finished warming up, and as he did he looked at Mike and said, 'You'd better loosen up. It's not going to take me very long.' "

Brett's first meeting with Saberhagen came during the Royals' 1984 spring golf outing. Jones had suggested that Brett put Saberhagen on their team, saying "We may not win, but we'll have a lot of fun."

Brett never had met Saberhagen, but they became fully acquainted, so to speak, on the first par-5, a water hole. The first two members of the team hit their drives in the water. As Brett was getting ready to hit, Saberhagen told him to go ahead and use his driver because he would play a safe shot and lay up if Brett went in the water.

Brett hit his ball in the water and then turned to see what kind of an iron Saberhagen was going to hit.

"The next thing I know the kid is getting out a 4-wood," Brett said, "and I'm thinking, 'He's going to lay up with that?' He swung and his ball went right in the water."

After the tournament Brett and some other members of the Royals invited Saberhagen out to celebrate with a little tequila, only they drank shots of water while Saberhagen was drinking the real thing. After five or six rounds, including one double, Saberhagen said he wasn't feeling too well.

"He's coughing and gaging and sucking on a lemon," Brett laughed. "We told him, 'You can do it, let's have one more.' That's when he really got sick."

Blaylock recalls an incident in West Palm Beach when the Royals were playing the Braves. The National League does not use the designated hitter, so Saberhagen had to hit.

"Brett had a stiff back and wasn't playing," Blaylock said. "He had his jacket on and when Saberhagen went up to hit he pointed to the jacket and told George, 'Bring that to me when I get on first base.'"

When the Royals opened the season, Saberhagen and Mark Gubicza had trouble finding a place to live and moved in with Brett for about a month.

"They had been there about three weeks," Brett said, "and one day Gubie came to me and said, 'Is it all right if I use the phone?' I said, 'Yeah, call anybody you want. Call your parents if you'd like.' He said, 'Oh, no. It's just a local call.' While he's doing that, Saberhagen is in the closet going through my clothes to see what he wants to wear. That's how different they are."

How did Saberhagen become so good after only one year of pitching in the minors?

"He knows how to pitch," Blaylock said. "He knows how to set up hitters and move the ball around. That usually takes a long time to learn. They talk about the sophomore jinx, but I don't think it will bother him. I don't think it enters his mind."

Quisenberry thinks Saberhagen has an unusual mental makeup that helps him cope with the pressure.

"It helps a lot for him to be flaky," Quisenberry said. "He's just a natural flake. Each guy deals with the pressure in his own way. Sometimes it helps if you don't think too much.

"He's a natural athlete. He loves to compete and I don't think the sophomore jinx will bother him. Pitchers sometimes have a bad second year because they think they have to do more, that they have to throw the ball harder and make it sink more."

For all of his confidence, Saberhagen said he did not expect to make the Royals' staff last season. He added that Brett's willingness to share his home helped to make him and Gubicza feel comfortable and a part of the club.

As for the possibility of pushing himself too hard and falling victim to the sophomore jinx, Saberhagen said he learned about that sort of trap in high school. He batted .426, tried to do even better the following year and wound up having a bad season.

"I like to compete," Saberhagen said, "Whether it's baseball or basketball or tiddlywinks, I want to win. I am not a good loser."

It would be unfair to Saberhagen to project him as a 17 or 18-game winner this season, but if he puts another solid season on top of last year, the Royals will be safe in concluding that Saberhagen, like Hunter, is one of those extraordinary pitchers who has achieved maturity without going through the conventional learning process.

CHAPTER 6

GOLF

The Young Tom Watson

Tom Watson and Charles Digges were relaxing over a beer following their second-round match yesterday in the Missouri Amateur Golf Tournament. A woman passed by their table, gave them a surprised look and said, "Is your match over already."

Digges, who has lost to Watson, 7 and 6, looked up, laughed and said, "Good lord, is it over?"

Watson had a surprising amount of trouble in the first round before he disposed of Red Hogan, 1-up. He played well against Digges, who also helped him out with an erratic performance. And so after two rounds Watson was still the man to beat as he sought his fourth Missouri Amateur title in the last five years.

It was seven years ago that Watson became the boy wonder of Kansas City golf when he won the Kansas City Golf Association Match Play championship at the age of 14. In those days people said he had a Huck Finn look because of his reddish brown hair, his sunburned nose and a gap between his front teeth. Today his hair is longer and he has grown a moustache ("A caterpillar crawled up there and died," Watson laughs).

Last Sunday he was graduated from Stanford with a degree in psychology and now, as a young man of 21, he has come to a turning point in his career. Like all young golfers Watson has been doing some thinking about the pro tour but he is not sure his game is that good. He plans to play an extensive schedule of amateur competition this summer. By the time he is through he expects to have the answer to his question.

"I can't decide whether I should try to develop my game out there (on the tour) or whether I would be better off trying to develop it before I go," Watson said. "I do know that my game is not good enough the way it is right now.

"My driving has been erratic and my irons are not good enough. My putting has been all right. If I had to pick out one part of my game that concerns me most it's the irons. Those are the clubs you really score with. Your irons get you up there for the birdie putts."

Watson recently played with John Brodie, the San Francisco 49ers' quarterback who is an outstanding golfer. Brodie impressed on Watson that if he hopes to improve his iron game he must develop a shorter swing.

"John told me I need to bring my irons back slower and to shorten my swing," Watson said. "That way I'll get finer with my irons and I won't get off line so easy. I'm going to go back now and try to accomplish this practicing.

"Another thing I have to find out this summer is how well I can do in good competition. You never know whether you're a good player unless you prove yourself in good competition. You can't play sporadic golf and win against good players. I'm fortunate to have enough money to go out and play this summer. If you don't have the bread you can't do it."

Watson had hoped to qualify for the U.S. Open. He survived the opening qualifying round in a playoff but missed out in the sectional qualifying. There was a playoff for the final berth and Watson missed the playoff by one stroke.

Since he couldn't spend this week at the Merion Golf Club, Watson set off on a 1,500-mile dash by car and plane to Kansas City for defense of his Missouri Amateur title.

"Our graduation exercises were Sunday," Watson said. "I drove all night and got to Phoenix the next morning at 9 o'clock. I wanted to leave my car there since the N.C.A.A. tournament is next week in Tucson. I had a 4-lane highway and I was fortunate there weren't any highway patrolmen around. I caught a flight from Phoenix that got me into Kansas City at 6 o'clock Monday night. When I got here I passed out."

Asked if it was worth that effort to defend his title Watson laughed and said, "If you're the defending champion you've got to play. You don't have to qualify, either, and I don't want to pass up a tournament where I don't have to qualify."

It was on June 21, 1964, that Watson created a sensation in Kansas City golf circles by winning the K.C.G.A. match play title. He defeated Bob Devine, 4 and 2, to become the youngest player ever to win the championship. Devine led, 3-up, after 19 holes, but Devine lost four of the final seven holes and Watson won the championship.

The following week Watson qualified for the Missouri amateur championship by shooting rounds of 71-76. His second round featured a spectacular 33 on the back side. Watson was eliminated from the tournament that year by Jim Colbert.

Yesterday Colbert shot a 69 in the U.S. Open and Watson was starting his quest for a fourth Missouri Amateur title. Both of them have come a long way in seven years, but Watson says his game has deteriorated in one area.

"I just wish I could chip now like I did when I was a kid," he laughs.

Watson
Replaces Nicklaus
at the Top

Jack Nicklaus is quite likely the greatest player in the history of golf, but he is no longer the greatest player in the world. Slowly but ever so resolutely Tom Watson has moved into that role.

There have been earlier challenges to the Golden Bear by a succession of young men with sun-bleached hair whose backswings ended in perfect arcs. They arrived in a burst of birdies and tournament victories and were proclaimed as the young lions of the tour.

The pattern has been for Nicklaus to go on being Jack Nicklaus while in time the frailties of his challengers were exposed. More often than not they lacked the dedication, the discipline or perhaps the mental toughness that is required to play such a perverse game at its highest level over a period of years.

Once a professional has achieved a reasonable degree of skill, golf, to a great degree, becomes a game of the mind. It is a solitary game—one man against the field, the golf course, and on some days, the elements. It is a game that destroys the insecure and makes the even the strong apprehensive.

The swing that is pure today can go awry tomorrow. A Ben Hogan can lose a U.S. Open playoff to a Jack Fleck. A Sam Snead can come into the 72nd hole of the Open needing a 5 to win and take an 8. An Arnold Palmer can win the 1964 Masters at the age of 35 and never again win a major championship.

Even a Nicklaus can be humiliated by this game, a point he made before the start of this year's Masters.

"Six weeks ago I was playing so poorly I wanted to slip off the course without anyone seeing me," Nicklaus said.

Watson is a different type of challenger than Nicklaus has faced before. The 29-year old native of Kansas City is reaching his peak at a time when Nicklaus is 39 and perhaps less motivated than he once was.

Today the most fascinating question in golf is whether Nicklaus will make the effort required for a last stand against the only young golfer who has shown the capacity for greatness. Can he reclaim the throne from the man who outdueled him to win the Masters and the British Open in 1977?

Watson did not come streaking across the golf scene shooting 62s and 63s as Johnny Miller did. His progress has been slow and methodical. He has studied himself and his game with great care. Among his fellow pros, Watson is known as a grinder, a man who never lets up on a shot.

One of Watson's first public statements concerning his ambition of becoming the best golfer in the world was made in December of 1974 when officers of the Western Golf Association came here for a trophy presentation.

Pursuing the subject a few days later Watson said, "I meant what I said in the sense that I have enough talent for golf so that it can be developed to the point I can be the best in the game. There are a lot of roadblocks and I'll have to see if I can overcome them.

"I'm a great admirer of Gary Player. He doesn't have as much talent as some of the people on the tour, but he has taken his game and made the best of it. What I see in him I'd like to see in myself. He has a great desire to play and a great love for the game. The great thing he has going for him is his determination....

"You can't luck into success. You have to set high goals. Not many people have an opportunity to set high goals for themselves. That's why I feel that I'm fortunate. I have the talent, the time and the people to help me."

The season following those statements, Watson won his first major championship, the British Open. He did not win a tour event in 1976, but the next year he won the Masters and his second British Open. Last season he became the first player in history to sweep the tour money title, the Player of the Year Award and the Vardon Trophy two years in a row.

Nicklaus remains a superb golfer, but his is playing less each year and there are signs that his skills are declining. He appeared in 18 tour events in 1977 and 15 last year.

"The week-to-week tournaments can't excite me any more," Nicklaus said. "I've got to be building toward the Masters or some other major event."

It is understandable that Nicklaus can no longer get butterflies about playing in the Greater Greensboro Open, but there is reason to question whether he can cut back his schedule to 14 or 15 events a year and still retain the competitive sharpness necessary to win the major tournaments.

Age brings about a deterioration of physical skills and concentration. Most athletes say they have to work harder as they get older just to maintain a normal level of ability. Nicklaus may not be willing to make that sacrifice.

His position in golf is secure if he never sets another ball on a tee. His wealth is estimated at $30 million or more and he has numerous outside interests. He takes an active role in his course architectural business and, according to friends, he closely follows the financial condition of all of his enterprises. His teen-age sons play high school football and basketball and he saw all but four of their 31 games, once flying home during a tournament.

How well Nicklaus plays from this point will depend largely on how much time he wants to devote to golf, but for the first time since he displaced Arnold Palmer, he is only the second-best golfer in the world.

Palmer, Nicklaus and Fun at Dub's Dread

When Jack Nicklaus approached the first tee yesterday at Dub's Dread he looked at the spot where he and Arnold Palmer would be teeing off. Then he looked 50 yards ahead where Byron Nelson and Jug McSpaden were waiting to hit.

"Is this handicap based on how old we are or how old we feel?" Nicklaus asked.

"In that case I'll move up to the front stake," Palmer said.

On the second hole Nicklaus turned to his partner and said, "Arnie, have you noticed we're hitting all the upslopes and they're hitting all the downslopes?"

McSpaden, who was in hearing distance, laughed and shouted, "Haven't you got the message?"

"No, but I'm getting it," Nicklaus replied.

On No. 3 Palmer stood on the tee, surveyed the expanse of greensward in front of him and exclaimed, "Now I remember why I got so tired last year."

Despite their good-natured complaints, Nicklaus and Palmer played Dub's Dread as if the layout measured 6,800 yards instead of 7,800 yards. They succeeded in shrinking the dimensions of the course with some awesome long ball hitting that brought gasp after gasp from the crowd of 1,500.

Nicklaus, who shot a remarkable 69, had only one bogey and won long ball honors for the day. Palmer, aching hip and all, had a 71 and was almost as long as Nicklaus off the tee. Even Nelson got long-ball fever. After Palmer and Nicklaus closed out the match on No. 16 Nelson accompanied them to the back marker on the 614-yard No. 17.

McSpaden, who was already at the front marker, looked at his partner.

"I'm going to hit from back here," Nelson said.

"Are you out of your mind?" McSpaden needled.

As it turned out, Nelson knew exactly what he was doing. He cut the corner on the dogleg hole, was on in 2 and sank a 12-foot putt for an eagle. For those who find fun in nostalgia, it was the most memorable hole of the day.

A year ago Palmer and Nicklaus struggled to a 1-up victory over the Gold Dust Twins of yesteryear, but on this occasion they won decisively. They held a 3-up lead after eight holes and Nelson and McSpaden were never able to cut into it.

Nicklaus and Palmer, who shot 71s a year ago, improved on their performance while Nelson and McSpaden had their problems and played their best golf only in spurts. Nelson, who is bothered by arthritis, was not as effective with his irons, but hit the ball well off the tee.

More than anything else, the fans came to see Nicklaus and Palmer hit the long ball and they were fully rewarded. Arnie and Jack averaged about 280 yards with their drives and hit several of 300 yards.

One of the big moments of the day came on No. 11, a lake hole that measures 266 yards from the back tee. A year ago Nicklaus drove the hole with a 1-iron. Palmer, who had started to use a wood, switched to a 1-iron and was short to the left.

When Nicklaus and Palmer came to No. 11 the fans were ready.

"Get your 1-iron, Arnie," a spectator called.

"You'd better get your 3-wood," another shouted. "Why don't you pick up?" someone else yelled.

Nicklaus, using a 1-iron, lashed the ball within 14 feet of the pin.

"I'll show him," Palmer said, drawing a 1-iron from his bag. He glared at the ball, swung and sent it hurtling toward the green. The ball hit a few feet short and kicked off to the right.

As Nicklaus and Palmer started down the fairway, Jack turned to Arnie, shook his head and said, "I just didn't catch mine whole." Palmer chose to ignore his partner.

At No. 12, a 577-yard hole wrapped around a lake, Nicklaus asked how he should line up his shot. A dispute developed among the fans as to where he was on his tee shot a year ago.

"I know where I was last year," Nicklaus said, "I just want to know where I should be."

He then proceeded to hit a tremendous tee shot. Seven or eight seconds had elapsed when some spectators far down the fairway let out a cheer.

"It just came down," one of the fans at the tee quipped.

At No. 16, a 260-yard lake hole, the question arose as to whether Nicklaus should hit a 1-iron or a 4-wood.

"I don't think a 1-iron is enough," Nicklaus said.

"Jump on it, Jack," Palmer needled.

Nicklaus took the wood from his bag. Palmer motioned for a 1-iron. McSpaden, 50 yards ahead, booed.

"What are you going to do, lay up short of the lake?" Nicklaus said to the grinning Palmer.

Nicklaus hit his wood solidly, but sliced it.

"There's another great shot," he said. "I'm going to try a 1-iron now," he called to McSpaden. "I want to see what you yelled boo about."

Nicklaus's shot hit the front part of the green, dug in and stopped about two feet inside the fringe. It was the sort of thing the spectators loved.

Nicklaus and Palmer closed out the match on 16 and then surrendered the center stage to Nelson, who thrilled the fans with his eagle on 17.

Nicklaus, reflecting on his 69, said he didn't feel the course played as long as it did a year ago.

"As I recall it had been raining a lot when we were here last year," Nicklaus said. "There was water in some places on the course and there wasn't much roll.

"I don't feel the course is excessively long. The greens are all big and that keeps everything in proportion. If you have a short course the greens are smaller. With a long course like this they should be big. You could make some of the greens smaller and make the course a lot tougher, but then you would be defeating the whole idea of the course."

Racial Barrier Falls
at the Masters

Lee Elder: Age, 40. Joined Professional Golf tour in 1968. Became the first black to qualify for the Masters Tournament when he won the Monsanto Open in Pensacola, Fla., last April. Finished 30th on the 1974 money list with earnings of $71,986. Has not played well this season. Tied for 36th place in Tucson, withdrew after three rounds of the Crosby and missed the cut in his next three tournaments. His best showings this year have been a tie for 17th at Jacksonville, Fla., worth $1,806 and a tie for 12th last week at Greensboro, N.C., worth $4,219.

AUGUSTA, GA.—The ordeal of Lee Elder began at 2:10 o'clock yesterday afternoon. The weather was spectacular—sunny, crisp with only a few long, thin clouds strung across the sky. A red Oldsmobile with a black vinyl top entered the circular drive at Augusta National Golf Club, its tires making a sticky sound against the pavement.

"Here he comes," someone said. A deputy sheriff, his gun sitting conspicuously high on his hip, said, "Wasn't that Lee that just come in?"

Writers, broadcasters and photographers walked across the parking lot to intercept Elder, the first black man to play in the Masters, a tournament with an antebellum flavor and a reputation for being hostile or at best indifferent to the idea of integration.

Elder is something of a Flip Wilson look-alike. Normally he is a friendly man who smiles easily and is courteous to interviewers, but yesterday was not a normal day. Accompanied by his wife, Rose, and a friend, Dr. Phillip Smith, medical director of Martin Luther King Hospital in Los Angeles, he walked unsmilingly through the parking lot toward the registration building.

"I'm not talking," he said in reply to a question. Another interviewer tried. "I'm not talking," he said. "Every time I talk I get in trouble." He walked on briskly, ignoring a question as to what kind of trouble he meant. Elder and his wife entered the building, leaving Dr. Smith to talk with newsmen.

"We just flew up from Charlotte," Dr. Smith said pleasantly. "He's relaxed. He seems to be in good spirits."

Rose Elder emerged from the registration center and was asked about her husband's sudden reticence.

"He talked from January until last week," she said. "Now he's asking for a week to concentrate on golf. He's having a press conference at 3 o'clock tomorrow. He thought that would be the fairest thing for everyone."

A short time later Elder went to the clubhouse while his wife waited outside. She was asked if she would be glad when the ordeal was over. "Absolutely," she said. "It has been pressure packed since January." Asked about the significance of the Masters she said, "It's another major championship and Lee would like to play well in it."

But of course this is not just another major championship. This is the Masters with all its Southern tradition and Elder is a symbol, a standard bearer for his race.

Elder quickly left the clubhouse and walked off toward his car, this time leaving his caddy, Henry Brown, to talk to the press. Henry, it developed, was not reticent.

"I'm the best golfer in Augusta, black or white," Henry said, Masters week presumably excluded. "Any man wants to beat me can come out and try. Why haven't I been on the tour? That costs money. If I had all that it takes I'd be out there."

Brown said he had asked to caddy for Elder two years ago when he thought Elder might qualify for the Masters. "He was my choice of all the blacks out there who had a chance," Brown said.

Asked how he would feel if he were Elder, Brown replied, "If it was me in this position I don't think I'd feel too much pressure. I'd just play it as if it was another tournament."

Forty minutes after arriving at Augusta National Elder drove away, but he told his caddy he would return in an hour. He was back at about 4 o'clock, but this time he made it to the clubhouse almost unnoticed. He went to the practice tee to hit iron shots, but soon the photographers gathered again.

At 4:45 p.m. with the shadows beginning to spread over the rich green fairways of Augusta National, Elder went to the first tee by himself to begin an abbreviated practice round. Only a few reporters and photographers were following and he was relaxed and smiling.

Elder played 1, 2, 3, and 4 and then cut across to finish on 7, 8 and 9. He hit most of his shots well, but on two holes he was short with approach shots. As he finished No. 7 a barefooted girl asked him for an autograph. As he signed she began to sneeze.

"What's the matter, catching cold?" Elder said solicitously. "You got to put on some shoes."

As he trudged uphill to hit his second shot on No. 8 he laughed and said, "Whew! You got to be in shape to play this hole."

As he completed 9 a black man in the gallery said, "I follow you everywhere you go. I sure hope you go to heaven when you die."

The man asked Elder to pose with him while a friend took some pictures. Elder did, then he signed autographs. As he walked toward the clubhouse a reporter with a tape recorder asked him a question. "I'm not talking," he said.

Thus Elder's first day at the Masters ended as it began.

For Robert Lee Elder the next few days will be difficult, if not impossible. Not long ago he said, "I go to bed thinking about the Masters, I wake up thinking about the Masters."

In a first person story written for the *New York Times* he said, "I would like to see another black player qualify for the Masters. I've said that publicly. I think then the situation would turn pretty much to him. I wouldn't have everybody running out and addressing me solely."

Unfortunately, Elder is a man alone. No one expects him to win the Masters, but there is great pressure on him to make a respectable showing. Earlier in the season he was playing poorly. Recently he has shown improvement. Many great golfers have had poor rounds at Augusta, but for Elder, failing to make the cut would be a personal calamity.

Shortly before 6 o'clock yesterday Elder and his caddy came walking down No. 9 fairway alone, the pine trees rising in columns on either side. It was a scene rich in symbolism.

A Wild Opening
for the
TPC

PONTE VEDRA, FLA.—Golf is thought of as a tradition-encrusted sport played at elite country clubs under rules of decorum set down by stuffy old men, but there was nothing dull about the Tournament Players Championship, which ended Sunday with Jerry Pate winning the first prize of $90,000.

This was a tournament that had everything except the San Diego Chicken.

You like alligators? They've got alligators. You like snakes? They've got snakes. You want to see a commissioner pushed into a lake at the 18th green? The next splash you hear will be that of Deane Beman. You want to see a tournament winner and a golf course architect pushed into a lake? The next splashes you hear will be those of Pate and Pete Dye.

You want to see Arnold Palmer roll his jet over the course after missing the cut? Just look skyward. You want to see Lee Trevino run to the parking lot after purposely taking a disqualification? Look quickly because there he goes. You want to see a golfer who had to arrive by helicopter to keep his tee time? Check out Ray Floyd.

You like wisecracks? How about this one from Pate, who was asked if he brought his $90,000 check with him when he came to the press room:

"I gave it back to Pete so he can build some new greens," said Pate, one of the outspoken critics of the greens at the Tournament Players Club.

If you don't like that line, then how about one from Tom Watson, who is critical of the course but admires the La Quinta Hotel course Dye built in Palm Desert, Calif.

Asked if he had talked with Dye this week, Watson said, "Yeah, I saw Pete. I told him, 'You birdied the La Quinta course. You bogeyed this one.'"

Or how about another line from Pate who was asked if he would rank the course here as one of the best in the nation.

"It's one of the toughest we play," Pate said, "but you can't rank it. It's not old enough. It would be like ranking girls when they're born."

By now you should have the idea that the TPC was not just another routine golf event.

The tournament did not produce any scoring disasters or near hurricane-force winds such as those seen when the tournament was held at nearby Sawgrass, but it was an interesting event with an atmosphere all its own.

The tournament, played under almost ideal weather conditions, was highly successful and produced some exciting golf as Pate overtook Bruce Lietzke and birdied 14, 17 and 18 on his way to a round of 67 and an 8-under-par 280 for the tournament.

The opening of the course to tournament competition and the controversy over the severity of the greens almost overshadowed the TPC itself, but while Beman may not have liked the public complaints, the controversy gave the course instant identity.

"This might be the most difficult golf course in the world," Beman said.

Quite likely the severity of the greens resulted from that concept on the part of the commissioner, who discovered that the high scores and wind conditions at Sawgrass attracted national coverage and interest.

"I think some of the problems came about because they were concentrating on making this the toughest course in the world," Watson said. "You can afford three or four greens with big contours, but not as many as they have here. I think they will make changes and I think they want player criticism.

"I was critical this week, but I think it will be a better course because of it. I would never be that critical of someone else's course."

Public acceptance of the course appeared to be good because of the view provided by the numerous spectator mounds. One fan at 17 turned to another and said, "This is the best spectator course I've ever seen."

The marketing of the Tournament Players Club is off to a swimming start.

The Gold Dust Twins

Byron Nelson and Jug McSpaden.

The names are inseparable.

They were the Gold Dust Twins of the 1940s. They were close friends, as well as rivals. They traveled together, won together and dominated the pro golf tour together.

By today's standards the gold was only a trickle, but as McSpaden said, "In those days you could buy a loaf of bread for a nickel."

On May 21 the Gold Dust Twins will be reunited at Jack Nicklaus' Memorial Tournament in Columbus, Ohio. Nelson will be the honoree this year, and McSpaden will take part in the ceremonies.

It will be a nostalgic occasion, and for McSpaden the past will offer a pleasant refuge from the harsh realities of the present.

In the last few years McSpaden's work of a lifetime has turned to ashes, literally and figuratively.

McSpaden has suffered business losses he estimates at $3 million. His home burned and he and his wife, Betsy, were fortunate to escape alive. Trophies and mementos representing his many accomplishments in golf were reduced to globs of gold and silver. He was burned in the fire and lost the sight in his left eye, but his vision later was restored through surgery.

A lesser man would have been destroyed. McSpaden has suffered some emotional scars, but he hasn't quit. McSpaden was never a quitter.

The first time McSpaden went on the pro golf tour he quickly exhausted his skimpy savings and had to return home. He went back to work as an assistant pro, went on the tour again and failed a second time. He also failed a third time, and a fourth. On his fifth try, he made it. In 1934 he won seven tournaments and, ironically, became know as "an overnight sensation."

"I wanted to play," McSpaden said. "I practiced six days a week, six to eight hours a day for four months before I went out in 1934. All of a sudden I had it together. I didn't think there was a man on two legs who could beat me."

When McSpaden was an assistant pro at Victory Hills in Kansas City, Kansas, he dreamed of owning the course. He made the dream come true. That and much more. In 1964 he purchased 237 acres of land in western Wyandotte County and began construction of the world's longest golf course, a layout measuring 8,000 yards from the back tee. Appropriately, he named it Dub's Dread. In time he bought more land, started a second course (McSpaden called it Dub's Delight), built an elaborate clubhouse and started a housing development.

He ran bulldozers, installed watering systems and even promoted golf exhibitions. The 14-hour day was routine for McSpaden.

In time McSpaden became overextended, and in 1977 the project was foreclosed by banks and an insurance company. McSpaden also was forced to sell Victory Hills. Before the sale was completed, his home, located on the course, burned.

The only mementos McSpaden has left are two lamp bases made from trophies he won in 1925 and 1926, when he was the Kansas City, Kansas, champion. He had given them to his sons, who returned them after the fire.

The McSpadens have rebuilt their home on the same site, retaining the property as part of the agreement made when Victory Hills was sold to its members.

When McSpaden was younger he responded to adversity by attacking. No one was going to keep him down for long. Today he is 71. He has only a few gray hairs at the temples and looks surprisingly robust, but it is scarcely an age for starting over.

In McSpaden's view, neither is it an age for quitting.

"I'll never give up," McSpaden said. "I'm still strong. I won't say I'm young. I'll be 72 in July, but I intend to live to be 100. I've got a sweet gal, I've got my sight and every morning I say, 'Thank you dear Lord.'

I made some 6-footers in my day and I missed some. I made a 40-footer to beat (Ben) Hogan and a 20-footer to win Tam O'Shanter. I'm a poor caddie boy out of Rosedale, but I still got it done.

"I won 26 tournaments, but I went past that. I ran the Palm Beach Co. I helped build it into a $350 million company. They appreciate what I did. The president still calls every few months.

"I lost $3 million, but I thank the dear Lord for my eyesight and I thank the dear Lord for my life."

McSpaden's voice sometimes wavers with emotion as he talks about the fire and the loss of vision in his left eye.

"You know what I had left from the fire?" he said. "A towel and a pair of rubber boots that were in my Bronco. And the towel wasn't very big. When I came out of our bedroom and saw the smoke, I got a fire extinguisher, but it didn't do any good. I ran back and told Betsy to get out. Then I went to the garage and got four fire extinguishers. I could see the flames going up the kitchen wall. When I opened the door to the kitchen, it was like walking into the biggest flamethrower you ever saw.

"All my golf clubs are gone, the ones I shot the 59 with and the ones I used to win the Canadian Open. All of Betsy's things are gone. I had Kenneth Smith make her a new set of clubs, but she's so discouraged she's hardly hit a shot yet."

The loss of vision in McSpaden's left eye came gradually, but one morning he woke up and found he could not see. As a result, he decided to undergo surgery.

"What choice did I have?" McSpaden said. "They did a plastic implant. I went in on a Thursday, they did the surgery on a Friday and Saturday they took the bandage off.

"The first thing I said was, 'I can see.' Betsy was there and she said, 'Bless your heart, honey. I can't believe it.' "

The forthcoming trip to Columbus for his reunion with Nelson has lifted McSpaden's spirits.

"When Byron came out on the tour, you knew he was going to be a fine player," McSpaden said. "We became very good friends. We traveled a lot together. He was a very religious guy. He gave 10 percent of everything he won to his church. Me, I didn't go very often.

"In all the years I've known him, I've only seen Byron mad a couple of times. Once was when I beat him in Phoenix. Another was in Richmond, Calif. We were playing on a miserable course. Every time you hit the ball on the green it would roll back. Byron was disgusted with his game, the golf course and himself. He was so mad he could spit, and he said he was going home. I said, 'Byron, there's no way.'

"I used to keep him together. I knew his game backward.

"Things were tough in those days. Today any young guy who plays good, some doctor or businessman is willing to invest in him. I remember one time in Oakland someone stole the tires off Hogan's car and we all had to come up with a little money to help him."

Although McSpaden enjoys looking back, he also is talking about getting his game in shape. He no longer needs glasses following his eye surgery, and he has erected a practice net on his patio.

"I'm still strong," McSpaden said, "and I'm going to start hitting some balls. All I have to do is work at it and I can still move the ball out a little."

Adversity has wounded Jug McSpaden, but it hasn't broken him. The poor caddie boy is still competing.

Golf's Greatest Shot

Sports writers are sometimes accused of being careless as well as extravagant in the use of adjectives. Fortunately, the charge has less validity than it once did, but stimulated by the immediacy of an event there is a temptation to call it the greatest upset, the greatest comeback, the greatest shot or the greatest collapse.

Experience teaches us that it is preferable to err on the side of restraint and there is nothing cowardly in using the qualifying phrase "one of the" in association with the word "greatest." Only with the passing of time is it possible to clearly judge the historical significance of an event.

A case in point is the U.S. hockey victory over Russia. Time has reinforced the magnitude of that accomplishment because it turned out that most of the players on the team had only minimal talent when judged by professional standards. A strong case can be made that this was the greatest upset of all time in an event involving an American team.

Although we have arrived in a roundabout manner, this brings us to the point of today's column. Thursday Tom Watson will begin his defense of his U.S. Open championship, a title he won on the 17th hole at Pebble Beach by holeing a wedge shot from about 20 feet that he hit out of high grass to a slick green that sloped downhill.

At the time Watson's shot was equated with Gene Sarazen's double eagle in the 1935 Masters, Jerry Pate's 5-iron in the 1976 U.S. Open and Jack Nicklaus' 40-foot putt in the 1975 Masters as one of the greatest golf shots of all time. Now, a year later, there is no longer much question that it is the greatest shot in the history of golf.

My ground rules for making such a judgment are that the shot must come in one of the four major tournaments, that it be difficult, that the consequences of failure be severe and that there be little or no chance to recover if it fails.

Sarazen's double eagle probably is the most storied shot in golf, but it involved little pressure. Sarazen hit a 4-wood from a difficult lie on the 15th hole. He eventually won the tournament in a playoff. Sarazen was three shots behind at the time, he was not expected to win at that point and he hit the shot with no thought of making it.

Nicklaus' 40-foot putt came on the 16th green and gave him a 1-stroke lead, but even if he had missed he still would have had a good chance to win.

Pate hit his 5-iron out of a severe rough to within two feet of the pin to win the Open. It was a 194-yard shot over a lake in front of the 18th green. Pate had a 1-shot lead at the time and could not lay up, but if he had hit the ball in the water he would have lost the tournament. It was an extraordinarily difficult shot made under extreme pressure.

Sarazen's shot was more difficult than Watson's and probably Pate's was, too, but Watson's shot is in a class by itself because so much was riding on one swing of the club.

Watson knew that if he made the shot he almost certainly would win the Open. If he missed, he would have gone far past the hole and would have had virtually no chance to win. He was competing not against just anyone, but against Nicklaus, a four-time U.S. Open winner widely regarded as the greatest player in the history of the game.

In Pate's case, he was a tour rookie and not expected to win. Watson was the No. 1 player in golf and had never won an Open even though he had made the Open his top goal. With each passing year, the pressure on Watson was growing and more was being written about his inability to win the Open. In this respect, he was being compared to Sam Snead.

The Open is a tournament known for unhappy endings. Snead could have won in 1939 by shooting a 5 on the final hole. Instead he took an 8. Harry Vardon went 7-over par on the last seven holes in 1920 and lost by a stroke.

The Open being the Open, it would have been no surprise if Watson's shot had gone off the green. Instead he told his caddy, Bruce Edwards, he was going to make the shot. And he did.

Never before has so much pressure been involved on one shot, unless, of course, your game is Russian roulette.

Nicklaus Moves into the Twilight

"He's the best I've ever seen play the game. Jones, Hagen... if Hogan had played against him, he might have gotten discouraged and gone home. He's the best who ever had cleats on. Another will never come by either...."

—Lee Trevino on Jack Nicklaus

BIRMINGHAM, MICH.—Time is a thief that robs even the most gifted athletes, stealing their strength, their agility and their skills in such a stealthy manner that they have difficulty comprehending what is happening to them. The greatest athletes are time's most incredulous victims.

They have overcome adversity so often and the will to win is so strongly ingrained in their character that they will not—no, they cannot—accept that they are something less than what they once were.

Muhammad Ali could not understand that he was through even when he lost to someone such as Leon Spinks. An angry Warren Spahn, charging that his manager would not give him a chance to pitch, went off to Mexico in a futile attempt to prove he was not finished. Early in the 1982 golf season, when Arnold Palmer had gone more than eight years without winning a PGA Tour event, his eyes burned defiantly at the mere suggestion that he might be unable to win tournaments.

The final stages in the decline of a great athlete never are pleasant to watch, and that is especially true if the athlete in question is Jack Nicklaus.

He is the greatest golfer of all time, and Trevino may be right when he said that we will not see his like again. But there is more to Nicklaus than his ability to play golf. Win or lose, he has conducted himself with unsurpassed grace. He is a symbol of all the best things to be found in golf. Even in his worst moments of defeat he never has lost sight of the responsibility he carries.

The decline of Nicklaus has taken place in several stages. In 1977 Tom Watson displaced him as the best player in golf. After winning four tournaments in 1978 Nicklaus went throught his first winless season, in 1979.

His obituary was written widely, but he reworked his game and for one lovely season he was the Jack Nicklaus of old, winning both the U.S. Open and the PGA championship in 1980.

He seemingly had won his cherished fifth U.S. Open in 1982 until Watson holed an almost miraculous wedge shot on the 71st hole. He had a chance to win the 1983 PGA but was beaten out by Hal Sutton.

Since the start of the 1981 season he has won only two tournaments, the 1982 Colonial and the 1984 Memorial. But like Palmer before him, Nicklaus could not allow himself to think he had lost his ability to win. If he had, he would not have been Jack Nicklaus.

Friday a landmark development took place when Nicklaus missed the cut in the U.S. Open for the first time in 22 years.

As reporters gathered around him, he looked up at them and said, "I don't know why you're all here. What do you want to talk about?"

But of course Nicklaus knew exactly why so many reporters had come to talk with him after he had shot rounds of 76-73 on a course that was being abused by players named Tze-Chung Chen, Jay Haas, Andy North, Denis Watson and Rick Fehr.

For a while he talked about breaking his driver and the fact that he rarely has played well at Oakland Hills. He talked about the necessity of getting more strength back in his left knee after undergoing arthroscopic surgery. He talked about losing weight on the "Eat to Win" diet and the necessity of building strength in his upper body.

Then he came to the question that he knew everyone wanted to address.

"Maybe after today I'm not competitive any more," Nicklaus said. "I've got to find that answer myself. That's why you guys are sitting here. But I'm stubborn enough to keep trying.

"I've had that question in my mind for 15 years, ever since you guys started writing about it—since you wrote my first obituary. Please send me all of the articles you write and get me mad. Then Trevino will get mad at you guys for waking me up.

"I can either try or quit and I'm not about to quit. I'm too dumb."

But the more Nicklaus talked, the more evident it became that he has been doing a lot of thinking about his future as a competitive golfer.

"I might say at the end of this year that I've been selfish enough and I should start thinking of spending some Saturdays and Sundays at home with my family," he said. "Or my family may give me a kick in the rear and say they want to spend some time with me out on the tour on Saturday and Sunday.

"I don't know what I'm going to do. I don't see myself playing the Senior Tour. I'm not going to be playing anyplace if I play like I did today ."

As he talked about the possibility of giving up competitive golf, Nicklaus sounded much like a 65-year-old businessman who is contemplating retirement but is not sure what he will do with himself.

"I've often said if I quit playing tournament golf, I would have to find something to do," Nicklaus said. "I happen to enjoy doing golf courses, spending time with my family and doing a little bit of some other stuff that I do. But that doesn't fill a thimble of my time.

"Why do I want to quit doing something I enjoy doing? There will be a time when I can't compete. Maybe a physical thing will come along and stop me. But right now I happen to like playing golf more than anything else I can do."

But while Nicklaus doesn't want to quit, he has said many times he does not want to be what he calls a ceremonial golfer, and he concedes he is not playing well.

"I haven't hit the ball well for a long time," he said. "I haven't hit the ball really well all year even though I have had a couple of good tournaments. I played pretty well last year except for the majors."

Nicklaus said he was optimistic coming into the Open and was thinking in terms of 1980 when he won at Baltusrol.

"When I came in here, I felt a little like I did at Baltusrol," he said. "I felt like I was getting where I wanted to go. I think I'm going to start playing well pretty soon.

"No matter where I was in the golf tournament, I tried as hard as I could. The day I stop trying is the day I'll stop playing. That would not be fair to myself or the spectators."

Perhaps the most compelling remark Nicklaus made had to do with the 65s shot Thursday by Chen and Friday by Denis Watson.

"A 65 is amazing," he said. "I don't know how they shoot scores like that on this course."

The words were those of a 45-year-old man marveling at the prowess of the young.

CHAPTER 7

DEPARTED FRIENDS AND HEROES

Bill Veeck

"It's not the high price of stars that's expensive. It's the high price of medi-ocrity."

—Bill Veeck

If I were asked to name the three most interesting persons I ever met, one would be Bill Veeck. Through most of his adult life he smoked three to four packs of cigarettes a day, drank too much beer, stayed up too late and worked too hard. He read voluminously. He gave sleeping a low priority.

If you were a friend, his generosity was unlimited. If you were an enemy, it was best to give him a wide berth. Even in matters of love and hate, Bill Veeck did nothing in moderation.

A nonconformist, he refused to be bound by the rules of life that apply to most mortals. His extraordinary energy enabled him to do superhuman things, but it also was a destructive element in his makeup. How he survived to the age of 71 is a physiological mystery of the first order. Veeck detested pomposity, elitism and those whom he judged to be abusive of authority, wealth or position.

He was a champion of minorities and the underdog. He brought the first black player into the American League and hired an aging Satchel Paige to pitch first with the Cleveland Indians and later with the St. Louis Browns. When Curt Flood challenged baseball's reserve system in court, Veeck testified in Flood's behalf, thereby infuriating the baseball establishment.

He was inventive, a stimulating conversationalist and knowledgeable on any subject from the Federal League to Teilhard de Chardin. Genius has been defined as knowing everything about something and something about everything. If that is a valid standard, Bill Veeck was a genius.

Since his death we have been reminded repeatedly that as the owner of the St. Louis Browns he sent a midget to the plate. That is merely one humorous incident in a remarkable career, but in his wisdom Veeck recognized that this incident would follow him to the grave.

"What I really will be remembered for is sending a midget up to bat," he said in 1981. "Everything else I've ever done in baseball—forget it. I don't mind. As a matter of fact, I don't mind if they put it on my tombstone—'He helped the little man.'"

It would be a fitting epitaph because it is pure Veeck—a wry touch of humor combined with something he felt strongly about.

University of Kansas Chancellor Gene Budig recalls that following the appearance of the midget he wrote to Veeck from his home in Mc-Cook, Neb., to ask for a tryout. An exchange of letters followed, and while the tryout didn't come about, Veeck invited the youthful Budig and his father to a Browns game, where he introduced them to all of the players. Thus began a long friendship.

This type of thoughtfulness and generosity was typical of Veeck.

Veeck never wore a tie. That might not seem so unusual today, but Veeck grew up in an era when there was much more emphasis on conventional conduct and attire. Occasionally he wore a turtleneck shirt, but that was his only concession to formality. He never wore a topcoat, even in the coldest weather.

He lost part of one leg during World War II, and when he was sitting, he used the hollow in his artifical leg as an ash tray. It was Veeck's way of making light of his handicap.

He insisted that all of us take life much too seriously.

He gave us the exploding scoreboard. He taught baseball owners how to save millions of dollars in tax money by depreciating their players. He advocated moving teams to the West Coast four years before the Dodgers went to Los Angeles and the Giants went to San Francisco. He invented the portable fence that he moved back and forth depending on the power of the visiting team.

"I never tried to break any rules," Veeck explained airily. "I just wanted to test their elasticity."

He entertained baseball fans with flagpole sitters, clowns, livestock giveaways and unusual promotions. When his Cleveland Indians were eliminated from the pennant race in 1949, he put on a top hat and drove a horse-drawn hearse to center field, where the 1948 pennant was buried to the accompaniment of a funeral dirge.

Veeck was the first major-league owner to incorporate Abner Doubleday with Ringling Brothers, Barnum & Bailey. He believed that baseball should be sold as entertainment, not on the basis of a team's record. Human nature being what it is, he never was able to make this concept a total success, but he had a lot of fun trying.

Always the showman, he carried his entertainment philosophy into horse racing when, for a brief time, he operated Suffolk Downs, a Boston race track. One of his big promotions there was an event he called the Gen. Custer Memorial Stakes that was to have included a re-enactment of the Battle of the Little Bighorn. When the event was rained out, Veeck wryly observed, "Custer should have been so lucky."

Veeck, who owned the Chicago White Sox twice, was forced to sell the club the first time because of ill health. He began to suffer blackouts, lost 16 pounds in one month and his doctors advised him to get his affairs in order. They thought he was suffering from a brain tumor or a series of strokes. He retired to Easton, Md., and in time his ailment was diagnosed as an aneurysm near the brain.

Veeck spent his so-called recuperative period giving speeches, appearing as a commentator on "Wide World of Sports," writing a syndicated column and doing book reviews.

His columns, which were published in *The Star*, were delightfully irreverent. Writing about baseball's search for a commissioner following the retirement of Ford Frick, Veeck stated: "I'm afraid the owners will carefully screen all 180 million people in this country, weigh all of the qualifications carefully and then select either a relative or close personal frind of Walter O'Malley."

When the American League owners blocked Charles O. Finley's attempt to move the Athletics from Kansas City to Louisville, Veeck wrote: "Gentlemen, I salute you. You behaved magnificently under fire, refusing to be intimidated, coerced or conned. You even lived up to your fiery pre-meeting statements. And instead of charging into the conclave like tigers and voting like tabbies, you came out like lions."

The range of Veeck's talents was truly extraordinary.

Veeck learned the baseball business from his father, a former newspaperman who became president of the Cubs.

Like most baseball operators he had his successes and his failures. He won a pennant and a World Series in 1948 at Cleveland and set what was then a home season attendance record of 2,620,627.

He sold the Indians after the 1949 season and three years later purchased the lowly Browns. His promotions helped attendance for a time, but when he saw he could not survive in St. Louis, he attempted to move the team to Baltimore.

His nonconformity had angered many owners in the league, especially Del Webb and Dan Topping of the Yankees, and the move to

Baltimore was blocked. Veeck was forced to sell, and the new owners were allowed to move the club.

Veeck purchased the White Sox on April 30, 1959, and the club won the American League championship that season. His second ownership of the White Sox was a grim experience.

As usual, Veeck was short of funds. He had to buy the team under unfavorable conditions to prevent the American League from moving it to Seattle. To meet the league's requirements, his group had to set up a corporation instead of a limited partnership. As a result, the owners were not able to get the direct advantage of depreciation.

"We were playing with 100 percent dollars, and the Steinbrenners and Turners were using 50-cent dollars," Veeck lamented.

Free agency increased Veeck's financial problems, the club struggled and Veeck's health began to deteriorate. He suffered from emphysema and began to make more and more trips to the hospital. The financial rules of the game were changing, and Veeck had no outside millions to fall back on.

Adding to his discomfort was a promotion known as Anti-Disco Night that turned into a disaster when rowdy fans could not be removed from the field and a game had to be forfeited.

In September of 1980 Veeck sold the club.

In his first book, "Veeck as in Wreck" which was written after his first sale of the White Sox he concluded by saying, "Look for me under the arc lights, boys. I'll be back."

This time he knew there would be no return. In 1981 Veeck said, "I look in the stands today and I see underlying it all a tincture of violence. I look at the field and I see greed. I am not unhappy to be unemployed."

Life did not cheat Bill Veeck. It is a shame that all of us cannot live life as fully as he did. Even so, I am filled with a great sadness to think that this remarkable man won't be coming back to Kansas City to have lunch at Arthur Bryant's or drink beer at our kitchen table.

Ernie Mehl

This eulogy was delivered at the funeral of Ernie Mehl, who was sports editor of The Star *and the person principally responsible for bringing major league baseball to Kansas City.*

Through the years I heard Ernie Mehl speak on many occasions. Sometimes he was inspirational. Sometimes he was humorous. Sometimes he was profound. But whatever his subject, anyone who heard Ernie came away uplifted and with a joyous heart.

Joy, faith, optimism, love—these qualities were the essence of this truly extraordinary man.

Being called on to speak about someone who spoke so eloquently is intimidating. I'm not even sure where to begin because, you see, there were so many Ernie Mehls. There was Ernie Mehl the family man and devoted husband, Ernie Mehl the distinguished journalist, Ernie Mehl the lay minister, Ernie Mehl the civic leader, Ernie Mehl the youth leader, Ernie Mehl the nationally known speaker. And, yes, there was Ernie Mehl the friend, the willing counselor, the man who could not say no to anyone in need.

In this vein I remember an incident that took place in spring training when one of our children was born. I saw Ernie at the ball park that day and told him the good news. The first thing he said was "Do you need any money? Is there anything I can do?" That was Ernie. Always giving, never taking.

Some men and women are memorialized in stone. Ernie's memorial can be observed in the lives he touched and the changes he helped to bring about in Kansas City. His memorial is a living, growing thing.

A stone thrown into a lake sets off ripples and because of the energy released the lake never again will be quite the same. Ernie's life set off ripples, and in his case the ripple effect will be endless. The lives he influenced in such a positive way in turn will influence other lives on through the years.

Ernie Mehl was a complex man and although we worked closely together for almost 20 years I would not be so presumptuous as to try to define his personality. Even so, let me offer a few insights into Ernie's more private side.

We traveled thousands of miles together covering baseball. He was a colleague, a friend, at times even something of a father figure. Working with him was one of the greatest experiences of my life. He was my boss for 14 years, but in all that time I was never conscious that I was working for him.

I wrote my share of klunkers in those days, but he was never critical. I never recall him raising his voice to anyone he supervised.

Ernie and I never discussed it, but I knew that he never enjoyed being an administrator. He was quick to praise, but he did not like to reprimand or intrude in the lives of others. Ernie was sympathetic and compassionate. He hated to say no.

Never have I known anyone who could write so well so fast. The one disconcerting thing about working with him was his speed. He was closing up his typewriter and leaving the press box while I was still fumbling for a lead.

Ernie had a self-deprecating sense of humor. He loved to tell about the time he guarded Milt Singer in a high school basketball game and was totally embarrassed. He liked to tell about playing tennis with Bill Tilden and suffering a similar fate. He delighted in telling about the parakeet he and Blanche had that learned to say, "Mr. Mehl is impossible."

Ernie and I frequently discussed religion and philosophy over dinner. Ernie talked freely about his belief in God and an afterlife, but he never went into details of his religious beliefs. Denominations meant little to Ernie. His was not a religion of dogma and theology, but rather a religion of love. He was equally at ease with Catholics, Jews and fundamentalists as he was with Methodists.

He wanted to inspire people, to elevate their thinking and convince them that with faith and perseverance all things are possible. He greatly admired Norman Vincent Peale and the positive bent of Peale's religious message.

Ernie Mehl was many things, but above all he was a visionary, both practically and philosophically.

Kansas City went into a period of stagnation following the end of World War II. Through the decade of the '50s, the only major civic breakthrough that took place in Kansas City was the acquisition of major league baseball. That happened because of Ernie Mehl.

Once the Braves were moved from Boston to Milwaukee, Ernie became convinced that Kansas City could support major league baseball.

Unfortunately his enthusiasm was not shared by many of the business and civic leaders in Kansas City. One of the most prominent bankers in Kansas City said, "Sure, Ernie, I'll help you. I'll give you $10,000."

Day after day I saw Ernie come back to the office after getting negative responses. But he wouldn't give up. He had become a good friend of Del Webb, who at the time was co-owner of the Yankees, and Webb told him the Athletics would be for sale. Webb suggested he call Arnold Johnson, the president of Automatic Canteen who had purchased Yankee Stadium. Johnson said he knew nothing about baseball and was not interested. A month later Ernie called again. Johnson still was not interested. Later Ernie was going through Chicago and decided to give Johnson one more call. Johnson said, "Ernie, I'm glad you called. I've been trying to get hold of you. I've changed my mind. I'd like to buy the Athletics."

At that time Kansas City claimed a population of 1,200,000, but that figure probably took in Topeka and Wichita. Nonetheless, because of Ernie Mehl, Kansas City became one of only 13 cities in the nation that had a major league baseball team.

The acquisition of major league baseball changed Kansas City's image nationally and it changed the way Kansas Citians thought about themselves. In 1963 the Chiefs came to Kansas City and four years later they played in the first Super Bowl. The Athletics were moved in 1968, but with Ernie's help Kansas City found a new owner in Ewing Kauffman and obtained the expansion franchise that became known as the Royals.

With baseball and football serving as the foundation, we have seen construction of the Harry Truman Sports Complex, Crown Center, the airport and the building boom that is taking place in Kansas City today.

In closing I would like to leave you with one other image of Ernie. Whether it was at the office or the ball park, I always looked forward to seeing Ernie. He had a remarkable quality about him because you always felt better when you saw Ernie and talked with him. He had an infectious sense of humor and a contagious optimism. He lifted your spirits, and if you had a problem it didn't seem quite so bad after you had discussed it with Ernie.

It is hard to say goodbye to someone who has meant so much to all of us, and yet I know Ernie would want us to leave this chapel today with soaring spirits and joyous hearts.

The noted philosopher and paleontologist Pierre Teilhard de Chardin theorized that love is the greatest form of what he called radial energy, the energy that radiates from inward self perfection. The other form of energy is that which we expend as physical human beings. He believed that death, in the light of Christ's resurrection, frees man from the constraints of his humanity and allows God's love to grow unfettered in him.

Ernie Mehl's entire life represented an ascent toward this highest form of love.

Satchel Paige

Satchel Paige was buried Saturday, and after the services the thought occurred to me that I had come to know this unusual man better in death than I had in life.

I saw Paige pitch near the end of his career, I attended dinners and meetings where he was honored, and I interviewed him from time to time. But as much as I admired his accomplishments, I had trouble relating to him.

To me, he seemed improvident and self-centered.

He treated contracts and money casually. Punctuality was not one of his virtues. He spoke guardedly on racial matters although he obviously took pride in the accomplishments of the players who played in the Negro leagues and the success of the black players in the majors. His ego perhaps can be explained best by saying that Reggie Jackson is not the first player to see himself as the straw that stirs the drink.

In today's vernacular, I never quite knew where Satchel Paige was coming from.

Since his death I have reread books and newspaper clippings about him, I have talked with people who knew him and have listened to friends tell stories about him. Gradually I have gained some insight into the personality of this man who had a remarkable understanding of life and who developed an ego and an independent spirit that enabled him to survive the bigotry that denied black athletes a proper forum to display their talents.

Mary Frances Veeck, the wife of Bill Veeck, the man who brought Paige to the majors in 1948, remembers Paige as a man with a gift of resignation, a person who changed the things he could change and learned to forbear the things he could not.

"I think he was like so many people who have known injustice or tragedy," she said. "At some point you have to accept that this is the way it is and go on living the best you can. It's the only way to preserve your sanity."

At Paige's funeral I talked with a physician who had performed major lung surgery on Paige several years ago, and he told a story about his patient that offered insight into the ego and pride that were so much a part of Paige's greatness.

In the days immediately following the surgery, the doctor would come into Paige's room on his morning rounds, and Satch would be sitting in a rocking chair with a hood pulled over his head. Each morning the doctor urged Paige to get up and move around, explaining that it was important for him to exert himself and cough as much as he could. Satch's response was to nod and wave him away.

On the sixth day the doctor came to Paige's room and found the door closed. He knocked and Paige answered. He was dressed in a suit and tie and appeared to be in perfect health.

"Doctor," he said, "I'm going home."

Paige preceded Frank Sinatra in doing things "my way."

At Paige's services Saturday, his longtime friend, Buck O'Neil, offered one of the eulogies and said he wanted to tell a story about Satch he never had told before. The story had to do with Paige's attitude toward the material things of life.

Paige was pitching in Miama, Fla., of the International League at the time and asked O'Neil and Luke Easter to go fishing with him. Easter was a famous Negro league player who finished his career in the minor leagues after some good seasons with the Cleveland Indians.

Paige caught a fish and so did Easter. Paige caught another for O'Neil, who was not fishing, and said he needed one more to take home to his wife, Lahoma.

"He had a double hook on his line, and he actually caught two fish on it," O'Neil said. "He took them both off, but he threw one back in.

"I said, 'Satch, why did you do that?'

"He said, 'Because that's all we need.'"

Unlike most of us who are worried about storing up life's possessions, Paige took what he needed but not much more. Becoming wealthy didn't interest him, and neither did contracts nor schedules. He understood that as long as he could draw people to baseball parks he always would make money.

Satchel Paige was a pitcher, an entertainer, a man of great pride who changed the things he could and accepted the things couldn't.

Joe Delaney

On occasion all of us who are non-swimmers or who have limited proficiency probably have wondered what we would do if we were confronted with a situation in which someone, especially a child, were drowning.

Would we stand and watch, paralyzed by horror? Would we run for help that almost assuredly would be too late in arriving? Or would we attempt a rescue and quite likely die in the attempt?

It is a question no one can answer without actually facing that terrifying moment.

Wednesday in Monroe, La., that moment came for Joe Delaney when he heard the screams of three youngsters.

They had been playing in a pond near a recreation area. Swimming is prohibited in the pond, but youngsters are oblivious to hazards and to a child ponds are alluring on a warm summer day. The muddy bottom felt soft and reassuring as they frolicked, but suddenly they lost contact with the bottom. Without warning they had come to a 35-foot dropoff and they were drowning.

There is some confusion as to whether Delaney could swim. At best his proficiency probably was poor. But faced with the most frightening decision of his life he chose not to stand on the bank weighing personal risks or options. He did what he knew he had to do, and in attempting to rescue the boys he lost his life.

Self-preservation is an instinct that runs deep in all of us, and as a result there are few individuals who, when confronted with tragedy, are willing to risk their own lives to save the lives of others. Those who do elevate the stature of the human race.

What Joe Delaney did was not the result of careful decision making. It was a reflex action, but that reflex action was conditioned by his personal values and the way he lived his life. He was an honest, loving, unassuming man. As a small running back playing in the National Football League he was accustomed to taking risks.

Delaney did what he had to do, and he did it without thought of personal safety. That, of course, is the essence of heroism.

Delaney reacted to tragedy just as Arland D. Williams did at the time of the Air Florida crash in Washington. Williams, who recently was honored posthumously by President Reagan at the White House, helped rescue five survivors from the icy waters of the Potomac.

Williams passed a life ring from a helicopter to the survivors, who were unable to help themselves. Finally his strength gave out, and when the helicopter returned for him he could not be found.

In time it would be fitting if Joe Delaney were honored in a similar manner.

Delaney's death is another in a series of almost eerie tragedies that have taken the lives of Chiefs players.

Stone Johnson, a rookie flanker from Grambling College, died from an injury suffered in a 1963 exhibition game in Wichita. Johnson was blocking on a kickoff return and suffered a neck injury. He was paralyzed when he was carried from the field. The injury was diagnosed as a compression fracture of the cervical vetebrae. A week later Johnson died.

Mack Lee Hill, an outstanding running back, died near the end of the 1965 season after undergoing surgery for a knee injury. Hill suffered a ruptured ligament catching a pass against Buffalo in the next-to-last game of the season. He underwent surgery two days later. As the operation was being concluded, his temperature shot up to 108 degrees and two hours later he was dead.

In 1980 Mel Johnson, a wide receiver, underwent surgery for a wrist injury. Complications developed during the operation and Johnson suffered cardiac arrest. He was put on a life-support system but died five days later. An autopsy was performed, but the reason for the cardiac arrest never was determined.

Another player, Bruce McLenna, a free-agent running back, was killed in 1968 during Army Reserve summer camp in a Jeep accident. He was to have joined the Chiefs' training camp a short time later.

One of the Chiefs' greatest players, Jim Tyrer, took his own life and that of his wife, Martha, following his retirement.

Delaney's career with the Chiefs lasted only two seasons, but for a few weeks in 1981 he gave a performance unsurpassed in franchise history. He became a regular in the fifth game after Ted McKnight was injured, and he went on to gain 1,121 yards and set four Chiefs rushing records. He had his greatest game against Houston, running for 193 yards.

Following that game the Oilers Elvin Bethea said: "I've played against the best...O.J. (Simpson), Gale Sayers, Walter Payton, and he ranks right up there with them. He is great with a capital G."

Delaney was not a back who waited for holes to open. He anticipated where the hole would be, and when it opened at the last instant he would burst through. He paid a price for his recklessness that only his teammates could appreciate fully, but he never complained.

Little did he suspect at the time, but 1981 was to be the best year of his life. Delaney had to undergo retina surgery on both eyes in the off-season, and although he kept up a cheerful front he understandably was apprehensive. His performance last season dropped sharply from that of his rookie year, but friends said he was returning to summer camp this year determined to regain the heights he had known in 1981.

Because he placed the lives of others ahead of his own, Delaney will not be returning to the Chiefs this summer. But whatever he might have accomplished in the National Football League pales beside the courage and compassion he displayed Wednesday on the bank of a muddy pond in Louisiana.

(Editor's note: One youngster reached shore safely, one drowned and the third died later in a hospital.)

Red Smith

I'm not quite sure how to begin a column about the death of Red Smith because he handled the English language with such purity and grace that anything written about him will be clumsy and inappropriate by comparison. Writing about Smith is like being called on to sing at Caruso's funeral.

I suppose the best thing is to come right to the point and say Smith is the greatest talent our field of journalism has produced. No one—Damon Runyon, Paul Gallico, Grantland Rice—has written about sports with the humor, inventiveness and literary skill of Red Smith.

Those of us making this judgment are not without authoritative support considering that when Ernest Hemingway was searching for the ultimate sportswriter he named Red Smith.

Like all writers Smith had his peaks and valleys, but over the course of his lengthy career no one has written so well so consistently. If someone picks up one of his anthologies 50 years from now, Smith will be as delightfully readable then as he is today.

I first began to read Red Smith when he joined the old *New York Herald Tribune* in 1945 and I was a struggling apprentice at the *Tulsa World*. He immediately became one of my heroes. I was imitating other writers in those days, a phase every writer goes through in developing a style of his own, but unfortunately Smith's skills were so exceptional they defied imitation.

I first became acquainted with Red more than 25 years ago. The Dodgers and Yankees were playing in the World Series and the Dodgers had their hospitality room in the Bossert Hotel in Brooklyn.

I introduced myself to Red there, and he invited me to sit down and have a drink. That was typical of Red Smith. Red was not without ego, but he abhorred pretense and was one of the most approachable celebrities I have ever known.

Through the years we became good friends. Not close friends, but good friends. Red was a delightful raconteur and he spoke with a gracefulness and wit that matched his writing. Staying late at the bar with Red Smith was one of life's most enjoyable experiences. Red despised hypocrites and bullies and could lacerate his enemies with words honed to a sharp edge.

Speaking of a writer he disliked, he observed, "It's hard to understand how such a small brain could nurture such a large ego."

A mild strain in our relationship developed in the early 1960s when Charles O. Finley courted Red and persuaded him to write several favorable columns about Finley's efforts to move the Athletics out of Kansas City. Later, when Red developed a better understanding of Finley, he recognized his error and from that time on he was Finley's unrelenting adversary.

One of my favorite Red Smith lines has to do with his definition of chutzpah, the Yiddish word for nerve. Red defined it as "a man who kills his father and mother and throws himself on the mercy of the court because he is an orphan."

There is no "best" Red Smith column because so many of them were so good, but the quintessential Smith can be found in the opening paragraphs of his story on the 1944 Notre Dame-Army game:

"Quiet country courtyards from Killarney to Kimberly gave off a strange, whirring sound this afternoon as departed Irish whirled and spun and did flipflops under the sod.

"In the most horrendous Gaelic disaster since the Battle of the Boyne, the Celtic Szymanskis and Dancewiczes of Notre Dame were ravaged, routed and demolished by Army's football team by the most garish score in history—59-0."

Smith saw nothing demeaning about committing his talents to sports writing and contended that if athletes have been blown up into false heroes they are not alone.

"When you go through Westminster Abbey," Smith said, "you'll find that except for the Poet's Corner all of the statues and memorials are to killers. To generals and admirals who won battles, whose speciality was human slaughter. I don't think they're such glorious heroes."

Red had a way of putting everything in perspective. With his passing, a luminous talent has been extinguished.

Jackie Robinson

Jackie Robinson died yesterday at the age of 53. The stories of his death stated that he broke the baseball color line in the major leagues when he joined the Dodgers in 1947. To a younger generation this is a bland statement of historical fact, but there was nothing bland about the bean balls, the threats, the hostility and the challenges Robinson met when he entered professional baseball.

Branch Rickey, revered by many as a baseball genius, signed Robinson to a minor league contract on Oct. 23, 1945. Happy Chandler, a native of Kentucky was commissioner of baseball. Not surprisingly, he refused to comment on the signing. Today this may seem like a strange position for a commissioner to take but his attitude was enlightened compared with that of other officials.

Since Robinson was signed to a Montreal contract it had to be approved by Judge William G. Bramham, the commissioner of the minor leagues.

"Father Devine will have to look at his laurels," the angry Bramham said, "for we can expect Rickey Temple to be in the course of construction in Harlem soon. Nothing contrary appearing in the rules that I know of, Robinson's contract must be promulgated just as any other."

J. Alvin Gardner, president of the Texas League, joined arms with the law for protection from this terrible threat.

"I'm positive you'll never see Negro players on any team in the South as long as the Jim Crow laws are in effect," Gardner declared.

When Robinson went to spring training in 1946 he joined the Montreal club in Sanford, Fla. Sanford civic groups reacted angrily and finally forced the management to send Robinson to Daytona Beach, Fla., which was Montreal's main training base. A short time later the Montreal club went to Deland, Fla., for an exhibition game with Indianapolis and Robinson was exposed to another example of democracy in action.

Robinson slid across the plate in the first inning and as he got up he found himself facing a policemen who said, "Get off the field or I'm going to throw you in jail."

Robinson turned and walked to the dugout. His manager, a Mississippian named Clay Hopper, walked out to meet the policeman and asked what was wrong.

"We ain't havin' Nigras mix with white boys in this town," the policeman replied. "Tell that Nigra I said to git."

There was nothing for Robinson to do but leave.

The pitchers in the International League threw hard and often at Robinson's head that season, but instead of intimidating him they made him a better hitter. A Syracuse player held up a black cat and shouted, "Hey, Robinson! Here's one of your relatives."

Rickey made frequent trips to Montreal to talk with Robinson, urging him to avoid fights and other forms of retaliation. "Always you will be on trial," Rickey told Robinson. "That is the cross you must bear."

Despite his fiery temper Robinson had the intelligence to understand what Rickey was saying and realize that his behavior would determine the future of other Negroes in baseball for many years to come.

Robinson joined the Dodgers for spring training in 1947. Dixie Walker tried to get the other members of the club to join him in a protest but he received little support.

Carl T. Rowan, in his book, "Wait Till Next Year," wrote: "How could the fans sense the strain on a young ball player circling the bases after Dixie Walker has hit a home run behind him, wondering whether to follow custom and stop at home plate to shake Walker's hand or congratulate him in the privacy of the dugout so as not to embarrass him by putting him in the position of having to shake hands with a Negro before 30,000 people."

Ben Chapman of the Phillies rode Robinson so hard that Chandler finally intervened and put a stop to it. A Chicago Cubs player called for a strike but was unsuccessful. The St. Louis Cardinals attempted to organize a strike on May 6, the date of their first meeting with the Dodgers that season. They also tried to promote the idea of a general strike in the National League.

Their plans were thwarted by Ford Frick, then president of the National League. In a directive to the players Frick said, "If you do this you will be suspended from the league. You will find that the friends you think you have in the press box will not support you, that you will be outcasts. I do not care if half the league strikes. All will be suspended...This is the United States of America and one citizen has as much right to play as any other."

The strike threat was broken by Frick's strong stand and from that time on Robinson's position in the majors was established. Even so the 1947 season was a terrible ordeal for him. Pitchers threw at him, he was kneed and he faced the daily hostility of some of his own team-mates. He managed to keep his composure and said nothing.

One of the players who helped make Robinson's life bearable that season was Pee Wee Reese, the shortstop and captain of the Dodgers. Reese was from Kentucky but he was not a man given to racial prejudice.

Reese's first reaction to the signing of Robinson was concern about his own job.

"The first time I heard Robinson had been signed I thought what position does he play?" Reese said. "Then I found out he was a short-stop and I thought, 'there are nine positions on the field why does the guy have to be a shortstop.' Then I figured some more. Maybe there would be room for both of us on the team. What then? What would the people around him think about me playing with a colored boy? I figured maybe they wouldn't like it and I figured something else. The hell with anyone who didn't like it. I didn't know Robinson but I knew he deserved a chance the same as anyone else. It just didn't make any difference what anyone else had to say."

By 1948 the tension was beginning to ease but there were still hotels in the major leagues that would not take a black and when the Dodgers scheduled an exhibition game in Atlanta the Ku Klux Klan warned Robinson not to play.

By 1948 Robinson's position had changed to the point that he was arguing with umpires. In time he became a bench jockey in his own right and engaged in shouting matches with newspapermen. Robinson remained controversial throughout his career.

Ralph Kiner once observed, "You have to hand it to him. He has come a long way and he has taken a hell of a lot but he has never stopped coming."

On Oct. 15 Robinson was honored before the World Series game between the A's and Reds. It was to be his last public appearance and he used the occasion to remind baseball that the time was overdue for a black to be named to a managerial position.

Unfortunately he did not live long enough to see his dream realized.

Phog Allen

Dr. Forrest C. Allen, who died yesterday at the age of 88, was one of basketball's all-time great coaches. He was also a football coach, an athletic director, an osteopathic physician, a colorful phrase maker and a man drawn to controversy because of his strong convictions.

His activities were so wide ranging that his file in *The Star* library fills nine envelopes, the greatest number for any sports figure. The first clipping is dated 1905 and reads, "Forrest Allen of Independence, Mo., manager of the K.C.A.C. basketball team last year, has enrolled at the law school of the University of Kansas. He does not expect to do much in football this year, but he will be making a good basketball team at K.U. this winter."

A man as strong-minded and as outspoken as Allen was certain to have enemies. His eastern critics sometimes called him the Big Wind of the West and the Kansas Hayshaker, but in verbal exchanges Doc, as his players called him, gave much more than he got. His flair for phrase making made him a favorite with sports writers.

Once in a Kansas City speech he attacked Col. Harry Henshel, then chairman of the U.S. Olympic Basketball Committee, saying : "Col. Harry Henshel—he's probably a colonel in the Brooklyn band."

Henshel was so incensed that he filed a libel suit.

"You have popped off one time too many," he fumed in replying to Allen. "I intend to make you pay dearly for one indiscretion too many." Allen filed a counter suit, but later both suits were dropped.

The A.A.U. was Allen's favorite target. He attacked it saying, "The A.A.U. is neither amateur, athletic nor a union. It is an eastern clique." He also said, "The A.A.U. is an archaic, decadent, high-handed, heterogeneous oligarchy." He once sneered, "I like the A.A.U. about the same way that a fellow likes garlic for desert." He called Olympic officials "Quadrennial trans-oceanic hitchhikers."

Before he had big men on his teams he referred to them as mezzanine peeping Toms. Allen campaigned for years to have the baskets raised to 12 feet and once said in frustration, "For some strange reason, the height of the basket has become somewhat sanctified, like motherhood."

When one of his centers, B.H. Born, failed to hustle enough to suit him Allen observed, "Born stood around like a Christmas tree, and out of season at that." In a game at Colorado Born fouled out and was hooted as he left the court. Later Allen said, "During those frenzied moments at Boulder my mind kaleidoscopically swept across ages past wherein I could see a captive and tortured prisoner being fiendishly dealt with at the hands of his heathen gloaters."

When a basketball scandal broke out in the East Phog commented, "There are a lot of rotten eggs in eastern basketball, but we only smell them occasionally when one gets broken."

Speaking on the subject of sportsmanship he said, "The father who takes his son to a basketball game and boos the officials is teaching that son the principles of bolshevism and communism."

Among Allen's attributes was his sense of humor. When he was asked why Clyde Lovellette, the giant center from Terre Haute, Ind., had enrolled at Kansas Allen explained that Lovellette had come to Mt. Oread because of his asthma. "The poor boy suffers from asthma simply terrible back there," Phog said. When Wilt Chamberlain announced that he would enroll at Kansas Phog dryly observed, "I hope he comes out for basketball."

Allen was largely responsible for the construction of Memorial Stadium on the K.U. campus, although when it was built critics called it Phog's Folly, claiming it was too large. When Allen Fieldhouse was being planned Phog insisted that it have 20,000 seats. A strong movement developed to limit the seating capacity to 12,000, but Phog finally achieved a compromise. Another of Allen's accomplishments was the establishment of the Kansas Relays.

Many of the rule changes and innovations that Allen campaigned for in basketball have come to pass. His major disappointment was his inability to sell his peers on the merits of the 12-foot basket. But he did succeed in keeping the dribble in basketball at a time when the rules committee proposed to eliminate it because the game was becoming too rough.

Despite his strong convictions Allen showed amazing flexibility in his personal relationships and his coaching.

For years Allen disliked Sparky Stalcup, the Missouri basketball coach. Their relationship changed completely in the course of one game at the Municipal Auditorium. Lovellette stepped on Missouri's Win Wilfong. For a few moments a riot seemed to be in the making, but Stalcup personally calmed the crowd and from that time until Stalcup's death he and Allen were close friends.

In his coaching Allen changed with the times and proved that he could win with all types of personnel. He coached for 39 years at Kansas and won 24 conference championships.

George Mikan of DePaul was the first big man to dominate collegiate basketball, but Allen would have pioneered with the big man except for a freak accident. In the late 1920s he had a center who stood approximately 6-10, but the young man drowned in a summer accident without ever playing for K.U.

Ted O'Leary, a forward who Allen ranked as one of his all-time great players, recalls that in the '30s Kansas played a rather informal style of basketball that stressed the skill of the individual.

"We didn't have any plays, except for out-of-bounds plays," O'Leary recalls.

In the '40s the introduction of the block and the pick changed basketball and Allen changed with the times.

When Mikan and Bob Kurland of Oklahoma State, then Oklahoma A.& M., established the era of the big man Allen recruited Lovellette, who in the early '50s was the most dominant player in the history of collegiate basketball. After Lovellete graduated Allen proved his coaching genius by taking a relatively small team and going to the N.C.A.A. finals in 1953, losing the championship game to Indiana by one point. The success of Allen's team was predicated on quickness and the use of the half court and full court press, which at the time was a newly emerging technique in college basketball.

When Wilt Chamberlain became the most sought-after player in the country Allen recruited him for K.U., but unfortunately Allen was forced to retire before Chamberlain's sophomore year.

While Allen's technical competence was extraordinary, perhaps his greatest asset as a coach was his ability to motivate players and establish a winning attitude. "Somehow he convinced you that when you played for Kansas you were supposed to win," O'Leary says. "If you didn't, it was a fluke. He was a very enthusiastic positive man and he made you share his enthusiasm."

Today all who knew him share a great sense of loss.

Elston Howard

Today's column has to do with racial matters and the death of Elston Howard, a friend of many years who played for the Kansas City Monarchs and Blues before becoming the first black to play for the New York Yankees.

Howard and Hank Bauer had adjoining lockers in the Yankee clubhouse and Bauer, who makes his home here, remembers Howard with great affection.

"He was a real gentleman and one hell of a player," Bauer said. "People said it took the Yankees a long time to get a black player, but when they did they got a great one."

Nearly everyone liked Elston Howard, a man of integrity, compassion and class.

Howard could not be called a leader in breaking down racial barriers in athletics, but he was among the pioneers, and his death is a reminder of the profound changes that have taken place in the last 25 years.

Those of us who comment on racial matters in newspapers usually do so from a crisis perspective. As a result we concentrate on the problems of the present and the future, usually ignoring the progress that has been achieved.

For a younger generation, it probably is difficult to realize that as recently as 1955 Howard was not welcome to eat in the Hotel Muehlebach or, for that matter, any other leading downtown hotel. This was the same year Vic Power, who played first base for the Kansas City A's, was removed from a team bus in Florida by sheriff's deputies following an argument with a white gas station attendant over a 2-cent deposit on a pop bottle.

Major-league baseball came to Kansas City in 1955 with the transfer of the Philadelphia Athletics. The city went wild about going major league, but the leading hotels were not wild about housing teams that were coming to town to play the A's. The problem was that most of these teams had black players.

All of the teams except the Yankees made arrangements to stay at the old Town House Hotel in Kansas City, Kansas. The Muehlebach agreed to take the Yankees. Howard, of course, was allowed to stay a the Muehlebach, but he soon discovered he was not welcome to eat there.

Arthur Bryant, owner of Bryant's Barbecue, was a close friend of Howard's and Howard often ate with him.

"I remember that very well," Bryant said. "Elston told me he didn't want to be embarrassed trying to eat at the Muehlebach. He said he'd rather just come out and eat with his friends."

In time the hotel racial barriers fell, giving way first to the quiet dignity of an Elston Howard and later to the law of the land.

The incident involving Power took place following an exhibition game. In those days the A's trained in West Palm Beach and usually played eight or 10 games a spring with the Pirates, who were in Fort Myers. The roads between the two cities were rough and winding, and the trip usually took about three hours.

The Clewiston Inn, operated by the United States Sugar Co., was the only restaurant between the two cities that would serve blacks. As a result, the team usually tried to return to West Palm Beach to eat. On this occasion the bus made a brief stop at a gas station between Fort Myers and West Palm Beach. Several players, including Power, bought pop. As Power returned to the bus with his pop the attendant accused him of not paying the deposit on the bottle. Unpleasantries were exchanged and the bus pulled away.

Several miles down the road the bus was stopped by two carloads of sheriff's deputies who removed Power at gunpoint. He later was released, but only after the governor's office intervened.

On Monday, Dave Winfield, a black outfielder, signed a contract with the Yankees worth a potential $25 million. Twenty-five years ago Howard could not eat at the Muehlebach. Today Winfield could buy it.

The nation's racial problems remain deep and complex, but even so we are living through a period of great change.

Roe Bartle

H. Roe Bartle will be remembered for many things, among them his philanthropy, his Scout work, his dramatic oratorical style and his long love affair with Kansas City. His interests were as expansive as his girth and his personality, spreading into every aspect of community activity.

Bartle, who died Thursday, was a confirmed sports fan and of all his accomplishments perhaps none brought him more enjoyment than the role he played in bringing the Chiefs to Kansas City. Bartle did a remarkable selling job on Lamar Hunt and had it not been for his persuasiveness Hunt unquestionably would have taken his team elsewhere.

The Dallas Texans, the team that was to become the Chiefs, won the A.F.L. championship in 1962, but attendance was poor and Hunt made up his mind that Dallas was not big enough to accommodate the Texans and the Cowboys of the National Football League. Quietly he began looking for places to move his team.

Bartle, who was then mayor of Kansas City, was in Atlanta on a business trip when he heard of Hunt's desire to move. Hunt was checking out Atlanta as a possible site and despite his efforts to maintain secrecy Bartle learned of his plans. Bartle reasoned that a man of Hunt's wealth and reputation would be a desirable addition to the Kansas City sports scene. Since Bartle regarded Kansas City as "the greatest, the most magnificent, the most dynamic city in the universe," Hunt obviously stood to benefit by relocating his team here.

Bartle called Hunt and made an appointment to meet with him in Dallas. The meeting went well and Bartle invited Hunt to Kansas City, but Hunt declined, saying he was afraid someone would learn the purpose of his trip and he was not ready to fully cut his football ties in Dallas. Bartle swept this objection aside by outlining a plan that would assure Hunt complete secrecy.

On the day of the trip Hunt purchased a coach class ticket to Kansas City under an assumed name. Since Hunt always travels in the coach section he should have purchased a first class ticket for a foolproof cover, but a man does not get to be a James Bond overnight. He arrived in Kansas City and caught a cab to the Muehlebach Hotel. He checked in under an assumed name and made one phone call.

A short time later he left the hotel through the 12th street exit. A blue limousine pulled up. In the back seat was a big man smoking a cigar. Hunt entered the limousine and was taken directly to 22nd and Brooklyn. At this point only Bartle and his chauffeur, Carroll Dean Lassiter, were award of Hunt's presence in Kansas City.

Bartle and Hunt toured Municipal Stadium. When Bartle felt compelled to introduce Hunt to anyone he reverted to what he called an old southern custom and referred to him by his first name, introducing Hunt as Mr. Lamar.

Reynolds D. (Pete) Rodgers, Bartle's assistant, was later informed of Hunt's trip. Mail relating to the possible transfer of the Dallas franchise was sent to Rodgers' home. It was addressed to Reynolds Rodgers, U.S. Army Reserve. All mail sent to Hunt was taken from city hall and mailed elsewhere.

Hunt was also seriously considering New Orleans as a site, but the Sugar Bowl was not available and there was no other facility that Hunt regarded as suitable. As a result his interest turned more to Kansas City. Hunt made additional trips to Kansas City and was accompanied by his general manager, Jack Steadman. Bartle continued to introduce Hunt as Mr. Lamar. He introduced Steadman as Jack X, who he said was in the city doing investigative work.

Bartle's introduction of Steadman was so convincing that in time the word spread that he was with the FBI or the Internal Revenue Service. Bartle relished the deception.

On one occasion Hunt and Steadman were in Bartle's office and told him they wanted to get the reaction of one or two outsiders to the possibility of an A.F.L. team coming to Kansas City. At the same time they did not want to give away their identity. Bartle called Ernie Mehl, then sports editor of *The Star*, and William E. Dauer, general manager of the Chamber of Commerce, on a speaker phone. The five men discussed the situation, but Mehl and Dauer did not learn until much later that they were talking with Hunt and Steadman.

Hunt announced on Feb. 9, 1963 that he was moving his team to Kansas City. Later, in discussing the reasons he selected Kansas City he said, "I was impressed with Mayor Bartle. He spoke highly of Kansas City and I felt he believed what he said even though he said it in a flashy way. We were looking for a home where we would be welcome and he just made me feel we could do well in Kansas City.

Steadman, who worked with Bartle on a day-to-day basis in the period that the operation was being established here, said Bartle's influence was decisive when the final decision was made.

"He was totally instrumental in the decision to move here," Steadman said. "He wanted the team very badly. He said it could be accomplished and he set about accomplishing it. Without his influence we never could have put things together.

"He worked out so many problems for us. For example, when we were trying to locate our practice field in Swope Park there was some question that this might void the Swope will. Roe remembered that the city had purchased additional property in Swope Park. We found out where it was and that's the reason we selected the location we did for our office and practice field.

"When we had our name the team contest we had a lot of entries and one that turned up frequently was Chiefs. Roe, of course, was know as The Chief and I finally told Lamar, 'There's just no other name we can select.' "

The Chief is gone, but the Chiefs remain as a living testimonial to Roe Bartle's faith in Kansas City.

Bill Vaughan

Three days have passed since the death of Bill Vaughan, but it will take much longer to adjust to the reality that he will no longer be with us to inject laughter into a trying day or make some observation about a foible of human nature that we had assumed was a personal secret.

The mind, in the interest of self-preservation, buries some of the harsh realities of life deep below the surface of our consciousness. Thus, I permitted myself to assume that Bill would always be writing for *The Star* and that he would be forever available as a luncheon companion and a wise friend.

Even now, when I turn to the editorial page, I have some inexplicable feeling that maybe, after all, his Starbeams column will still be there.

Readers have often asked me if Bill was as funny in person as he was in print. The humorist, as opposed to the comedian, is an introspective person and many humorists are morose men, but Bill was equally as witty and stimulating in conversation as he was at the typewriter. His humor did not follow a formula. It was an exercise of the intellect, a wry reaction to the world around him.

When he visited with friends over a drink or two, his humor might be a little more biting. Unstuffing stuffed shirts was a specialty. But Bill's humor was never cruel. He had the gift of making us realize that there is a little bit of Congressman Sludgepump, Cousin Fuseloyle and the Office Grouch in all of us.

Bill was a genius by any definition of the term. Because he wrote so well, he inspired the rest of us to attempt to work up to his level. The end result was to make *The Star* and *Times* better newspapers.

When Bill made public appearances he was often asked, "How do you do it? Where do you get the ideas for your columns?" His answer was probably a one-liner, but the truth is that he sweated and dug and agonized.

He read extensively, he followed sports, he watched television and he was knowledgeable in the arts. There seemed to be no facet of life

220

that escaped his scrutiny. At the same time he understood the average man. A hard hat or a federal judge could read and enjoy Bill Vaughan.

It has been my observation that in any field—athletics, literature, medicine—the people who rise to the top do so because they are willing to work harder than anyone else. The talent has to be there, but it means little unless it is combined with dedication.

Bill Vaughan had talent, but he also worked harder than any columnist I have ever known. The three essay columns he did each week constitute a full workload for most syndicated columnists, but in addition he did five Starbeam columns a week.

Column writing is an unusually demanding occupation because you can never fully escape from it. Wherever you go you cannot close your mind to the fact that you need an idea for tomorrow's column. Roger Kahn, an author and former sports writer, made note of the next-column syndrome in writing about a friend, John Lardner, who at the time wrote a column for *Newsweek Magazine.*

Kahn and Lardner would meet once a week after Lardner had turned in his column and go to a nearby saloon. After a few drinks Kahn was puzzled to find Lardner becoming morose. Later he realized the source of the problem. Lardner already was starting to worry about his next column.

Whether Bill was reading papers in the newsroom or trying out ideas on his luncheon audience, I could recognize the symptoms of a fellow sufferer looking for an idea.

How Bill carried the workload that he did and maintained the quality of his writing was a source of amazement to his colleagues. We sometimes hinted, ever so delicately, that maybe he should ease up just a little bit. As we expected, he ignored us. The truth is that he was doing what he wanted to do. Like a great musician or painter, he found fulfillment in his work.

For many years Bill and I engaged in an exchange of spring training columns. The series began by accident when Bill wrote a column in which he scolded Ernie Mehl, then the sports editor, and myself for picking the A's to finish in the second division. Bill proclaimed that he was not among the doubters and picked the A's to win it all.

The idea was outrageously wonderful. It was pure Vaughan. In July of that season the A's were playing remarkably well and were only a few games out of first place. My fellow workers began to ask me why Vaughan was so much more knowledgeable about the true ability of the team than I was.

I responded with a column in which I wrote some Starbeam-type paragraphs and warned Bill that there would be more to come if he didn't quit poaching on the preserves of the sports department and jeopardizing the livelihood of honest working men such as Ernie Mehl and myself.

Following are a few paragraphs from Bill's first column. They reflect the deceptive simplicity of his style and the marvelous effect he achieved with words:

"As we poise on the brink of a new baseball season, a revolting aura of defeatism seems to have gripped even those sports writers we hold nearest to our heart.

"Ernie Mehl picks the Athletics for sixth and Joe McGuff moves them up only to fifth. In the cold light of reason that holds all wisdom to exist east of the Mississippi, these may seem to be daringly optimistic home town predictions. A New York paper, for example, says that the A's and the Washington Senators are the two worst teams in the major leagues.

"But the times do not call for pessimism and resignation. In an era when the president says the answer to the recession is to buy, enthusiasts wear saucer-sized buttons proclaiming the motto: 'Buy it now,' and our Chamber of Commerce is taking on new vitality and verve, what kind of communal patriot would settle for fifth or sixth?

"There is, in our opinion, no reason why the Athletics should not win the pennant this year. Ah, you say, this man is writing what he knows we want to hear. Not at all. As a matter of fact, you do not want to hear this. You want to hear that the team will finish fifth or below. You want to be able to grouse and complain all summer long. We know you and we are ashamed of you..."

From that season on the column and counter-column continued. It was great fun. Now the fun is over and life will be more difficult because we no longer have Bill Vaughan's humor and insight to sustain us.

CHAPTER 8

COLLEGE ATHLETICS

Larry Brown's Search

When you observe Larry Brown, the new University of Kansas basketball coach, in unguarded moments, his face reflects a quality of sadness, suggesting that the world has not been quite as he thought it would be. It is the look of a man who is resigned to being disappointed.

He comes across as something of a latter-day Sisyphus, the figure of Greek mythology who was condemned forever to push a heavy stone up a hill only to have it slip from his grasp at the last minute and roll back down. In Brown's case, he moves from coaching job to coaching job. He has been successful wherever he has gone, but even so, fulfillment keeps slipping from his grasp.

Brown's latest move has taken him from the New Jersey Nets, where he was earning approximately $260,000 a year, to Kansas. He will not be brown bagging it on Mount Oread, but his income from all sources will be substantially less than he earned at New Jersey. Obviously, the move was not financially motivated.

That leaves us with the fascinating question of why Brown would go from the Denver Nuggets to UCLA to the Nets to Lawrence, Kan., where a 10-minute drive in almost any direction will take you to a setting of bucolic tranquility. The one thing Brown is not, is a good old country boy.

Brown's numerous critics in the National Basketball Association will tell you his latest move was only another manifestation of his insecurity. They claim Brown is as careless with the truth as he is with contractual obligations and that in two years, or three at the outside, he will leave Kansas at the time of his choosing no matter how much the school might be inconvenienced.

Some people are compulsive gamblers, some are compulsive eaters and some are compulsive drinkers. Brown is a compulsive wanderer. When he becomes disillusioned with a job, he finds it easier to accept a new challenge rather than live with the consequences of his decisions.

Not everyone agrees with that view. There is the theory that Brown is at heart a teacher who stresses effort and team play and who can find fulfillment only as a college coach. He lasted only two years at UCLA, but he was not the first coach to find that situation unbearable.

Brown is close to Dean Smith, his college coach at North Carolina, and supposedly wanted an opportunity to establish the same type of identity and tradition at Kansas that Smith, a former Kansas player, established at North Carolina.

"I don't know if I'll ever be thought of like a Dean Smith," Brown said. "That would mean a lot to me. There's a family atmosphere at North Carolina and it doesn't end when you stop playing. It's something I'd like to have here."

Smith, who called Kansas Chancellor Gene Budig in an effort to save Ted Owens' job as coach, discounts the claim that Brown is too unstable to establish a successful, long-term program at Kansas.

"He's bright and he's a good teacher," Smith said. "I know he'll do well. He was a great competitor when he played. I've said before, if I had the choice of any player I've ever known to be on the foul line with us two points behind and one second to play, it would be Larry. His team will play hard and they'll play together. He'll do well."

The choice of Brown to replace Owens predictably has been controversial, but given the problems Kansas faced, it was a shrewd move on the part of Athletic Director Monte Johnson.

The firing of Owens could be justified only if a name coach were hired as his successor. Brown not only is a big name, but even his harshest critics concede he is an exceptional coach. Kansas needed a coach who could keep the present players from defecting and whose name would be a plus in recruiting.

Kansas needed someone to stimulate ticket sales. Brown should do that.

The worst thing that can happen to Kansas is that Brown will depart after two years, but by then the furor over Owens' dismissal will have subsided and the administration will have had time to think about Brown's successor.

The seach committee might consider holding a preliminary meeting about a year from now.

Don Faurot
a Man of Principle

Some remarkable men have left their imprint on the University of Missouri football program in the 73 years that the sport has been played by the Tigers. Among them are Paul Christman, Dan Devine, Bob Steuber and Gwinn Henry. But towering above them all is the lean, restless figure of Don Faurot.

Tomorrow the M.U. playing field will be dedicated to Faurot in ceremonies before the Missouri-Kansas game. Henceforth it will be known as Faurot Field. The dedication represents partial payment of a debt that Missouri can never fully repay.

Seldom has a man had such a total commitment to a university as Faurot has had to Missouri. Faurot was a 145-pound fullback on the M.U. football teams of 1923-24. He played on the basketball team for three years and was captain his senior year. He was a member of the baseball team for two seasons.

He was freshman coach in all three sports in 1925 and then left to become a coach and athletic director at Northeast Missouri State at Kirksville. Faurot was called back to his alma mater in 1935. The athletic program was $500,000 in debt and the football team had won only six games in five years.

Faurot's first M.U. team had a 3-3-3 record. In 1936 the Tigers were 6-2-1 and defeated Kansas, 19-3. It was the first time Missouri had scored on Kansas in seven seasons. In 1939 the Tigers, led by Christman, won the Big Six championship and went to the Orange Bowl. The Tigers also won conference titles in 1941 and 1942.

To pay off the athletic debt, Faurot began upgrading the M.U. schedule. At the beginning of his regime the Tigers had such a poor reputation that they were unable to schedule strong opponents, but with typical Faurot perseverance Don pursued the teams he wanted and finally got them on his schedule.

226

The big breakthrough came in 1941 when the Tigers began a long rivalry with Ohio State. Every game was played in Columbus, O., and the Tigers won only once, but as Faurot said, "That series got us enough money to pay off the debt on our stadium."

When Faurot retired as athletic director in 1967 he left a flourishing athletic program and an impressive bank balance, but as important as those things are his greatest legacy to M.U. was integrity.

At at time when college athletics were being swept along in a tide of cheating and hypocrisy, Faurot remained a man apart.

One time a wealthy alumnus offered Faurot some money to sign an outstanding high school prospect who was being sought by many other schools. Faurot responded by saying, "You're asking me to break the ethics of my profession. You wouldn't break the ethics of yours, would you?"

Devine likes to tell the story about the time Jim Tatum brought one of his Maryland teams to Columbia. The night before the game Tatum called Faurot and said he thought the tarp should be out on the field. Faurot said he had called the weather bureau and that there was no rain in the forecast.

Maryland had great speed and Missouri stood to benefit by playing on a wet field. It so happened that it did rain. The game was played on a soft field and Missouri nearly upset the Terrapins. Afterwards Tatum told Faurot, "If anyone else had pulled this on me I would be mad enough to fight him, but if you say you called the weather bureau I know you did."

In 1967 Missouri opened its season with Southern Methodist. Faurot, serving his last year as athletic director, was informed the game would be put on national television if Missouri would agree to move it up from Sept. 23 to Sept. 16. Although a substantial amount of money was involved, Faurot refused, saying that he felt the university owed it to the students not to play the game before they were back on campus.

Wayne Duke, former Big Eight commissioner and now commissioner of the Big 10, once summed up his respect for Faurot by saying, "If everybody in collegiate athletics was Don Faurot, then collegiate athletics would be what it is supposed to be."

Nowhere did Faurot's character come through more clearly than in his willingness to share the split T with his colleagues. Faurot invented the formation in 1941 and it revolutionized college football. He used the split T for two seasons at Missouri and then went into service. He coached Iowa Pre-Flight in 1943 and the Jacksonville Fliers in 1944. Wherever he went he taught the split T.

Among the coaches who learned the split T under Faurot were Tatum and Bud Wilkinson. Both were to use it against him later on with devastating effect. Apparently it never occurred to Faurot that he could have taught some other formation while he was in service and kept the intricacies of his invention to himself for a few more years.

"People were interested in what I had so I showed it to them," Faurot said. "That's the way I believe. Nothing gets to me more than to attend a clinic and have the speakers hold back. That isn't right."

Although Faurot was deadly serious about football and ethics he has always had a remarkable ability to laugh at himself, an unusual quality in a profession where there are so many super egotists.

One of Faurot's favorite stories concerns an experience he had when he was coaching at Iowa Pre-Flight. Many of the players on the team were young but he also had some older players who were officers. Before the season started Faurot called the officers together and asked them to decide on a code of conduct. They agreed that when they were with the football team there would be no smoking or drinking, but at home they were free to live as they normally did.

On a trip home from a game Faurot learned that two of the veterans had been drinking in front of other members of the squad. He called them in the next day and told them they were off the team. One of the two, Perry Schwartz, shrugged his shoulders and said, "That's all right, I'm tired of your coaching anyway."

When the commanding officer heard of the incident he threatened to send the two players back to Great Lakes, where they would have suffered a reduction in rank. Faurot agreed to take them back rather than have that happen, but only with the understanding that they would not break the rules again. When the two players showed up in his office Schwartz smiled and said, "You know, I'm not nearly as tired of your coaching as I thought I was."

There are numerous stories about Faurot's inability to remember names. Devine said he had been at Missouri for five years and Faurot was still calling him Frank, as in Frank Bryoles. But there was one thing that Don Faurot never forgot—the real values and purpose of collegiate athletics.

Dan Devine's Inner Toughness

It is reasonable to assume that anyone who ranks second in victories among active college football coaches and eighth in winning percentage would not be lacking in toughness or competitive zeal.

Nonetheless, Dan Devine often is misjudged on these counts despite his success as a coach.

No one questions Paul "Bear" Bryant's toughness. Shoot, Bear is the kind of guy you'd like to have with you if you were in the Alamo when ammunition was running low. And Woody Hayes? Who wouldn't feel better riding up San Juan Hill with Woody close by?

But Dan Devine? Even with his Notre Dame jacket on he looks more like a parish priest in a Bing Crosby movie than a football coach.

Bryant, Hayes and others like them are not hard to read. Devine is much more complex. Although he is totally trusting with old friends, he is wary of those he does not know well. If you want to know Devine, you had better be prepared to invest some time and effort.

When Devine replaced Ara Parseghian as head coach at Notre Dame, some alumni complained that he did not relate to the public. The gregarious Parseghian was to the Irish alumni what Arnold Palmer was to his Army. Some of Devine's critics thought they could run him off, but they misjudged his inner toughness.

In 1977, Devine silenced his critics by winning a national championship. In 1978, the Irish went 9-1 and then defeated Houston 35-34 in the Cotton Bowl, staging what some regard as the greatest comeback in Notre Dame history.

Last season the Irish had an unusual number of injuries and slumped to 7-4. Predictably Devine's critics exerted pressure and hoped he would be forced out.

Devine had other problems. His wife, Jo, suffers from multiple sclerosis and has virtually lost the vision in her right eye. She was involved in an automobile accident during the season. She suffered six broken ribs and two crushed vertabrae. Ten days after the accident she was released from the hospital to attend the Notre Dame-Southern California game. There were other family problems, and by the end of the season a less resolute man might have walked away. Devine stayed and fought.

"It was a traumatic season," said Devine, who spoke at a dinner of the Kansas City Chapter of the National Multiple Sclerosis Society Saturday night. "We had the most injuries of any team I've ever coached. There were traumatic personal problems. It was the hardest year of my life."

Devine responded by stepping up his recruiting efforts.

"I worked harder at recruiting than I ever have before," he said. "Except on weekends, I was never at home. When you've been doing it this many years, the food is the same, the motels are the same, the travel is the same. But I've passed the test. I've never been more successful recruiting. I'm pleased with myself.

"The whole recruiting picture has changed. It used to be the assistants did much of the work. Now the head coach has to go out.

"If the time comes I should leave Notre Dame, I want to leave things in the best condition I can. The freshmen we signed a year ago are super. This was a super year. If in the future I should decide to do something else, I don't want to quit coaching two years after I quit recruiting. I didn't anticipate quitting at Missouri, and I didn't leave them as well off as I should have. Here we've really got the thing built up."

Last December Devine said he would like to try coaching in the pros again, although not immediately.

Devine's happiest years in coaching were spent at Missouri. He encountered unusual problems at Green Bay, where the ghost of Vince Lombardi filled the city. At Notre Dame he replaced Parseghian who resigned because the pressures were affecting his health. The personable Parseghian was Notre Dame's most popular coach since Knute Rockne.

Being subjected to comparison with one coaching legend is bad enough. Few coaches would be willing to endure the experience twice. In Devine's case, the criticism and his family problems have only strengthened his resolve. He may not project the image of a Bryant or a Hayes but no one should be misled about the toughness of the man.

Osborne
Makes the Safe Choice

Since shortly after 11 p.m. Monday I have been hearing, almost to the point of gagging, about the courage Tom Osborne exhibited when he elected to go for a two-point conversion in the Orange Bowl game after Nebraska scored with 48 seconds left and trailed Miami 31-30.

Those who worship at the shrine of macho would have us believe that Osborne has become some sort of an American folk hero. With college football's national championship at stake, he said damn the tie, only two will do. Or something to that effect.

Questioned in the dressing room after the game, Osborne said, "We didn't come here to tie." John Wayne couldn't have said it better. The next thing you know Osborne will appear in the Oval Office to receive a presidential citation for bravery.

The only problem is that all of this talk about guts is nonsense.

Whether Osborne made a good or bad decision in attempting a two-point conversion is a matter of individual judgment. Reasonable arguments can be made on either side. What Osborne did not do was make a gutty decision.

The gutty decision would have been to kick the extra point, finish the season with the best record in major-college football and hope the electors in The Associated Press poll would be fair enough to vote Nebraska No. 1.

Sure, Osborne personally would have been denounced from Maine to the border of Baja California. He would have been called a coward and people would have accused him of not playing to win. He would have been compared to former Notre Dame Coach Ara Parseghian who, for very sound reasons, played for a tie against Michigan State in 1966 and was villified for years even though Notre Dame won the national championship.

Making that kind of decision takes courage. Going for two points was the easy way out Monday night. No one among Osborne's coaching peers would dare criticize a macho decision. The entire football establishment would applaud his courage. Osborne clearly made a popular decision, but popular decisions are not always courageous decisions.

Those who will suffer for Osborne's decision are the players because they will be remembered for playing on a team that lost the national championship.

To put the situation in perspective, it is necessary to reconstruct the events of the fourth quarter. Nebraska trailed 31-17 and Mike Rozier, college football's best running back, was out because of an injury. The Huskers scored once, and with time running out Jeff Smith ran 24 yards for a touchdown. At this point Nebraska had established itself as Miami's equal on a night when a lot of things had not gone well and Miami was playing what amounted to a home game.

On conversion attempts, NCAA figures show that over the last five years the success ratio for kicking extra points is about 90 percent. The success ratio for two-point conversions is roughly 40 percent, although against an excellent defensive team such as Miami that figure probably is closer to 30 or 35 percent.

By kicking the extra point, Nebraska could finish with a 12-0-1 record. Miami would be 10-1-1 and Texas and Auburn would have 11-1 records. Any fair-minded voter in either of the wire service polls would have to make Nebraska No. 1.

Was it worth gambling a national championship on a play that probably had no more than a 35 percent chance of success?

"I never even thought about that," Osborne said when asked if he considered going for a tie.

Despite the odds, most coaches are resigned to going for the two-point conversion because of public reaction. SMU's Bobby Collins played for a tie in 1982 and was severely criticized. Arizona State's Darryl Rogers took a lot of alumni abuse after playing for a tie with UCLA this season.

Logically a coach should consider nothing more than the percentages and the risk-reward factor in determining whether to go for a two-point conversion. Unfortunately, football's macho image keeps getting in the way.

The First MU-KU Game

The 83rd renewal of the football rivalry between Missouri and Kansas will take place tomorrow in Columbia. The game will have no bearing on the national rankings or the bowl picture, but the intensity of the rivalry and the sense of history that surrounds the series sets this game apart from any other played in the Big Eight area.

Considering the imposing age the series has attained and the fact that it began in Kansas City, I have often thought of going through the microfilm file of back issues to find the story of the first game. Yesterday curiosity goaded me into taking on the project.

I did not know the exact date or whether *The Star* even carried sports news in 1891. After some skipping around I discovered the first game was played on Oct. 31. Overcoats were selling for $10, men's suits were $8, ladies shoes were $1 and the price of *The Star* was 2 cents. The corn market was strong, the stock market was down because of a bank failure in Boston and there was a threat of war between the United States and Chile. A reward had been offered for the capture of the Daltons and in Leavenworth a man named Jack Draves made a contract with the United States marshal to hand over a convict named Benson for $20.

One of the more intriguing stories of the day was from Chicago where the police had encountered a problem almost too big for them to handle. The story read, "Susie Conrad, a fat woman weighing 600 pounds who has been on exhibition at a museum, became ill yesterday and it was decided to remove her to a hospital. A call was sent for a patrol wagon.

"The two wagon officers who responded summoned five other officers and managed to get the woman on a stretcher. Then every bluecoat tugged until he was black in the face, but they could not budge the woman. Several citizens were called in and after a great deal of

233

pulling, hauling and shoving the woman was placed in the patrol wagon, which she filled completely."

So much for the events of the day.

The story of the first Kansas-Missouri game appeared in *The Star* of Nov. 2 since the paper did not publish a Sunday edition. It carried a head that read, "Rock! Chalk! Jayhawk! K.U." The story stated that some people had trouble understanding the game, but enthusiasm ran high, especially on the part of the Kansas fans who had a 22-8 victory to celebrate.

Following are excerpts from the story of the first game: " Exposition Base Ball Park was the scene of a football match Saturday between rival elevens representing Missouri and Kansas State (Kansas) Universities. It resulted in a well earned victory for the Jayhawks by a score of 22-8. The Kansans scored five touchdowns and a goal, while Missouri made but two touchdowns. In fact, the Missourians had the hot end of the game after the first 10 minutes of play, but did not shake off the trance they fell into until the closing quarter of an hour, when they seemed to realize their advantage of weight for the first time.

"The audience was rather mixed, being somewhat evenly divided between collegians, society people and base ball fans. The latter, of course, were not up to the fine points of the game, but the enthusiasm of the college youths seemed contagious and everybody warmed up to the game as it progressed and as the uninitiated began to catch on to the merit of the plays they became as wildly hilarious as the hundreds of young men who sported the crimson of Kansas or the orange and black of Missouri.

"The game was witnessed by a crowd of about 3,000 people. The Kansans were the first on the grounds and the delegation of enthusiastic rooters from Lawrence took possession of the west bleachers, which were just opposite the center, the goals being placed almost directly north and south from the left-field fence to the east end of the covered stand.

"The west bleachers became one waving mass of crimson and completely overshadowed the more subdued orange and black of the Missourians. Before the game the college cries of the rival universities filled the air and the lung power of the Kansans rang out particularly strong. They yelled themselves hoarse with their cries of 'Rock! Chalk! Jayhawk! K.U.'

"Just previously to the call of 'time' the Missourians were reinforced by a delegation of university alumni....This party had resurrected a lot of horns that had been expected to do duty for the late, lamented Blues at the close of the base ball season and they made good use of them. Their appearance was the occasion for a grand rallying cry and 'Rah, rah, M.S.U., Missouri University, rah, rah, rue,' was given with a lusty goodwill followed by a continuous tooting of horns that drowned out the Jayhawkers for a few moments."

The game began auspiciously for Missouri. Missouri won the toss and on the first play Bradley (no first names were used in newspaper accounts in those days) carried the ball into Kansas territory. Two plays later Shawhan scored on an end run. As it turned out, this was to be the high point of the day for Ol' Mizzou.

Kansas scored shortly thereafter and went on to run up a 22-4 lead. Picking up at this point *The Star* story reads: "At this stage the Missourians grew desperate and did what they should have done earlier in the game, go through by mere force of weight....Scrimmage followed scrimmage, but finally the weight of the Missourians told and Bradley, with the ball hugged tightly to his breast, rolled out from under the struggling heap of humanity and scored Missouri's second touch down. Anderson again failed to kick goal and shortly after the whistle sounded and the game was over with the score 22-8.

"A mighty yell went up from the Kansas delegation and they broke on to the field and carried off the victorious team while the Missourians quietly disappeared. During the evening the Kansas excursion, enveloped in crimson bunting, marched through the streets and rock! chalk! Jayhawk! K.U. is now as well known in Kansas City as the iridescent salesman or Jerry Simpson's socks.

"It is conceded that Kansas outplayed the boys from Columbia at every stage of the game. They were better trained, surer kickers, safer catchers and knew what to do with the ball when they got it. Their victory was marked by more team play and the victory was a well earned one. A return game is talked of for Thanksgiving Day."

Tomorrow 55,000 spectators will gather at Faurot Field to see these old rivals meet again. The principal concern of the Kansas and Missouri partisans is winning, but a little history will make the occasion more meaningful.

Don Fambrough
Looks Back

Don Fambrough is a symbol of Kansas football, having served the program for 37 years as a player, assistant coach, head coach and fund raiser. He was dismissed as head coach Dec. 3, 1982. At the time he was offered a job in the athletic department, but turned it down, advising Chancellor Gene Budig he was interested in serving the university, but in some other capacity. Fambrough agreed to the following interview, but with the stipulation that he did not want to comment on any of the controversial aspects of his firing.

LAWRENCE, KAN.—"It's a little cold in here, isn't it?" Don Fambrough said as he invited his visitor into the head coach's office. "No one has said I have to leave here yet, but it feels like they've turned the heat off. Maybe they're trying to tell me something."

Fambrough smiled, settled back in a chair and said, "Well, where do you want to start?"

Fambrough was advised that the public has been asking if he is angry or bitter over his dismissal and is interested in knowing what his plans are.

"I'd be telling a complete lie if I said I'm not angry," Fambrough said. "I have two years left on my contract and I wanted to complete those two years. More than anything else, I'm angry because I had to go out with the miserable season we had. That bothers me.

"In time it will fade away, but I didn't want to leave on this kind of a season. But all in all, as I reflect back, I knew what I was getting into. I started working here as a freshman coach for J.V. Sikes, and if anyone was seasoned for something like this, I was.

"It hurts now, but in time I'll look back and see how lucky I was to have spent all these years here and to have been head coach of my alma mater two times. I don't think many people have done that. I wanted my successor to be able to take over without all of this conflict. It's not good for the school and it's not good for the football program."

"What happens to Don Fambrough now? I don't know. Sure, I'm thinking about it. I'm 60 and coaching is not in my future plans. Lawrence is home and I hope to stay here. I don't know what I'll wind up doing. I'm too young to retire. I think I've got some good years left."

"Whatever I do, it will not be in the athletic department. If some other phase of university work was offered to me that was meaningful, I might take that. Or it might be something outside of the university.

"The university indicated to me they would like for me to remain in some position. I asked for some time to think about it. It's been a tough year and with all of the dramatic things that have happened lately I need some time to settle down. Hopefully, I'll find something for Don Fambrough to do.

"I went to work here for E.C. Quigley in 1948. He was the athletic director. He was a conservative man. Maybe some would call him frugal. He gave me $3,800 a year to coach the freshmen. J.V. Sikes went to him and said that with the cost of living going up that wasn't enough, that I had to get $4,000. Quigley finally gave in and that's what my first salary was."

Fambrough was asked why the Kansas football program has had such unusual high and lows. In answering, he alluded to the fact that he served two separate terms of four years each as head coach and both Pepper Rodgers and Bud Moore had served four.

"Someone asked me the other day if I had any advice for the next coach," Fambrough said. "I told him yes, I did, that the new coach should take a sabbatical after four years.

"This is a program that will always continue to have this kind of highs and lows unless they change the way they do things. Someone came by the office and told me that for the last 90 years the average length of time for a football coach at Kansas is 2.7 years. I guess I've got to feel good if this sort of thing has been going on for 90 years. Hopefully, one of these times we'll try something different. It's obvious that changing coaches every four years is not the answer."

Fambrough was asked what could reasonably be expected of the program if it were well run and there were coaching continuity.

"It's reasonable to think that if the program is well supported and the proper facilities are available you should be able to finish in the top half of the Big Eight most of the time and compete for the title once in a while," Fambrough said.

"Kansas cannot be a Nebraska or an Oklahoma. We're not even close. Why? I'd say it's the commitment those people have to football.

It's the total commitment that results in Oklahoma and Nebraska having winning programs. They're not going to let anything stand in the way—facilities, budget, whatever it takes. And when I say that I'm not talking about cheating.

"Let me give you an illustration. When we played Nebraska here this year we were riding to the stadium in our bus and I heard one of the freshmen say in a low voice, 'You wouldn't know whether we're in Lincoln or Lawrence. All I see is red.'

"If you played on the moon, those people would be there. You can't compete with those people just on the day of the game. You've got to compete year around. Maybe the people here don't want that, but let's make it known what kind of program we do want. Let's not talk about beating Nebraska and Oklahoma unless we're willing to make that kind of commitment.

"There are some other factors, too. One of them is population. Kansas is not a big state and there are three major schools playing football. There are three major schools playing football in Oklahoma, but OU gets what it wants out of the state and is able to go into Texas. Location hurts us, too, because everyone comes into the Kansas City area to recruit."

Fambrough regards Gale Sayers as the best running back he has ever seen.

"I never will forget one day in spring practice we had him playing safety and his belt broke," Fambrough chuckled. "His pants were sliding down and he grabbed them with one hand and intercepted a pass with the other. As talented as he was, he could play anywhere."

As the interview drew to a close, Fambrough spoke of what has meant the most to him in his long career at Kansas and the things that are sustaining him at this low point in his life.

"I know it sounds corny to anyone but an old coach, but I've got to say what I feel best about is the people I've been associated with," Fambrough said. "I told the team at our football banquet that if someone asked me about a game eight years ago, I'd have to look up the score, but I can remember people who were on the team and the things that went on on the practice field. My assistant coaches, the many people who stuck by me, the people who put the program first—I've got a lot of friends. Most of them are little people and I feel good about that.

Villanova vs. Georgetown

LEXINGTON, KY.—The conventional wisdom of the day holds that the championship game of the Final Four will be little more than a final bore. Georgetown has been acclaimed a team for the ages. Nobody seems to be quite sure what to make of Villanova, a team whose senior players will not cause punctures in the National Basketball Association salary cap.

Even so, the Villanovas of the world sometimes do win, so come with me and we will do a little creative work with the available facts and figures to develop a case for the Wildcats becoming the champions of college basketball.

As a starting point, Villanova is the type of team Georgetown would least like to play.

Because Georgetown has the best talent in college basketball, it likes to play all 94 feet of the floor for the full 40 minutes. The Hoyas' style is to attack. Villanova reduces the time and the dimensions of the court to match its limited talent.

If the Hoyas like to rock and roll, it is fair to say that Villanova dances to the music of Lawrence Welk.

With the Wildcats, it's not so much what they do, but what they don't do. They don't shoot much, they don't turn the ball over much, they don't foul very often, they don't make many mistakes and they don't allow many points.

They also don't do much to excite the fans, but basketball is not a sport in which points are awarded for artistic merit.

Georgetown defeated Villanova twice during the regular season, but the scores are significant. They were 52-50, in overtime, and 57-50. In only one other game was Georgetown held below 60 points.

With the shot clock turned off for the tournament, scoring against Villanova is even more difficult.

Not only is the championship game likely to be close and low scoring, but Coach Rollie Massimino thinks the Wildcats have pulled everything together and are playing better down the stretch than any other team he ever has had.

"They realize it takes the ultimate to be what they can be," Massimino said. "The last few weeks have seen an incredible transition in these kids."

Michigan's 55 points are the most scored against Villanova in five tournament games. Dayton had 49 points, Maryland 43, North Carolina 44 and Memphis State 45. These teams have shot only 41 percent.

The Wildcats, in keeping with their unusual personality, regard the officials as their best friends. The Wildcats are so adept at drawing fouls that in their last four games they have made 50 more points from the free-throw line than their opponents. Villanova has gone to the line 92 times and made 69 free throws while the opposition has been to the line only 28 times and has made 19.

"We look bad, but we make the other team look worse," said forward Harold Pressley on this ugly-is-beautiful approach.

Villanova uses 10 or more defensive sets, and Pressley said the Wildcats finally got comfortable with all of them just before tournament time.

Psychologically the Wildcats are in the best possible position. If they lose, they will have been defeated by a team rated among the best of all time. For Georgetown, a loss would be a disaster. To a degree, Georgetown finds itself in the position of playing not to lose.

"We've been in that position several times this year and it's not the most comfortable situation in the world, to tell you the truth," Georgetown Coach John Thompson said. "We feel more comfortable when the other team is favored."

Villanova also has a bit of recent history on its side. Two years ago Houston was acclaimed as one of basketball's all-time great teams. The Cougars played lightly-regarded North Carolina State in the championship game and lost 54-52.

And so you see, all Villanova has to do is keep the tempo nice and slow, get Patrick Ewing in foul trouble and the next thing you know, the Wildcats will become National Collegiate Athletic Association champions. And if they do, the next column in this space will explain how the Afghanistan rebels are going to defeat the Soviet Union.

[Editor's note: Villanova won, 66-64.]

Walter Byers
and the Search
for Sanity

Attending a Walter Byers news conference is a stimulating experience if for no other reason than to enjoy the artistic merit of the performance.

Byers, the executive director of the National Collegiate Athletic Association, is informed, has a command of the language that even William Buckley would appreciate and escapes from difficult questions as deftly as the celebrated magician, Harry Houdini, slipped out of straitjackets.

Last Tuesday, Byers appeared before a gathering of reporters to explain how the presidents and chancellors of the nation's colleges are going to do collectively what they have been unable or unwilling to do individually, to wit, bring honesty to college athletics.

Sin will be legislated away and college athletics at last will be a gleaming symbol of purity. Or something like that.

Byers said he has a "good feeling" about the NCAA Presidents Commission that has been established to deal with this problem. It will hold a special meeting in June.

"We have been whipsawed too long by unscrupulous minorities," Byers declared.

At another point he returned to this theme, saying that the question to be decided is whether policy will be set by the chief executive officers of the institutions or "a minority of coaches and enslaved alumni and boosters who think the order of the day should be (maintained) at any cost."

The rhetoric was impressive. The overall effect was depressing.

Perhaps I am getting old and cynical. Perhaps I have spent too many years listening to well-intentioned but naive speeches about cleaning up college athletics. I have seen rule piled upon rule until today a financially disadvantaged athlete living 1,000 miles from home isn't allowed to call home or fly home at the school's expense even if there were an emergency in the family.

These things smack of the rules so beloved by the late Avery Brundage in his heavy-handed effort to purge the Olympics of professionalism.

Don Canham, the Michigan athletic director, has said, "The most discriminated-against single group of people I know is the collegiate athlete."

As the size of the rule book has grown, so have the number and severity of the violations.

"It's just like the black market," the Los Angeles Rams' Eric Dickerson said recently. "All you can do is accept it. You can't make an example out of everyone that's doing it. If you make an example of them all, they'll have no college football."

Marv Harshman, who is in his final season as the University of Washington basketball coach, gave a forlorn commentary on college athletics when he recently said, "Now the bottom line is money. Everybody needs money to run their programs. It's simple: The more you win the more people turn out and the more money you make so you can finance those programs that don't make money. The pressure on college basketball coaches today is enormous."

Now we are being told that the college presidents and chancellors are going to solve the problem by shaking their fists and enacting tougher legislation that will include rules making it harder for many minority athletes to get into school.

Interestingly, the head of the NCAA Presidents Commission is John Ryan of Indiana University, who has endured the outrageous conduct of his basketball coach, Bobby Knight, over the years without so much as a word of personal reprimand.

"To the best of my knowledge, Ryan has never publicly chastised Knight for anything Knight has done," said Wayne Fuson, sports editor of *The Indianapolis News.*

After Knight threw a chair on the court Feb. 23 and was ejected from Indiana's game with Purdue, Ryan said, "As far as I'm concerned, the key thing is to recognize that that particular incident is wrong."

It should be noted that he did not say Knight was wrong or that Knight embarrassed the university, he merely said that what Knight did was a no-no.

On another occasion he said, "The Lord is satisfied with sorrow and an intention of amendment, and I'm satisfied I've got that from Coach Knight."

Said Vernon Scheiner, a retired faculty member and a former dean at Indiana, "In another department, he (Knight) would be taken out of his position."

The whole incident is typical of the years at Ohio State when the president was afraid to challenge the outrageous behavior of football coach Woody Hayes.

But even if the NCAA Presidents Commission had a leader of demonstrated fearlessness, it would face an almost-impossible task.

College football and basketball are out of control for the fundamental reason that the people who run college athletics insist on enacting amateur rules to govern what are fundamentally professional sports.

Over and over we have seen that where large amounts of money are involved in a sport, amateur rules are impossible to enforce. Tennis, hockey, track and skiing are just a few examples. Even a person as powerful as Brundage lost this battle in the Olympic movement, as well he should.

In a sport where coaches earn $250,000 a year and colleges are fighting each other in court over television money, the athlete has a justifiable reason to feel that he should get his fair share. And one way or another he will.

The *Los Angeles Herald Examiner* recently quoted Bill Rees, the UCLA recruiting coordinator, and Artie Gigantino, an assistant coach, who explained that some schools avoid detection by having alumni set up a trust fund in the name of an athlete's relative. At the end of four years, the alums get their money back, the relative gets some money and the athlete takes the proceeds of the trust.

The NCAA is swimming against the tide of history, and in the end it will lose.

To Byers' credit, several months ago he discussed the alternative of opening up college athletics, the premise being that the infractions are wrong, not because society says they are, but because the NCAA rules make them that way.

"The NCAA has rules that say you can't do certain things," Byers explained. "Is it worth the effort to maintain these recruiting and financial-aid rules, or should we make permissible some of the things people want to do?"

Byers said the idea received no support in the college community, and if anything, administrators who responded said they were rededicating themselves to making the system work.

And that will continue to be the response as long as the administrators are unwilling to confront the fact that they are in the professional athletic business.

If the profit-making motive were eliminated from college athletics, the rules would work. The problem is that the administrators, in the tradition of Avery Brundage, want the profits and amateurism, too.

St. Benedict, you were a man of peace.
You walked the paths of peace your
whole life long and led all who came to
you into the ways of peace. Help us,
St. Benedict, to achieve peace:
peace in our homes, peace in our sorely
troubled world. Through your
powerful intercession with God help
us to be peacemakers. Aid us to work
for peace, to take the first step in
ending bitterness, to be the first to
hold out our hands in friendship
and forgiveness. Beg God to let peace
permeate our lives so that they may be
lived in His grace and love. And at the
end of our lives obtain for us the reward
of the peacemakers, the eternal blessed
vision of God in Heaven. Amen.

Benedictine Sisters
Clyde, MO 64432-9700